The Portugal Journal

SUNY series, Issues in the Study of Religion

Bryan Rennie, editor

The Portugal Journal

MIRCEA ELIADE

Translated from the Romanian
and with a Preface and Notes by
Mac Linscott Ricketts

This publication has been made possible by a grant from the Prodan Romanian Cultural Foundation of London.

Cover image of seashell © Kasia Biel/iStockphoto.com

Published by
State University of New York Press, Albany

For information, contact State University of New York Press, Albany, NY
www.sunypress.edu

Production by Diane Ganeles
Marketing by Michael Campochiaro

Library of Congress Cataloging-in-Publication Data

Eliade, Mircea, 1907–1986
  [Jurnalul portughez. English]
 The Portugal journal / Mircea Eliade ; translated by Mac Linscott Ricketts.
      p. cm. — (SUNY series, Issues in the study of religion)
   Includes bibliographical references and indexes.
   ISBN 978-1-4384-2959-5 (hardcover : alk. paper)
   ISBN 978-1-4384-2958-8 (pbk. : alk. paper)
   1. Eliade, Mircea, 1907–1986—Diaries.   2. Religion historians—United States—Diaries.   I. Title.

BL43.E4A3 2010
200.92—dc22   2009017903

10 9 8 7 6 5 4 3 2 1

In Memory of Mary Park Stevenson
1920–2007

Contents

Translator's Preface

A well-written private diary (or "intimate journal") was one of Mircea Eliade's favorite forms of literature. In his own journals he often mentions reading such a book for pleasure. There is no doubt that he assigned an important place to journal writing within his numerous and varied activities as an author. In his memoirs, he recalls his first journal, which he dates to 1921 (when he would have been fourteen).[1] He used a school copybook, on the cover of which he wrote *Jurnalul* [The Journal]. Throughout his life, with the exception of only a few years, he faithfully recorded his activities and thoughts in notebooks. Four autobiographical novels—*Romanul adolescentului miop* [The Novel of the Nearsighted Adolescent], *Maitreyi*, *India*, and *Şantier* [Work in Progress]—draw heavily upon his journals.

One of his greatest regrets—and ours—was the loss of the diaries of 1932–40 that occurred during the Second World War, while he was abroad on diplomatic service. Upon leaving Romania in April 1940 for London, he entrusted them to his cousin, Gicu, but when Nina, his wife, came to Bucharest in the summer of 1943, she placed the journals (by prearrangement) in the care of N. I. Herescu, professor of language and literature at the University of Bucharest and secretary of the Romanian Writers' Society. Only a year later, Herescu fled the country as a refugee and left Eliade's journals and many of his own papers with a friend of his. Somehow, in the turbulent years of the early Communist regimes, they were lost.[2]

Speaking of "The Portugal Journal" in his *Autobiography*, Eliade says, "If it should ever be published in its entirety, the reader will find many facts and much information useful for understanding the era."[3] This is true, but for the person desiring to know more about Mircea Eliade, the significance of the book lies in the "many facts and much information useful for understanding" the author that will be found there! The importance of the phrase "in its entirety" cannot be overemphasized. For the first time it is possible to read a journal text of Eliade's that was not subject to his editing for publication. The original manuscript totals about 435 pages, much of it written in a small, neat hand with very few obliterations or corrections.[4] This would suggest that it was transcribed from pocket notebooks and loose pages (to which the journal in fact sometimes refers), and in this process some changes probably were made. However, although the text may have been "polished" when copied, the reader does not have the impression that the material has been "censored"; there is a surprising candor in many of the statements it contains.

Did Eliade plan to publish this journal, or at least selections from it, during his lifetime? The text makes several passing remarks about its future readers, although the author underscores that he is writing it first of all for his own benefit.[5] The clearest statement on the matter is dated 5 February 1945, where he indicates he had been planning to publish the journal in 1967, at age sixty, but now he is considering releasing it sooner. The thought makes him hesitate: "[W]ill it intimidate me so much that I won't dare confess everything?" he asks. He concludes that he will not be intimidated—since in any event he would publish only excerpts.[6]

In 1972, when Eliade was five years past the age of sixty-five, some excerpts from his onetime friend Mihail Sebastian's journal were published in Israel—excerpts chosen in part to embarrass Eliade by revealing his "Legionary past" and including a passage about how Eliade seemingly had snubbed his friend when he visited Bucharest briefly in July 1942. When the selections from Sebastian's journal appeared, a close colleague of Eliade in the history of religions, Professor Gershom Scholem of Jerusalem, wrote asking for an explanation. Eliade answered point by point the incriminating passages from Sebastian's journal, saying, among other things, that in 1942 he had had a "long interview with Salazar." Concerning it, he said, ". . . I still cannot give details—but [they] will be read in my *Journal*."[7] Here, Eliade seems to promise that he intends to publish "The Portugal Journal" soon, since Scholem was then seventy-four. But Professor Scholem died in 1982, and Eliade himself died four years later (22 April 1986) without having made any preparation for bringing out that journal. He had, however, in the meantime, written the second volume of his memoirs, chapter 18 of which is devoted to his time in Lisbon.[8]

Why did Eliade not publish at least selections from "The Portugal Journal," as he did from the journal notebooks of other years? The most likely answer is that it contains too much material that he would have found embarrassing to see in print. On the one hand, there were personal things: his outpourings of grief after Nina's death, his recurrent attacks of "neurasthenia" and melancholy, expressions of personal religious sentiments and belief—subjects he always refused to discuss in later years—revelations about his sexual problems, disclosures of personal secrets. On the other hand, there were "exposés" relative to his "past" that would have been difficult for him to explain, after having endeavored to keep them secret all these years: the extent of his relationship with the Iron Guard and his hopes for a victory of the Axis (born of his terror of what a

Allied victory would mean for his country: its inevitable engulfment by the Soviet Union). Had he been making selections for a "Portugal Journal" that he could have published, all the above things would have had to be set aside. In addition, there are a number of journal entries in which Eliade makes statements that readers might consider expressions of hubris—statements he surely would have modified or deleted entirely before publication. What would have remained would have been essentially the sorts of things found in chapter 18 of the *Autobiography*—which was written, obviously, with the journal in hand. Here, routine biographical and historical events are recorded, meetings with important persons duly noted, and references made to books planned and/or published. This remnant, although longer than the chapter in the autobiography, would not have been enough to merit issuing as a book.

In fact, he *did* publish a few "fragments" from his journal of the Portugal period (and from a special journal) for his fellow exiles in a mimeographed periodical with a very limited circulation, *Caiete de dor* (Paris), nos. 5 and 8 (1954–55). Mircea Handoca also included them in his edition of Eliade's *Journal* (*Jurnalul*, vol. I, Bucharest: Humanitas, 1993), 10–18. These have been incorporated in this volume where appropriate, as indicated in the notes.

The value of this text cannot be overstated. It is the most important journal volume for the reasons stated above, and others. The biographer will find it the most reliable source of facts for these years of Eliade's life. The literary historian will prize it for the information it provides on the background of the books Eliade published during the war, especially *Salazar*, plus several older ones he reread for new editions. For historians of religions, most precious is what this journal reveals about the inception of his two major works in the field, *Patterns in Comparative Religion* and *Cosmos and History*, and the importance he assigned to them. But for anyone who wants to gain insight into the enigmatic and multifaceted personality of Mircea Eliade, this "Portugal Journal" will be a treasure.

In addition to the journal proper, four "appendices"—documents by Eliade having an autobiographical character from the "Portugal era"—have been included in this volume. The "Journal of the Novel *Viață Nouă* [New Life]" began to be written in Oxford, England, while Eliade was still serving as press secretary there, but the majority of the material was written in Lisbon. This little diary records the inception not only of a novel that was never finished, but also of the volume that became *Patterns in Comparative Religion*. I have grouped some travel notes from Eliade's first months in his new post under the title "First Impressions of Portugal." Two communiqués of a rather personal nature that he telegraphed to Bucharest are found in appendix B. I have included, finally, the preface Eliade wrote for his controversial volume praising Salazar, the Portuguese dictator; it reveals much about its author and explains why he composed the volume.

If all the material Eliade wrote while he was living in Portugal were collected, two more volumes this size would not suffice. But I have chosen to add to the journal only those "extras" that seemed the most autobiographical. The notes are by myself, unless otherwise stated.

PART I

The Portugal Journal

The Journal, 1941

Lisbon, 21 April

I've been at Lisbon since 10 February. And it's been months since I've written anything, even intelligent letters. My private journal I interrupted when I left Romania—19 April 1940.[1] It would have been useless to write my impressions. I knew I wouldn't have been able to leave England with a single page of manuscript. Then, too, I was afraid of a search. If I'd kept the journal regularly and honestly, I'd have had to recall many important conversations with English political persons and many confidences, on which, if they were betrayed, a man's freedom or perhaps even his head could have depended. I keep trying all the while to refresh my memory on dates, in order to be able someday to write my memoirs of England.

I begin this notebook today for an entirely different reason. Nina[2] left for Bucharest a few days ago. For four or five weeks, I'm sure. The suspension of any responsible work for so many months, the pressure of politics under which I live, the mental sloth, the abandonment of my manuscripts and notes in Oxford, the intellectual poverty of Lisbon—all these threaten me with slow deterioration. I need to find myself again, to collect myself.

28 April

Great popular demonstration in honor of Salazar.[3] With difficulty, I make my way, an hour and a half before the appointed time, into Praça de Comercio. I have a seat on the balcony of the Ministry of Finance, on the third floor. An ocean of heads in the plaza. Enormous numbers of children and young people. For several hours, all sorts of cannons have been firing continuously, from the land and from the river. I give a start—remembering London.

At 6:00 Salazar appears. The whole living mass at his feet roars. With difficulty, leaning far out over the banister, I can make out his profile. He is wearing a simple, gray afternoon suit, and he smiles, saluting with his hand, deliberately, without gestures. When he appeared, baskets of rose petals, red and yellow, began to be poured out from above. I noticed later, when a young man was speaking from a platform in the middle of the square, that Salazar was playing pensively with a few petals still left on the banister. I watched him, then, as he spoke. He read, warmly enough but without emphasis, lifting his eyes from the page at intervals and looking at the throng. He raised his left hand weakly, thoughtfully. A voice never strident. And at the conclusion of the speech, when those below were applauding, he inclined his head, smiling. Seemingly, he failed to be aware of the overwhelming, collective might at his feet. In any event, he was not their prisoner; the thought didn't even occur to him.

30 April

The solemnity of the presentation of the letters of accreditation of the new minister, Iuraşcu. The first I've attended. The agony of dressing in tails and the shirt with the stiff front, which I had bought that fatal morning (cf. the letter sent to Nina with details about the route taken from Aviz to the Presidential Palace). Accompanied by motorized units. I was in the first car, with Antohi[4] and Norton from Protocol. Amused at being the only one with no military decorations—other than Salazar, of course, who accepts every kind of decoration but wears none. The scene at the Palace: old General Carmona, the providential president—who, instead of having Salazar shot, according to the Romanian custom, made him the dictator of Portugal—listened resignedly to the letter of Iuraşcu, nodding his head slowly every time he heard the word "Latinity." Salazar, standing beside him in a frock coat, seemed exceptionally modest, as if he were one of the President's secretaries. He listened without any apparent tension, without emphasizing his presence. I had the impression that he was more interested in the expression on Iuraşcu's face. I could see his eyes clearly now. They don't sparkle, nor do they pierce or intimidate you—but they pass through you without hostility. I'm sorry I didn't hear him speak. The minister presented us to Carmona. About me he said, "One of our talented writers." I believe the old gentleman doesn't hear well. He kept saying, "Merci, merci."

6 May

Today my manuscripts and note slips came from London. Vardala[5] telegraphed from here to the counselor at the Swedish Legation, and after almost four weeks the package has arrived.

My joy on opening it, finding the notes and manuscripts I'd given up hope of having in my hands again before the end of the war! A few German pamphlets have disappeared. I reread the five or six journal pages, the only ones I wrote, all having to do with *Viață Nouă*.[6] Oxford, with all its tragedy and beauty, I sense anew. And I sense again my sickness, depression, hopes, plans—the whole pathetic life I led from 8 September till 24 January. Now I don't know which work to take up first: the novel or *Introducerea în istoria religiilor*.[7]

7 May

Tonight I reread the seventy-five pages of the novel. In general, I found it good. Minor corrections in both chapters and some polishing of the text.

15 May

I dine this evening at the residence of Georges Oulmont, the French refugee writer whom I met at the Circulo Eça de Queiroz and whom I invited to our place for a meal some two weeks ago. He had told me he was living in a single room, very modestly, as a refugee, in a building of the Patriarchate—but I never imagined I'd find such sad misery. The only thing of beauty: the balcony, which overlooks the Tagus. A small room reached by passing through an auditorium in which every evening religious lectures are held, followed by stupid and porno-graphic chattering among the boys. (I myself could hear, without trying to listen, the inevitable lecturer raising his voice.) A bed and a sofa, a worktable with only a single plate on which I was served some stewed peas, then a slice of ham and salad, then a little cheese. A few cherries, a sweet, and a cup of coffee. It was not this, however, that was depressing, but the iron tableware, the dirty glasses (no two alike), the previously opened bottle of wine, the dried bread from a tin box, the tiny kerosene stove on which he heated the peas and made the coffee. And the rest of the room: the bed with the pajamas on it, the suitcase with the boots on top, the sofa where Mme Oulmont was lying that undoubtedly had bedbugs, because she got up scratching her arm, which looked suspiciously red, lit the lamp, and put the arm under the pump. In the room also were a clothespress, a washbasin, and a few shelves with books. Mme Oulmont fled France with a fur piece around her neck and a dog on her lap. He with the clothing he had on his back and his manuscripts. He tells me that he owns two houses in France, has a library of 6,000 volumes, silverware, paintings. Now he leads the life of a refugee. And yet we spoke only of nonmaterial things. He is depressed, however, by what is happening in France.[8]

29 May

How sad to discover that all men of culture and nearly all writers appropriate in their work the philosophy in fashion at the time in which they live, even in its most sterile and vulgar aspects! Eça de Queiroz[9] and all of his generation—Oliveira Martius, Theophilo Braza, etc.—were atheists, positivists, socialists, and the like. Eça's novels carry this inert theoretical mass of philosophy then in vogue. Pio Baroja writes that he professes materialism because "it is the doctrine most produc-tive for science." Examples can be multiplied. With great delight, all these men introduce defunct theoretical elements into their work. In fact, since science has been popularized, it has begun to be fashionable in the arts to borrow from the universe of contemporary savants or, even worse, the simple unverified conclusions of certain premises and methods valid (validated) for the generation—as was the case with positivism, materialism, physiologized medicine, etc.

How singular Goethe seems, who waged war against the science of his age! Or Dostoyevsky, or even Tolstoy who dared to rediscover the Gospels in the midst of positivism!

(Note at the time of transcribing, 4 August: a few days ago, while working on a chapter of *Viață Nouă* that is going hard, I copied a part of the above into the journal of David Dragu.)

4 June

Not until today did I realize that I could write anything so unsuccessful, so lacking in vigor, content, and zest as those eighty or ninety large pages of *Ştefania*! I remember that I had tried several times before to reread the manuscript, without succeeding. From the first pages I renounced it, depressed. Other than the chapters published in *Universul literar*,[10] there's almost nothing salvageable: not even episodes, "subjects," that could be melted down and recast. I wonder how I could have persisted for two months in such a sterile work. I wonder especially how I could have written so badly. Where was my fertile imagination, where my lively dialogues, where the intelligence of my characters? Everything in this book is dull, uninteresting, lamentable. I congratulate myself for having abandoned it definitively.

For *Viață Nouă* I'm forced to rewrite everything pertaining to Ştefania and Petru.

10 June

Magnificent outing with Aron Cotruş[11] to Arrábida and Letubal. This is the third time I've seen the Cornice of Arrábida and The Forest of the Solitary. A series of little notes, scattered through pockets and notebooks, waiting to be written up. I bought a special leather-bound notebook for keeping such notes, but I can't always carry it with me. Nor have I transcribed any of the trips to Porto, Coimbra, or Évora. I believe I still have somewhere the notes from Sintra. I ought to start writing them up, because later they'll lose their freshness.

13 June

Today I reread *Nuntă în Cer* [Marriage in Heaven][12] for a new edition. The first part moved me to tears. Never have I written anything more perfect, more moving, and more sincere. Too bad that the second, especially toward the end, falls well below that level. Otherwise, it would be the most beautiful novel of love in the Romanian language.

Two weeks ago, right after I returned from Madrid, I reread *Întoarcerea din rai* [The Return from Paradise] and *Huliganii* [The Hooligans].[13] I began the reading with anxiety lest perhaps these two books, which will find their fulfillment in *Viață Nouă*, would seem lamentable to me. But how interesting, how amazing they were to read again! Never have I had more clearly the sentiment that I am a great writer and that my novels will be the only things read, out of my whole production of 1925–40, a hundred years from now. So strongly did this sentiment take hold on me, so completely am I now convinced of my literary genius, that I sometimes wonder if this "discovery" might not mean the beginning of old age, if my power of creation might not be exhausted.

20 June

From the homeland I receive copies of *Ion* and *Întunecare*.[14] I'd requested them in order to refresh my memory, after an absence in time and space, from the Romanian novel. I began with *Întunecare*. I confess here that I'd never read more than three-fourths of volume I, as much as appeared in the first volume of the Editura Universul edition of 1927. About this portion I wrote a rather equivocal review in *Cuvântul* [The Word]. (I remember Pamfil Șeicaru's[15] fury: "You've practically condemned it!") But, actually, I had a rather good opinion of it, incomparably better than I had of the later novels. Mihail Sebastian never tired of teasing me about my excessive tolerance for *Întunecare*. Now that I've read both volumes, I understand him and see that he was right.

Several times while reading, I said to myself with sadness: Is this all we could give ourselves concerning the era 1916–26? I couldn't believe that this was the "fresco of national life" that so many reviewers and literary critics lauded. I console myself by saying that no generation can extol its own accomplishments, that no great historical event has been reflected in its true proportions by contemporary artists.

There are, nevertheless, certain good passages: the beginning of volume I, the description of the declaration of war, the retreat. Then, in volume II: scenes at the front, Comșa's visit to his natal village and his sister's sergeant, fragments from the electoral campaign. All that refers to "psychology" and "sociology" is false, strident, unconvincing. The theoretical dialogues are mediocre in the extreme. And it is incontestable that Cezar Petrescu has talent. What a splendid theme for a novel he had in hand, the way it began! . . .

22 June

I was on the Guineho Beach when Nina brought me the news of our entrance into the war against Soviet Russia. At first we heard only about our country and Finland, and we were afraid; we believed the Germans would help us, but not openly. Then we learned the truth, that the Reich is indeed fighting, and we are only a part of the German right flank.

I admit that I wasn't expecting this war in 1941. I believed that the so-called Russo-German collaboration would last longer. This means that the Germans have realized they can't win the war this year, and they're preparing for a long fight. In my opinion, the attack is a sign of weakness on Germany's part. Because, if they had been certain they could crush England this year, there would have been no need for them to attack Russia; the Soviets, after the final German victory, would have done everything Hitler would have asked. Before reading Churchill's speech and seeing what the Americans said, I had hoped (very faintly, it's true) that perhaps on the back of Russia it would be possible to make a compromised peace. But I see that my imperialist at London is howling that the Russians are fighting for freedom and they must be helped to resist the Hitlerite invasion. Once again, how ridiculous the ethics of this British war seems to me! You don't say anything when the Soviets take Bessarabia, the Baltic lands, half of Poland, part of Finland—you howl for the Danzig Corridor, and now you help Stalin in the name of democracy, liberty, and Christianity . . .

30 June

I finish reading the second volume of *Ion* with the greatest emotion. What an amazing book! I can imagine the surprise, the perplexity that Rebreanu's contemporaries felt when, in 1921, this masterpiece appeared, so very different from and surpassing all that had been published up to that time. The only "live" peasant in our literature and, undoubtedly, one of the very few authentic peasants in world literature.

There is an enormous number of actions, events, and people in this relatively concise novel (fewer than 800 pages). A book in which "time" intervenes without any artifice; you sense how it flows, how it consummates or releases.

✳

Yesterday, the first German communiqués from the Russian front, which calm me somewhat. My furious love of country, my incandescent nationalism, overwhelms me. I can't do anything since Romania entered the war. Can't write. Have abandoned the novel again. But, à propos the novel: I mustn't forget that time totalizes, it fuses extremes. This is the great lesson of my novel: that man cannot be perfected if he does not "totalize" all his extremes, if he does not succeed in loving his enemies, if he does not transcend his political positions, not through an Indian asceticism or through a skeptical-Olympian placidity—but through the living of the Christian message: "Love your neighbors." The great lesson of "time." . . .

20 July

I'd begun working on the novel and had written with some facility the Ştefania-Nadina-Barbu episode, when Pamfil Şeicaru arrived on an official mission and stayed eight days. I wasn't able to write another line. Everything was suspended: novel, intelligence, sensibility. From the time I met him at the station, a terrible sadness and spiritual drought overwhelmed me. Pamfil Şeicaru on an official mission! Our Pamfil—in audience with the Patriarch, with Salazar and Carmona—then with Franco, with Petain . . . I've reconciled myself to the new Romania of the General[16] and Ică Antonescu[17] (what a horrible resemblance to Armand! . . .)[18] because we are engaged in a terrible war—but the stormy and tragicomic appearance of Pamfil has gotten me down. All the massacres, all the prison camps, all the humiliations, all the rebellions, all the purifications, all the liberal programs—only to end up again with Pamfil Şeicaru, our eternal Pamfil, who has terrorized all our kings and all our governments, but always lands on his feet. Corneliu Codreanu dead, Iorga[19] dead; dead are Nae Ionescu,[20] Armand, I. G. Duca,[21] Moruzov[22]—dead all the Legionary leaders and all the executioners of Legionaries—while Pamfil is alive, dynamic, patriotic. Today, in the gravest hour of our history—because our very existence as a state is at risk—Pamfil Şeicaru is sent on an official mission. He tells me that he was offered the position of Minister of Propaganda, but he refused, because "all things in their time," and now it's beginning to be too late.

He abuses the Legionaries horribly. He abuses Nae, but in the face of my reserve and the superficial defense I make of him, he forgets what he has said and begins to praise him. He pretends to have great love for me. He promises me I don't know how many university chairs! Probably he likes my candor, my embarrassment at seeing myself praised so mightily by him. I pretend to be astonished: a poor man of books, in love with poetry and nature, who has no idea what life is ("Life, man, it's wine, women, music—the good life!"). I do all these things with an immense disgust for myself, for him, for the country, for everything. Nae died on account of the prison camp—while I'm forced today to escort Pamfil to Salazar, to introduce him to directors of newspapers, to writers, etc. And he talks, always, in a loud, firm voice, in a picturesquely incorrect French. António Eça de Queiroz[23] smiles, listening to him . . .

Of course, it's not Pamfil's fault if the government didn't send someone else. But he is to blame for speaking as he does about Romania. I persisted in publishing as much news and as many communiqués as possible about his visit to Portugal. I arranged for him to make statements for the press. Anything that can serve us is good. I defended him before the many Portuguese who met him and belittled him. But never will I be able to forget the torture of having to sit beside him in the car all the way to Coimbra, of sensing him nearby at Alcobaça, Batalha, and Busaco . . .

4 August

An enormous amount of time lost with the stupid "press and propaganda" work. It's true, I've managed, in five months, to write much about Romania in the newspapers. But what importance can all these have? Ephemera of no consequence. The translation of Eminescu and of Camões[24] would do more for the reciprocal knowledge of our countries than all the telegrams of press agencies.

But this, of course, no one can understand.

In the past weeks I've worked very little on the novel. I find no time. (See the notes in the journal devoted to the novel.)

5 August
    Together with the Iuraşcu family, we are invited to lunch with Senhora Ferro—Fernanda da Castro[25]—at her little *quinta* [farm] at Marimba. The three brothers, owners of a pine forest on the edge of the ocean, over thirty hectares in size, had the intelligent idea of erecting some twenty villas ("fishing cottages"), which they rent. Everyone does as he pleases there. There are no fences, no walls; one has the feeling of ownership. I spent considerable time outdoors, under the pines. The wind that began blowing several days ago in Cascais is not felt here.—Then, with the two Ferro boys, Giza,[26] and another girl, we went to play tennis. I notice how quickly I become absorbed in sports, games. Absolutely everything fascinates me.

12 August
    Tuesday evenings there is always a "whisky party" at Bolasco's. He's the new Italian press attaché who has a fine house in Mont-Estoril. I go regularly and meet interesting people. Then too, my current profession is chasing down news. . . . Almost the entire Italian Legation goes there. I've become friends with the son of Giovanni Gentile, second secretary of the Legation. His name is Bena-detto and he was born at the time of the friendship of Gentile and Croce.
    It was concerning him, in fact, that I began this note. He gives me a multitude of particulars about the life of Croce and the Croce-Gentile friend-ship. The most significant: Croce had a lady friend some 30 to 40 years ago, a beautiful woman, vivacious, who lived in his house—she too was a Neapolitan whom everyone called "Donna Angelina." Not even the Gentile family knew her surname, and when it was necessary for them to introduce her to friends, they would say simply "Donna Angelina." Croce was happy, he loved her; this woman renewed his life. When she died in 1910, Croce was utterly crushed for some time. A few years later, however, he married his present wife, a rigid, severe woman, a true bas-bleu. His new companion changed his life completely. Croce grew cool and withdrew from his former friends. In time, he became impassive, short-tempered, attacking everyone, disliking everything, finding fault with everybody. This is his post–First World War oeuvre.
    In this way Benedetto explains the cooling of the friendship between his father and Croce, as well as Croce's imperviousness to Fascism, in which, nevertheless, many of his own ideas could be found (antihistorical materialism, for example; antipositivism, etc.).

September
    The European political moment of 1930–40 helped a great deal to bring different kinds of people closer together as to mental structures—people who until then had been in conflict or impervious to one another. I think, for example, of Jacques Maritain, who, owing to the fact that his wife was Jewish

and that he had taken a certain attitude toward Communism and the Civil War in Spain, was forced, in later years, to mitigate certain of his hostilities (Bergson, Lévi-Bruhl, Gide). Likewise, I think of Gide, who, through his conversion to Communism, drew close to a group of Catholics toward whom he had always been reserved: Maritain, Mauriac, Benjamin, etc.

Today I see Portuguese Catholics taking up the defense of Communism, only because Hitler is fighting in Russia.

3 September

My notes on Portugal I have collected in another notebook. Now I'm sorry, because this journal has lost perhaps its most interesting part. But I wanted to make a book of my fragmentary observations, and at the same time I didn't want to have the sentiment that I was publishing parts of my journal.

The great enjoyment I'm having from swimming. I can go now, without effort, for 400 to 500 meters. Only one annoyance: I get cold quickly

15 September

This afternoon—reading, daydreaming, shaving—I had the idea for a long play in Romanian: *Tinerețe fără bătranețe* [Youth without Old Age].[27] Since, on account of illness, I interrupted work on *Viață Nouă* a week ago, I hope to begin writing it soon.

27 September

Sick for the past several weeks. My eternal autumn "cold," which coincides so suspiciously with the fever I had at Ciuc . . .

I've broken off work on the novel. Instead, when the fever isn't too bad, I've been reading Portuguese literature, Eça and Camões in particular. Several books are beginning to take shape in my mind, alongside the shelf of books long dreamed of, which God only knows if I'll ever have time to write. But one of them captivates me: a life of Camões, written freely, in which I can say all that I think about the ocean, colonies, India, Manuelin style, Goa, lyric poetry, destiny, Lusitanism, etc. A book without erudition, without notes, with many chapters and many subheadings: somewhat on the order of the biographies of Eugenio d'Ors,[28] whose technique I understand now. D'Ors does not have time to write in detail all he knows and thinks, so he creates a biographical sketch.

28 September

Reading today in *Os Maias* (vol. I, p. 143) about the plan of Ega's pretentious book, *Memoirs of an Atom*, I'm amazed to realize how much it resembles "Memoirs of a Lead Soldier" that I wrote in the fourth class of lycée and left unfinished—the manuscripts of which (some three notebooks) Radu Capriel took in 1928. Everything is identical, even up to the presence of the "author" (my lead) at the Crucifixion, the French Revolution, etc. I wrote these things when I was fourteen. Ega conceived it as a student at Coimbra (Ega is a character in *The Maia Family*; don't confuse him with the author of the novel, Eça de Queiroz). But it is curious that we are both situated in the same mental climate: positivism, prophetic scientism, etc.

29 September

Raining for many days. I can't get well in this adorable house, now a famous center for dampness and rheumatism.

Anyway, it seems a good idea for me leave Cascais now, in the midst of the rainy autumn. At Lisbon I won't be melancholy.

Lisbon, 9 October

Today I meet Reinaldo dos Santos. He receives me at the Museum of Modern Art, of which he is the director. I had heard of him long ago: the best surgeon in Portugal and an eminent art historian, a revolutionary in doctrines of the plastic arts. Among others, Eugenio d'Ors had spoken to me about him in Madrid; when I asked him to what extent a man of the Leibniz or da Vinci type is still possible, he gave me Reinaldo as an example.

The interview, set for a quarter of an hour, lasted almost two hours. We spoke especially about art and "maritime philosophy." I described to him my book about Camões. But I came around, as usual, to India, to the history of science, to symbolism and metaphysics.

I left the museum reinvigorated and yet feeling a little melancholic. Because, among other things, Santos asked me for clarifications about certain things in the history of the arts: for example, he had not heard of Saxl and Panofski, the Warburg Institute, etc. It was strange to see a great specialist taking notes from a layman. Back at home, I said to myself: What an extraordinary man I am! Into how many fields have I ventured—fields no one suspects because I've never written about them, considering myself a complete layman. And all these treasures, all my personal interpretations, risk being lost at any moment because I continue to waste time on trifles, and the best hours are no longer mine. How ridiculous they seemed to me then—the bulletin for the press that I draft weekly, the pasteups I do for the newspapers, etc. And my friend Leontin Constantinescu,[29] who at the office never forgets that he is "head of the press service," presents the bulletins with the following formula: "Composed by M. Eliade of the Press Service." The contrast between what I could be doing and what I have to do is tragicomic. Reinaldo do Santos, for example, proposed that I write a Romanian philosophy of history for the series in which he is writing on Portugal, Marañou on Spain, and the son of Charles Richet on France.

I've realized another thing: if I'd been living abroad, in the position I hold today, for five or six years, I'd have become a European writer. Even my books of essays and philosophy of religions would be known abroad today.

4 November

I recall that last year, about this time, I began the novel at Oxford. And with what enthusiasm, with what certainty that I'd finish it in a few years! And, lo, I've written only 222 pages. My illness, the tragedies in the homeland, the quarantine of the manuscript at the censor's (for three months), the annoyances of last summer, and finally the new illness (at Cascais) followed by the indisposition with which I've been struggling ever since I moved into this admirable third-floor flat on Avienda Elias Garcias 147—have contributed to the minimalizing, the "stunting" of the effort of creation. The work keeps growing in size in my mind, but the redaction is retarded, anemic.

Now I'm up to my neck in Camões—whose lyrical works I'm rereading, guided by the best commentaries and critical studies. I'd like to write a book about Camões' century: the maritime discoveries, Coimbra, the Portuguese "Renaissance," Infanta Dona Maria, the ocean, Goa, and Garcia do Orto—all of them centers for a philosophy of culture that I've not yet had the chance to formulate! This means, however, that the novel will be postponed once again.

Actually, since I was released from camp three years ago, I've produced almost nothing of consequence: *Secretul doctorului Honigberger* [Dr. Honigberger's Secret (a novella)], *Mitul reintegrării* [The Myth of Reintegration (history of religions)], *Ifigenia* [Iphigenia (a play)], a few studies, and the beginning of *Viață Nouă*. Three years of my maturity!

Since then, I make a great many books in my head, but I don't even take the trouble to start writing them. I began, long ago, *La Mandragore* [The Mandrake (folklore)] and *Introducerea în istoria religiilor*. I was ready to start *Comentarii la Legenda Meșterului Manole* [Comments on the Legend of Master Manole (folklore)], *Anthropocosmos* [The Cosmic Man (history of religions)], *Muntele magic* [The Magic Mountain (essays)]—and I postponed them, along with other, smaller works. Once I collected a large amount of material for *Prolegomena to the Study of Indian Religion* [in English] and I wanted to make a second, more courageous edition of *Yoga*. Here I've begun a book of impressions of Portugal—and I'm collecting material for a volume about Salazar and a large study about Eça de Queiroz. In addition, I've started writing several articles for Acção that I'd gladly publish in booklet form, in Portuguese.

This whole ocean of projects proves that I'm close to losing my profession.

7 November

An amusing, but nonetheless true story of the revolution of General Gomez da Costa of Braja, which opened the way to Carmona and, later, to Salazar—told last evening by Manuel Múrias and Correia Marquez, not only eyewitnesses but also the authors responsible for the success of that revolution!

It's a shame I can't use it in my book about Salazar, because, as is known, the official history gives a totally different version of the coup d'état of 28 May

1926. According to this version, the whole country was behind it from the first day, and the army passed over to the side of Gomez immediately. When I have time—or maybe in my Memoirs—I'll relate in full how things happened.

8 November

I'm going very slowly with the writing of the notes taken on trips.

Am reading an enormous amount about the monarchy and the republic, gathering material for the Salazar book. Last week alone I read some 600 pages of history and memoirs, besides Ferro's volume, which I reread, plus the five speeches of Salazar that I studied.

9 November

It's regrettable, both for me and for my country's culture, that the major ideas that have preoccupied me for many years, and which are not so chaotic in my mind as they seem at first glance, do not play an active role in my literary works.

10 November

A man I resemble very much: Menéndez y Pelayo.[30] Have just finished reading his *Historia de las ideas estéticas en España*, which I did not know. (I discovered Menéndez in Rome in 1928 when I was preparing my licentiate thesis at the V. Emanuel Library, and I read—learning Spanish at the same time—his *Historia de los heterodoxos* and *La Ciéncia Española*, along with two volumes of *Estudios* about Lope de Vega—and I believe that I was the first Romanian to have written something substantial, albeit emotional, about him: a column in *Cuvântul*, full of typographical errors.)[31] Like Menéndez, I have an immense thirst for knowledge. Like him, I have a passion for works that are broad and erudite, yet possess also an ample philosophical vision. Negatively, I have his whole, immense philological and bibliological learning. Positively, the talent of a narrative writer, and a philosophical originality. Likewise, I believe I've surpassed him in curiosity.

19 November

I'm in a period of enormous intellectual effort and yet one of mediocre creation. Have begun the foreword to the book on Salazar.[32] I've managed to write only a few pages, and in order to do so I've read twelve hours a day for the past two weeks. Again, the mania to know ten times as much as I need, in order to write a page.

28 November

I work hard and long on the book, *Salazar și contra-revoluția în Portugalia* [Salazar and the Counter-revolution in Portugal]. In addition to all the written information, I am using unpublished data obtained from Murias, Silva Dios, Correia Marquez, and others.

29 November

It's going hard, but the work must go on. Incredible effort—for me, who wrote so easily—just to finish a page or two per day. I wonder if my powers of creation aren't drained from so many abuses, and especially from the neurasthenia that has been hampering me for several months now. Then, there's something else: the leaving of Minister Iuraşcu is the occasion of endless luncheons, banquets, teas—in which I participate. I myself am "organizing" two massive meetings, for tomorrow and 2 December—ministers, etc. All these things exhaust me.

10 December

Among other things that annoy me in connection with this journal is the fact that I'm writing it on notebook pages, and since I'm forced to hide it, I try never to write more than a page, but not less, so I can take out that page and put it into its proper folder. (What a horrible sentence!)

11 December

My capacity for understanding and feeling culture, in all its forms, is unlimited. If only I were able to express even a hundredth part of all I think and know differently from the way others know it! I don't believe I've ever met a genius of such complexity—in any case, my intellectual horizons are broader than those of Goethe. I realize, for example, that I could write, easily, a book about Portuguese poetry of the nineteenth century. I'm not a scholar, or not only a scholar. Undoubtedly, there are others who know better than I the history of nineteenth-century Portuguese poetry. But I'm sure that I understand it and feel it more profoundly, more originally, more systematically.

14 December

Working rather poorly on the first part of the Salazar book. Have written approximately 60 pages, printed. I'm afraid to make an accounting of the year's activity.

17 December

Since America's entrance into the war, the atmosphere here has changed; the Portuguese are nervous, fearful, suspicious, etc. The Japanese naval victories have alarmed them. I was in a tobacco shop when I heard about the sinking of the *Prince of Wales* and the *Repulse*. Two citizens I overheard talking:

"If it goes on like this, with two battleships a day, we'll be . . . in for it!"

For several days—rumors started by the English: the Japanese have entered Macao, the Germans will occupy Portugal, etc. Today, they're talking about Timor, without saying anything specific.

✳

I almost never write in my "true" moments. That's why neither in the journal nor in my books is there reflected anything more than a neutralized part of my being—the balanced or compromised part, which comes from my refusing to take knowledge of myself, of reality.

18 December

The Dutch and the Australians have entered Timor.[33] Tomorrow Salazar is expected to address the National Assembly. People are in a paralyzing panic.

What a formidable game the English are playing! All these unfortunates believe that the Germans are to blame, that Hitler is the author of their colonial catastrophe.

I learn some interesting particulars, which I communicate to Totescu; then I send two telegrams in code. Young Totescu, chargé d'affaires, is terribly proud of his role in such a grave moment.

27 December

My old mania: I've scarcely begun the Salazar book and my mind flees to the history of religions! I'd like to live long enough to write *Mitologia morții* [The Mythology of Death] in several volumes. I read a great deal. Unfortunately, I don't record my thoughts any longer. Self-disgust.

2

The Journal, 1942

3 January
The writing of the book about the Portuguese counterrevolution is going rather hard.

I think how amusing it would be to compile someday an annotated catalog of my unpublished writings and a history of all my manuscripts.

11 January
A cold that has kept me indoors for several days has allowed me to write some fifteen compact pages. I'm up to the consulship of Sidonio Paes. But how many important, tragic, or merely amusing things I've had to leave out, in order not to spoil the general economy of the book! I realize now that it was for nothing that I read those thousands of pages of political memoirs from the time of the revolution, since I've related only a few scenes. As usual, the effort made to document is much greater than that employed in the writing of the work. When I'm fully clear about a thing, my only wish is to summarize it as quickly and as briefly as possible, in order to "escape" from it. Always I know much more than my books show.

My plan would be to finish the volume in March, and in April to start on Camões—and by fall to "liquidate" the Portuguese experience. Alternatively, I'd like to return to the novel.

I must do all these things in order to bear the thought that the war will last another eight, ten, twelve years.

12 January
I'm approaching my thirty-fifth birthday. The time for nonsense is past. Soon—an old man. My *oeuvre*—diffused, scattered, abandoned to the hand of a few mediocre critics and modest interpreters of my ideas in the history of religions, the philosophy of culture, and folklore—must find a point of support that will explain it, organize it, deepen it. To tell the truth, I'd need several points of support. They would be: (a) in the art of the novel, *Viață Nouă*; (b) in drama, *Tinerețe fără de bătrânețe*; (c) in morals, *Comentarii la legenda Meșterului*

Manole; (d) in the history and philosophy of religions, *Introducerea în istoria religiilor*; (e) in the philosophy of culture, *Symbole, mythe, culture*; (f) in folklore, *La Mandragore*; (g) in Indian studies, the second, recomposed edition of *Yoga* and *Introducere în istoria religiilor indiene* [An Introduction to the History of Indian Religions]; (h) in essay, *Muntele magic*. To all these are added other works, begun or planned: a synthesis of the origins of the sciences, a mythology of death, a mythic geography, a religious history of the Dacians. The rest—novels, studies, travels, modern dramatic events, politics—are details.

For the realization of at least a few of these works—from (a) to (d)—I'd have to have, at the minimum, five years of uninterrupted labor. But in the Lusitanian climate, it's hard for me to work. And the war, which keeps going on, paralyzes the documentation.

22 January
  You must decide: either [unfinished sentence].

10 February
  It's been a year today since I arrived in Lisbon. As yet, I haven't had time to write my impressions of England. Just some simple notes—and my memory.
  I ask myself what I've done in that year. Until April, walks and meditations. In May, I resumed work on the novel—and went to Spain. In the summer, I worked at the novel and read Eça de Queiroz. In the fall, I read Camões and a great deal of Portuguese literature. In November I began the book on Salazar. Winter—tremendous effort writing it.
  Today I took a brief inventory of the pages of manuscript. In Portugal I've written 75 large pages (equivalent to about 120 pages in book form) about the counterrevolution and Salazar, 140 pages of the novel, 25 pages of the book of impressions of Portugal, 40 pages of private journal, 12 pages of the journal of the novel, 10 pages of "Latina ginta e regina" [The Latin Race Is Queen] (my first article, which appeared a few days ago in *Acção*).[1]
  I've gotten through the worst sicknesses (October–January).
  I've read tremendously. I've suffered tremendously. I've meditated on my philosophical system. I've discovered the formula of the future center of Romanian missionaization that I want to establish.

16 February
  Three days in Algarve, in southern Portugal, to see the almond trees in bloom.
  Praga da Rocha—a place I want to visit again. (Notes in the black notebook.)

19 February

I have met Alfredo Pimenta,[2] the most learned man in Portugal. A splendid library: 20,000 volumes. Deaf. He is like a child. Sensitive, conceited. But he writes splendidly.

We become friends quickly.

22 February

Attacks of nerves return; almost hysterical. The rest of the time—I struggle with neurasthenia. The same things over and over: the lost youth, the banal life that oppresses me, the desire for strident, tragic adventures, such as I knew in 1928, 1930, 1932, etc.

I understand very well, in moments of lucidity, the cause of the attacks. The multiple demons that struggle inside me find their equilibrium only in my work; only in periods of creation are they at rest. Just now I'm writing the book about Salazar. I cannot realize myself totally in it; on the contrary, I try to be impersonal. The result—neurasthenia!

27 March

Yesterday, at António Ferro's, I met Ortega y Gasset.[3] Exciting conversation. Since he's spending some time in Portugal, I hope to form a true friendship with him. He told me about the book—horrible!—that he's writing now.

I read today *Kir Ianulea*. Depressed by the Slavo-Greek aspect of the language. Even worse, Caragiale,[4] by making fun of us, has done us much harm.

My nerves are even more fatigued. Seldom does a day pass without an attack.

Rereading Caragiale's notes on Eminescu, I find myself again, perfectly, in the ambivalence, nervousness, and irritability of the poet. Strange—the coincidence of our initials: M. E.

28 March

Relative to the cardiac attack of a few nights ago, the doctor has advised me to have an electrocardiogram.

I've started smoking denicotinized cigarettes.

The overwhelming mediocrity of Romanian cultural life and journalism. After what I read in the newspapers and magazines received from home, I want to cry.

I'm beginning to feel I'm alone in Romania.

31 March

Few books I've worked on have disgusted and exhausted me to the extent that *Salazar şi contra-revoluţia în Portugalia* has, ever since I began it. First, on account of the enormous effort expended in gathering the information, an effort that very few will be able to discern, since the book will not have notes and will contain only a summary bibliography. Second, because all the while I'm working I have the sentiment that I'm wasting my energy on a book that is not my own. True, I consider it improper to publish in wartime a book that has no relation to the political contingencies of my country. And the history of the Portuguese revolution and counterrevolution is not without interest and, especially, not without usefulness for Romania.

But I write reluctantly. I write badly. I think, among other things, that Ică Antonescu will make a new platform out of this book. The collaboration between Carmona and Salazar will seem to him a model for the collaboration between General Antonescu and himself: a general and a university professor of law, in both cases.

With much more enthusiasm could I write *Camões: Încercare de filozofie a culturii* [Camoes: An Attempt at a Philosophy of Culture].[5] But I've chosen Salazar in order to be of greater service to my country, to have at least the illusion that I'm doing my duty in a time of war. Through this book, the position of Romania in the Portuguese press will be strengthened. This thing seems important to me.

1 May

Nina and Giza left yesterday for Romania. I'm alone, and free, for at least three or four months. I've been looking forward to this interval, to be able to live at the mercy of all my emotional outbursts, to be able to understand myself, to verify whether or not my neurasthenia attacks of the past few months are due to the sentiment of inferiority, the presence of Nina and Giza, or simply disorders of my nervous system. I'm ready for any experience. Just one annoyance: the book about Salazar that I have to finish as soon as possible—and the book about Romania that Ameal[6] has asked me to do.

For the moment, I recollect myself by rereading and correcting *Huliganii* for a new edition.

2 May

Rereading *Huliganii*—what a curious melancholy! I relive the summer of 1935 on blvd. Dinu Golescu, my "drama" of that time, yet also the many regrets that tempt me (my strange love for Nina, the youth that has passed, the value it all has for me now—all that is linked to that heroic time, to that plenary, dramatic life).

If it weren't so late (2:00 a.m.) and I weren't so tired, I might attempt to describe more precisely this state of negative euphoria: the return of a time past that you love and hate at the same time.

3 May

How they gain in substance and significance—things, events, experiences that have been, that have a past. With what lucid delight would I abandon myself to a flight of memories of Cascais of scarcely a year ago, or to those of Oxford!

I'm beginning my third year abroad. I recall a curious thing that happened in India: in a dream, it seemed that I'd returned to the homeland and was on the point of going back to India, and this created a sentiment so troubling and confusing that it made me lose a sense of reality, even in the first minute after waking up. Sometimes it takes me a long while to realize where I am. I believe the same thing will happen in the course of this year too.

5 May

An excess in all the things heretofore forbidden, and I hope my neurasthenia will be cured. I start tonight.

6 May

And yet, no matter how I put the problem, I can't get beyond this one, fundamental fact: that I am mortal, that at any time I could die—thereby playing my card of salvation. The fact is, whatever I believe about the postmortem life, it *does* exist; if I accept the Christian belief and doctrine, then I must attempt to do at least something to save myself, I must at least do penance for some of my deeds. Or, if I accept the occultist (metaphysical) dogma, I still must *do* something, I can't live ad infinitum the way I've been living for the past several years: for readings, sex, writing, and passive contemplation. Both the roads that I know are forbidden to me—by my sloth, my sins, my neurasthenia. And yet not a day passes that I don't, for a moment at least, glimpse reality; and I could die *now*, passing into the great beyond, without any definite technique.

From the profane point of view, my situation as writer and as philosopher is equally sad. While I have access to the loftiest concepts, I've written nothing philosophical. Although I have literary genius, I haven't finished anything yet.

10 May

After a day of spiritual drought spent in pornographic and political conversations with young Romanians in Lisbon, I take from the shelf Nae Ionescu's *Istoria logicii* [History of Logic] and reread the preface signed by Vasile Băncilă.

Once again, Nae's presence. I'm projected into the Romanian world and the world of the spiritual. A sense of humiliation, realizing what an insipid and uncreative life I've been living for some time.

16 May

How strange—the sick pleasure I find in abandoning myself to an infinite melancholy, to a diffuse, musical sadness, nourished by remembrances of my dead youth and the futility of the life I still have left to live! At first, I did everything I could to avoid these attacks of melancholy, so frequent in adolescence and the first years of my youth. Now I abandon myself to them in full lucidity, I encourage them, I nourish them. I like facing up to nothingness and futility. Never more than then do I feel more clearly that everything passes, that everything is in vain. If, nevertheless, I love Nina so much, it's because we experienced the heart of my youth together, and the melancholic recollection of that dead love makes it all the more present, all the more necessary.

Now, at thirty-five, I'm reliving the sadnesses I had between ages sixteen and twenty. I am dying to a certain life.

17 May

I began to live, truly, in 1927, fifteen years ago. Then I was genuinely in love, then I went abroad for the first time—to Italy. In that year I wrote my first book, *Romanul adolescentului miop* (The Novel of the Nearsighted Adolescent). I was twenty years old. I'd become "famous" through *Revista universitară* and my columns in *Cuvântul,* the polemics of the young generation, etc. I was, it was said, the chief of my generation.

✳

My lack of interest for sociology, Marxism, and so forth is owing to the statement often made that these disciplines give you the illusion of having global explanations of history, while in fact they take account of nothing but the human mob. I have no doubt that thousands of inert and ruthless persons behave exclusively on the basis of economics, but by the same token one can say that they behave biologically or physically, as objects subject to the laws of gravity. The elect man—and any man can become elect when he is infused with spirit—moves on another plane. Actually, I learn nothing about the real man by learning economic laws that make him become proletarian or criticize his social institutions. I learn essential things about the real man by following the reaction of the individual vis-à-vis the spirit; man vis-à-vis death, vis-à-vis love: there is an object for research! The elect man, be he Goethe or an ordinary mortal in a sublime moment, has loved ones. Of course, man is integrated in a society and is subject to historical laws. But man likewise is composed of organs and is biological; he is composed of molecules and is physical.

23 May
  Terrible insomnia that began after I stopped work—at 3:00 a.m.—and ended at 6:00 or 7:00 this morning. The Pasiflorina no longer has any effect. I can go to sleep only after taking two or three Adalină pills. I got up at 2:00 p.m., and was hardly good for anything. With enormous effort, I succeeded in writing three large sheets (about eight printed pages) between 6:00 p.m. and 3:00 a.m. I'm finishing *Salazar* with my mental and physical powers in a state of total decrepitude. The days pass as in a dream without my being aware of them. I have no other wish than to finish that book.

24 May
  As usual, in order to break away from my work, I flee backward mentally—to ten years ago, to the summer of 1932, the most beautiful year of my life and of my generation. Afternoons at Floria Căpsali's, volleyball, preparations for "Criterion,"[7] Brezea, the outing to the Bucegi, the army duty at General Staff, Sorana, and so on. There are many things that I no longer remember whether they happened in 1932 or 1933. That era of my life attracts me more than I can say, although 1933 was tragic, a turning point. It's interesting to remark that in 1925–28 I fought terribly against the sick attraction to return to the past—adolescence, first love, Rica, etc.

25 May
  No, this journal will lose its meaning and purpose completely if I continue as I've been doing, writing it on loose sheets of paper. I ought to buy a notebook that I could keep on my work table all the time and carry with me on trips.
  Last night's hurricane reminded me of the cyclone that devastated Portugal a few days after my arrival in February 1941. And I had to write until 3:00 a.m. I took a good dose of Adalină then, and because I couldn't sleep, I read *Adela* by Ibrăileanu[8] in an Italian translation I had at hand. Any concrete contact with the homeland, with Moldavia (as I demonstrated with this detailed book), makes me infinitely melancholic. If I were at home now, on strada Palade, I'd have just one desire: to reread the boxes of letters and notes from lycée and write my memoirs from adolescence. Strange—this bitter pleasure of going back in time, of returning to the past.

28 May
  After two days of complete spiritual drought, of melancholy that advanced to the borders of nihilism—all of a sudden I feel the approach of equilibrium. Last night I lingered at a bar until 4:00. I returned home then on foot; that took almost an hour. The moon set. I thought of the Buddha, who nevertheless found the only natural solution to the problem of emergence from suffering, of escape from duration. The only possibility for man to escape from suffering,

from regrets, from melancholy, from the sentiment of lost opportunities, etc., is by nonattachment. How well I understood these things already in adolescence! What were my struggle against memories and my ascetic techniques from ages fourteen to seventeen but the attempt to live autonomously, without cadavers in my soul, without objects of passion in my existence? All I wrote in *Cuvântul* about "Medelenism"[9] and "Moldavianisms" of any form had a primarily therapeutic aim: to cure myself of the terrible melancholy in which I had spent my adolescence. In India I found again the same impulse to renunciation. How hard it was for me to recover after the loss of Maitreyi! But everything passes, and so passed also that fire in which I believed my whole being would be consumed.

I was thinking, returning home under the moon, that that which is irreversible in my life today—is Nina. The nine to ten years we've lived together can't be forgotten. I can be unfaithful to Nina, but two weeks later I feel that I can't live without her. The attacks of neurasthenia I have when she's near are transformed into attacks of melancholy when she goes away. At dawn, I arrived at the conclusion that there's nothing I can do about it.

But now I feel I'm approaching a state of equilibrium. Even the book about Salazar—which I've never liked—interests me. The Moldavian blood in my veins has grown weary. It's the Wallachian blood's turn to surge.[10]

29–30 May

It's 4:10 a.m. I've finished *Salazar*. Tomorrow I'll get up at 7:00 so I can take the manuscript to Hotel Tivoli, because the Romanians from Rio are leaving at 9:30. I can't believe that finally I'm free.

3 June

The great effort of the night of 29-30 May, together with the effort of the 30th, when I was invited to dinner at the French Institute and had to talk philosophy all the time—drained me. Since then, I've been even more melancholic. A loneliness that threatens to destroy me.

✳

Yesterday I received a telegram from Herescu asking me to catch the first available airplane to Romania, for a lectureship in the philosophy of culture, a new creation of the king. So far, I've hesitated to reply. I wouldn't want to return. Not yet. And for whom would I hold courses? All my colleagues and those younger than I are at the front. I'd go back to the country if I knew that I'd leave then for Russia.

6 June

> 5:30 a.m. The great monotony of debauchery.
> There's nothing else to do now.

8 June

> I receive a long letter from Nina via the diplomatic bag. At last I can find out many interesting things that couldn't be communicated through censored letters. Inter alia, Nina informs me that Sergiu Lecca, who left for Bucharest by plane immediately after her departure, being afraid that I was "plotting" against him—declares that he won't stop until I'm dismissed from my post at Lisbon. This Sergiu Lecca was named head of press services at Lisbon in February. He said he was sent here to make contact with the British, because he knows English. He is equally fluent in German and French. But he's an illiterate. And he is, of course, from the Secret Service. The poor man's almost demented. He's suffering from a persecution complex. Claims I've been working for the Germans. The truth is that the Italian journalists to whom I introduced him knew him well as a Mason, secret agent, spy, and, currently, in the service of the English.[11] I found out later that his wife, Austrian or Swiss and very good-looking, has also been a spy. Now, fortunately for him, she is deceased.
>
> Lecca receives 25,000 escudos per month. He lives in a single room and plays roulette all the time at Estoril.

10 June

> Antohi left today, moved to Rome as economic counselor. Also today the economic commission left for Madrid after spending two months in Lisbon.
>
> Have I written anything here about this famous economic commission? Especially about the engineer Pascal Popescu, its soul and creator, a gangster type—100 percent. A "strong man" who'd sell out the country for a thousand escudos! I'm afraid that my disgust for people—for Romanians, especially—and the melancholic moods that have dominated me for the past several months have kept me from writing anything in this journal other than screams of despair. But now, with the commission's leaving, I can't refrain from noting a few particulars for my amusement later.
>
> One of the most terrible business deals has been carried off in Romania. Each member of the commission—Pascal, the chairman Popescu-Benzina (or Redeventa), Antohi, and, to a lesser extent, Mircea Solacolu, representative of the National Bank—are today worth tens or hundreds of millions. From just one deal—25,000 kgs. of wool that they located in Spain—they gained around six million escudos, simply by virtue of the fact that they sold it at 2.60 escudos per kg. after paying 0.95 for it. This equals, at the real exchange rate, around 200,000,000 lei. The great gangster is Pascal, although the Lisbon market says

that the "wool deal" is the work of Chairman Redeventa (or Benzina). But the funny thing is that all the Portuguese and foreigners know about these deals—everyone but Ambassador Cădere.[12] Whenever someone calls his attention to the matter, he replies that he is "covered" and that he "has faith in Pascal." Moreover, some members of the Legation claim that the deals and thefts don't matter so long as the materials reach Romania. Now, the tragic thing is, no one knows if the goods will ever reach Romania, because Pascal and the others don't know how to transport them. We need the genius of a Bostanian—who makes gigantic deals with the Germans in order to pass many tons surreptitiously into Spain and France.

At one point I was ready to ask to be recalled, to avoid being a witness to the largest deals of the last several weeks (because the wool is just a "snack"; there is also sisal, rubber, wolframite, etc., etc.). But I realized that no one in the homeland would listen to me. I'd risk being arrested—as a Legionary or a terrorist. The commission covered itself well. They have fictitious contracts (with which they procure Swiss francs) and they have receipts from the Portuguese (paid for with millions) by which they can prove that they paid 600 escudos per kilo for the wolframite that they found on the market for 150–80 escudos. In addition, they have real genius. Tomorrow they'll rule Romania.

22 June

I'm writing less and less often in this notebook. Great disgust for the world. Melancholy. And in addition to these things, the troubles with Sergiu Lecca, that curious, demented representative of the Secret Service at the Lisbon Legation.

29 June

I've decided to to go to Romania on 10 July (taking a fifteen-day leave of absence). By plane, through Germany. I don't know why, but I have a deadly foreboding. Maybe it's just fatigue.

1 July

What did I do in the month of June? Almost nothing. My struggle with melancholy and orgy. The love that binds me to Nina—more powerful than any desire for freedom. Meditations for the little book about Romania for which J. Ameal has asked me. Boredom, sterility.

But out of this hell will come the light that will save me. I'd like to be able to write *Tinerețe fără bătrânețe* or at least *Comentarii la Meșterul Manole*, in order to heal myself and find myself again.

3 July

I've decided to leave for the homeland in a few days. I don't know if I ought to be happy or not. I've been away for two years and three months. I'd promised myself not to return unless I was recalled. This time I want to clear up a number of things: my transfer to Rome, the revision of *Mitul reintegrării*, my being named cultural counselor, which will give me a long-desired autonomy, etc. The fifteen-day leave that Minister Alexandru Marcu[13] cabled me in code (why?) resolves all these things. I leave on the direct flight from Lisbon to Berlin. From there, either by plane or train.

7 July

Yesterday evening António Ferro called to inform me that I would be received in audience today by Salazar. It was a warm day, and although I began looking for a taxi at 4:00, I didn't find one until 5:00. I arrived at the São Bento Palace out of breath, with my mouth dry from excitement—not because I was meeting Salazar, but because I was afraid of being late.

I climb the steps with haste. The doorkeeper asks me where I'm going. "Senhor Presidente." He points me to the stairway in the rear. "Two flights up, on the right." This is how one gains entry to the dictator of Portugal! On the third floor I inquire of some senators, who direct me to Salazar's office. I pause two minutes in the outer office and ask for a glass of water, in order to be able to talk. Salazar has not yet finished with a commission of colonial administrators. Then I go in, and he receives me himself at the door, pronouncing my name very precisely.

A modest office with a large wooden desk, bare of papers; to the left of it, a little stand for the telephone. While speaking with me, Salazar moves the telephone slightly from time to time. These are his only gestures.

He is less rigid, seen at close range. When he is listening, he squints slightly and his face brightens, radiating great kindness. There is something candid, fresh, virginal, in this face so finely chiseled and so masculine. His eyes are moist, shadowed, and they seem to be looking at you from a great distance; now and then his gaze glides over you, passing beyond. He has a warm, unique voice, different from the voice I've heard many times on the radio. He speaks rather proper French, with a Portuguese accent, groping sometimes for the right word. But he is by no means embarrassed by the inadequacies of his French conversation.

He listens with interest to what I tell him. He asks me what I have done so far in my life: India, the University of Bucharest, literature, my Portuguese experiences. I speak about the book I've just written, and he seems surprised at how much historical information I possess. He has a great talent as a listener, urging the other by his facial expressions and his gestures to elaborate his thought. When I described my thinking about Camões and the unlimited capacity for assimilation that the Latin genius has—he listened attentively and considered my ideas well-founded, but then he brought the discussion back to the point from which I had digressed.

I asked him several questions to which he responded quite willingly. One of them: the historical moment of the revolution of the Estado Novo was realized immediately after the consummation of the last phase of decomposition of the liberal-democratic structures. (I've written this sentence horribly, but the reader of my Salazar book will know what I mean!) Is it not perhaps true that the New State is an inevitable consequence of that process of decomposition? Or, in other words, could the New State have been realized if the old liberal-democratic structure had not passed into a state of decomposition? Could the revolution, and Salazar, have come about if the Republic had not known all its phases, from the initial enthusiasm to the final anarchy?

Salazar's response: Evil is not creative. The simple fact that a thing disappears does not imply the appearance of another living thing in its place. Of course, the historical moment made possible the revolution, but it did not create it. Democracy has entered the phase of decomposition in other countries (for example, the case of France after its defeat), but because the germs of another social order did not exist, what followed was decay and indifference, not revolution. (I'll write these things from my conversation with Salazar more fully later, which I will publish in a book.)

Salazar asks me if there exists in Romania an *esprit de front* group that alone would be able to save the country after the war, because it would be the only spontaneous, total, suprapolitical organization. The Romanian leaders have a great responsibility, because the loss of this *esprit de front* could be more serious than even the sacrifices of blood that they have made. The case of France after the other war, which did not know how to organize this spirit and allowed it to be scattered among various parties, lost the only possibility of remaking the unity of the country, and the results were seen in 1940.

He believes very strongly in the elite. It isn't necessary that a revolution be understood and supported by the masses. An elite suffices to transform a country. The masses are responsive only to a few constants: national dignity, equilibrium, internal peace, and so on—and if they are respected, the masses will embrace any revolution.

What a great importance the internal economy of a country can have! The savings of the Portuguese, as well as their large fortunes, were all deposited in foreign countries. In the moment of international crisis, seeing that the escudo held up while the pound fell, the Portuguese brought their money back to the homeland. Portugal is the only nation that has profited as a result of the crisis. But it is not possible to say that the "historical moment" did this, because if it were not for the internal equilibrium (obtained with efforts and sacrifices), the savings would not have been returned to the country.

He speaks also about Catholics, about Integralists.

The audience had been set for fifteen minutes, but when the secretary came to inform him that the time was up, Salazar made a gesture with his hand. The secretary came again at thirty minutes; the same gesture. Finally, at fifty-five minutes, I gave signs of impatience and made as if to rise several times. Salazar stood up somewhat abruptly, wished me a safe trip, and shook my hand calmly.

Outside, in the waiting room, I found Castérau, exasperated: his appointment had been for 5:30.

Bucharest, July

I arrive Monday, 13 July, after a two-day stopover in Berlin. The Berlin visit depresses me. Everyone at the Legation with whom I speak is pessimistic and Anglophile. The conquest of Voronezh[14] is not taken into account. Someone tells me that the day Tobruk[15] fell, our whole Legation in Berlin had headaches and asked the servants for aspirin . . . After five years I find Berlin sadder. Not many people on the streets, and all appear to be "preoccupied." I see and I spend almost all my time with the young men of the press service. Amzăr[16] tells me to watch my step in the homeland, because the Secret Service detained him for six weeks before giving him an exit visa. More serious than this, the courier Voinea, with whom I shared a room at Eden, tells me that it is a disgrace what is happening at home: on the Secret Services, mainly for tracking down Legionaries, almost a billion is spent per year . . .

At Budapest, Vardala comes to see me at the station. I learn from him that Nina, caught in the rush of Hungarians at the baggage area, missed the train, and Giza traveled alone, without visa and passport, all the way to Bucharest.

✳

July, Bucharest

Hardly arrived, I am summoned into audience with Mihail Antonescu. It is only twenty-four hours since I set foot on the platform at North Station. I owe this exceptional "chance" to Micky Boceanu, who, after meeting me at the station and coming to strada Palade 43 for a cup of coffee, went to the preşdinţie to inform Ică of my arrival "with an important message from Salazar."

The audience takes place at 8:00 p.m. Bucharest with its lights camouflaged makes a strange impression. On the tram, especially, life acquires wretched, larval aspects. I see Ică at the Presidenţie. I am received immediately after the minister Barcianu, whom the President ad interim[17] detains for just three minutes.

In his famous office, Ică begins by saying he knows me from *Cuvântul*, from the time he came to see Nae Ionescu, and that he is not in the habit of forgetting people he knew "beforetimes." We sit facing each other in easy chairs beside the desk. I give him Salazar's message, and I have to interrupt him several times in order to be able to continue. We talk for an hour. We might have gone on longer if a woman hadn't called him on the telephone (I heard her voice perfectly—and also her tone!)—the same woman whom I passed, waiting for him, when I was leaving. He said many things that, while not lacking in intelligence, were rather banal and, especially, too oratorically delivered. I realized that Salazar's idea—an *esprit de corps* group composed of men returned from the front—did not convince him, because he said: "I know what military men are like; they have a pragmatic spirit and they can't lead a country."

Since he made no impression on me, I didn't always listen to him. I was rather familiar in my gestures. It wouldn't have surprised me if I'd slapped him on the knee and said, "Never you mind, Ică old boy!"

As I was leaving, not knowing what to say, I managed: "It's been very good to meet you!"

At home, several friends were waiting for me; they were amused at the interview, but also disappointed: they had hoped that the audience would have a political meaning (that Ică would attempt, through me, to reach an understanding with the Legion).

✳

I hadn't expected that the Marshal would be so unpopular as he is. As for Ică, I don't believe anyone in Romania surpasses him in unpopularity.

✳

Our war is not present in Bucharest. Almost no one—outside of the Legionaries—realizes what's in store for us if the Anglo-Russians win. I begin to be in dread of the future, because if we lose we will perish both as a state and as a nation. I observe that I'm less nervous here in the homeland than I was this spring in Portugal.

On the other hand, I tire quickly. After a few hours of talking with friends, I seem drained of substance. At night I fall asleep exhausted. True, I'm running around a great deal; every morning and afternoon I'm at the Ministry.

✳

I'm having difficulty acclimatizing myself, even though people have stayed the same. I am aware of one thing, though: that what's happening on the front is the decisive matter, and my absence from there separates me in a certain sense from my generation. The common experience that begins at the Prut is forbidden to me. My writing won't have the same echo after the war. Another man will have to come who will feel and think in the way he discovered there.

✳

I find my parents more aged. Father is very feeble. Mother now has gray hair.

And yet I sense that they're glad that I'm stationed far from the home country, perhaps because they know I'm safe from the police, the front, etc.

I work at the final revision of the text for the little volume *Mitul reintergării*. *Salazar* is not yet in the press. In September, for sure.

I continue making inquiries among my Legionary friends: what happened, and why, on 25 January?[18] More and more I'm convinced that a trap was laid for them into which they fell like naive fools.

I observe that among the townspeople the refrain "robber-rebels" has disappeared.

Actually, Emil Bulbuc[19] is right: "Show me a single Legionary who got rich under the Legionary regime!"

An interesting expression of my friends: "The so-called Legionary victory of 6 September."[20]

There is much talk about the worsening illness of the Marshal. I'm horrified, but there are some who believe that nothing will happen, that the regime will continue under a general or under Ică.

Titu Periclu tells me that the last time the Marshal had an attack, Ică prepared several decisions that began, "We, Mihai . . ."

At Mircea Vulcănescu's,[21] at Mitu Georgescu's, and then, invited by Paul Sterian, at P. Grant's[22] villa at Snagov—I see all my friends from Criterion.

It is, undoubtedly, the most serious group within our generation. Outside of Paul Sterian[23] (about whom I don't know what to think), all the others are well established in their professions.

A vehement discussion at Mircea Vulcănescu's between Dinu Noica[24] and all the others, concerning the Legion. Dinu accuses them of making themselves a comfortable bed under the shelter of the formula, "We're content to be technicians and serve the state under whatever form it may have." Dinu demands: "What did you do when Codreanu was killed? When you voted for the Constitution? For the Plebiscite?" etc.

I intrude episodically in the discussion, declaring that I, although a Legionary, have suspended any judgment concerning internal politics so long as the war with Russia lasts. Dinu replies that the war is not a decisive thing. Decisive only is the moral question—of participating or not in a state that today is led by a Carol II, tomorrow by a Marshal, the day after tomorrow by a Soviet, and fitting yourself in without any qualms of conscience, telling yourself simply that you are a "technician."

The violent response of Mircea, who accuses the Legion of creating a new Dreyfusism.[25]

✳

1942, Berlin

Gorneanu [a member of the Legation] takes me today to Carl Schmitt,[26] who has wanted for a long time to know the true story about Nae Ionescu's philosophy. A house in Dahlem, with very un-Germanic furniture, several modern paintings, and a library rich in old books. Carl Schmitt is a small man with a face not very impressive but luminous, animated. He speaks fluent French. I tell him that of his books I know only *Die romantische Politik*, which influenced Nae Ionescu, Țuțea,[27] and others very much. But instead of beginning a discussion about Nae, he asks me about Salazar, about Portugal, about maritime cultures—and we talk for three hours. He is writing a book about "land and sea," and he has read enormously concerning aquatic art, culture, and symbolism. He says that *Moby-Dick* is the greatest creation of the maritime spirit after the *Odyssey*. He shows me several curious paintings by a modern German artist whose name I promptly forget: underwater, cosmological visions.

Since for many years I too have been studying such problems (*Mătrăguna*), I let myself be drawn into interpretations of Austroasiatic symbols and myths that might interest him. I promise to send him *Zalmoxis*, vol. II, where I have published "Notes sur le symbolisme aquatique." What impresses me about Schmitt is his metaphysical courage, his nonconformism, his breadth of vision. He reminds me of Nae [but with a more solid culture].[28]

He offers us a bottle of Rhine wine. He is delighted to have met me and he regrets that I'm leaving tomorrow for Madrid. He says the most interesting man alive today is René Guénon[29] [and he is happy that I agree].[30] He escorts us as far as the metro station, talking about aviation as a "terrestrial" symbol.

✳

[Lisbon] August

The truth is, I'm no longer the man I once was. If I work sixteen hours, I have insomnia till three in the morning. Of course, the climate is to blame, also Ciuc and England, but it's the fault also of my age. Added to the other great tragedy—the loss of memory—this fatigue will force me in time to modify my life. Without doing so deliberately, I shall depart from pedantry. (It's high time, anyway!) In my head I carry several books on the philosophy of culture, without notes. Not that they wouldn't have any notes; however, I've begun to lose faith in them. More serious is the fact that I can work so little, just now when I'm beginning to see things clearly.

3 September
The second major article of mine, "Camões e Eminescu," appears today in *Acção*. A whole page. One of the few works of good propaganda that I could do. And I begin immediately writing the third article: "Vida e obra de Mihai Eminescu" [The Life and Works of Mihai Eminescu].[31] Although I'm writing very carefully, I find myself obsessed with a single thought: to finish it as quickly as possible, so that we Romanians will be present in the Portuguese press! How crushed I am by this inferiority complex of a little culture, compelled to make itself known by any means and as quickly as possible! How fortunate are the English and the French, who don't feel any need to make themselves known—but only to be well-understood.

5 September
Basically, the tragedy of my life can be reduced to this formula: I am a pagan—a perfect, classical pagan—trying to make a Christian of myself. For me, cosmic rhythms, symbols, signs, magic, sexuality—exist more largely and more "immediately" than the problem of salvation. The best part of myself I've devoted to this problem, but without being able to take one step forward.

September
To live with newspapers means to become an imbecile. That's what I'm doing—an unfortunate duty of my profession of press attaché. Now, at least, I don't have to read more than one newspaper, in the morning. Never again will I agree to cast my eyes on those horrible things after twelve o'clock! Last year I was reading seven or eight Portuguese papers daily.

That which characterizes me: the desire to reconcile the *philosophia perennis* with the "experientialism" of the most luxuriant individualism. From this comes my bizarre passion for symbol, traditionalist metaphysics, occultism, and ethnography—and, if not concomitantly, then alternately, my no less significant passion for all my "lived experiences," for all that is linked to the moment, to experience, to fulgurant drama. (Cf. also my unquenched interest in Gide and Kierkegaard, my unhealthy curiosity for the lives of others, for certain heroes of the spirit or great humbugs: D'Annunzio, Papini, etc.)

To all these things is added an unlimited capacity for candor, spontaneity, innocence, even vulgarity that fools those around me so well that I don't believe there is one person in the world who has understood me rightly. Everyone judges me according to my continual boasting. Those who know me flatter themselves that they recognize me in some of my books. But they don't recognize me in those pages in which I have been most myself.

12 September

I'm rewriting a chapter of the book *Mătrăguna* for volume III of *Zalmoxis*. Once again, the passion for the history of religions. I have so many studies in my head, and yet I content myself with amorphous fragments written years ago . . .

I intuit a new interpretation of death in the case of the Indo-Europeans.

15 September

A sudden attack of melancholy.

The only thing that matters—my status as a mortal, a waiter-for-death—I'm forgetting. I'm wasting my time in an idiotic labor at the Legation and with pointless studies.

We are experiencing a cosmic catastrophe. This is the only meaning of the war: it must be regarded as my ancestors regarded drought, earthquakes, epidemics. There's nothing you can do about it. You must wait—and prepare for death, by praying, being reconciled with our neighbors. Any other attitude is ridiculous.

Only during attacks such as this do I realize the tragedy of my life: I have made culture, works of art, creations—and all of them are vanities on the metaphysical plane, and they are absurd in the historical moment in which we are living.

22 September

Picky Pogoneanu[32] arrives by plane from Madrid and heads immediately for Estoril, because the terrible disease from which he suffers does not permit him to come to Lisbon. I go to see him today. We meet again after six years. He's an invalid, suffering from a strange malady: the marrow of the spine, a progressive paralysis, etc. The doctors have condemned him. For four years he has struggled to be rid of it. He even went to Lourdes. He's here to see a metapsychic, a French *guérisseur* [faith healer].

But his moral stamina is formidable. This boy who can't move without painful efforts (it takes him five minutes to cross a room) has an extraordinary morale. For five hours we talk, laugh, make philosophy and politics. He is full of new things, because, although he has a post in Stockholm, he has just come from Paris where he stayed two months and saw Emil Cioran daily. He tells me that Emil has learned English, is writing a book about France, has a German lady-friend, that he's studying Portuguese now in order to read Antero de Quental—and that, bad as conditions are there, he prefers to stay in Paris. He refuses to contribute anything to German newspapers, in order not to compromise himself in the eyes of his French friends. Cioran, like all the others, foresees the fall of Germany and the victory of Communism. This is enough to detach him from everything.

23 September

Once again, the sentiment of the futility of any effort has taken hold of me. The truth is that there is absolutely no point in my attempting to realize myself in culture. I know full well that I'm living at the end of a historical cycle, and that I won't be able to integrate myself into the paradisal chaos that will follow. Besides, I wouldn't be allowed to. The new Anglo-Soviet world won't accept men like me into its bosom. But it's not my personal case that concerns me. It's all the same to me if I live or die, if I'm shot or not shot by the Communists (I might very well have been shot by Carol and Armand Călinescu, or even by General Antonescu). This is not what concerns me. On the contrary: to die knowing you leave behind you a world that will carry further your thoughts, that you are dying meaningfully—is a death I've always desired. What makes me tremble, however, is the nothingness I see ahead of me: Latino-Christian civilization foundering under the so-called dictatorship of the proletariat, actually the dictatorship of the most abject Slavic elements.

And if this is the truth—because that's what both Churchill and Roosevelt want, and they're the strong ones—then what purpose does creation in history and culture have? Only two attitudes can still find justification: mysticism and orgy—belief in holiness or cynical disintegration in voluptuousness. And you realize then how useless have been the sacrifices for Romanianism, made for so many centuries.

25 September

For the past several years, ever since I've been occupied almost exclusively with ethnography and the history of religions, I have maintained that such studies find their justification in the problematics of modern philosophy. Today there occurs to me still another coincidence between "modern problems of philosophy" and primordial metaphysics. Kierkegaard sought "his truth"—subjectivity identical with the truth. This position corresponds to the tendency in Indian philosophy to find the absolute in the subjective; when man discovers the self, the ātman, he discovers and at the same time coincides with the cosmic Absolute, Brahman.

This isn't the first time I've found themes from archaic thought in Kierkegaard.

⚹

. . . And it is enough for me to close my eyes, to think for a moment about death (as I conceive it, or as others do), and everything seems infantile to me. More than that: I have the sentiment then that I am betraying myself, that I'm running away from my duty to know reality and look it in the face.

How suspect it seems to me sometimes—my passion for diverse readings, my inclination toward hard work . . .

26 September

I have felt the most terrible despair and *angoisse* in moments when I realize that certain things *have passed*, irremediably; that *no matter what may happen*, it will never be possible to live them again. This sentiment lies at the center of my melancholy and despondency. I'm not frightened about anything that will or will not be, that will or will not end, etc. Nor am I frightened by anything that will happen in the future (death) or that is happening in the present (passing), but how terrified I am by that which will never be repeated! Then I realize the human condition: tragedy, religion, suicide, dementia—I understand them all then.

⚹

My religion:

Very seldom do I feel a need for the *presence* of God. I don't pray and I don't know how to pray. When I enter a church, I try to pray, but I can't tell if I succeed or not.

But often I have religious "attacks": the desire for isolation, for contemplation far from other people. Despair. The desire (and the hope) for asceticism.

That which is constant: a passion for the objective, eternal forms of religion—for symbol, rite, myth. I believe that my religious vocation is realized on these paths: to show the experiential validity of things considered dead. For me, a spiral or a "tree of life" is quite as full of sacrality as an icon. I have access, especially, to metaphysical formulas of religiosity ("metaphysical" in the primordial, not the modern, sense of the word). I "live" [*trăiesc*] these formulas that in appearance are dry and rigid.

29 September

Yesterday I began to write, in French, the little book about the Romanian people for which Ameal asked me last summer. I'm writing now about the Dacians, and I'm writing slowly—on the one hand, because of the language, on the other because I want to say as many of the most important things as I can in 80–100 pages.

But that isn't what I wanted to write about here. Rather, to note that the thought has occurred to me to compose, in Romanian, a book about the Romanian philosophy of history—a book written by a nonspecialist, but not devoid of importance. There are several observations that I don't believe have been made before by anyone else.

12 October

My readings of history in recent days make me regret that I failed to acquire an education all of which I could put to the immediate use of the nation. How good it would be if I had been fascinated, in youth, by archaeology or Slavic studies! Today, I'd be able to engage in polemics with our adversaries.

Only now, reading their theses, have I realized how absurd is the position of Hungarian historians. And there are foreigners of good faith who still take them seriously.

October

The weather has been beautiful for a whole week. A splendid Portuguese autumn. I've written certain things in the notebook of impressions.

I talk with Picky Pogoneanu about occultism (India, Guénon, etc.). The Costes, who are present too, tell me about a curious American who has traveled in strange places, knows secret things, etc. Once again I verify an old observation of mine: that interest in the occult is more widespread, even among more lucid people, than is commonly believed. It's just that they're all afraid or embarrassed to talk about it. You have to provoke them in order to discover it.

How imperfect and fragmentary my "published oeuvre" seems to me! A great many works that are unimportant from the viewpoint of "doctrine"; therefore, sensational from the biographical point of view.

I'm attempting a grandiose thing: a new synthesis of world culture. I count myself today among the few who have access to obsolete myths and symbols, to the spiritual meanings of the life long since superseded in the mental evolution of humankind. In addition: ordinary experience (which contemplatives do not have), the passion for the ephemeral and the insignificant (an essential of the

European), the sense of history (nonexistent in the Orient), the egocentrism of great despairers (the genre Kierkegaard), etc., etc. In addition: *affabulation*, journalism, essay writing. To which are added a great seriousness toward facts, respect for documents, etc.

15 October

I am equally attracted by the philosophy of culture and by metaphysics, art, and occultism. Just now I'm experiencing a period of an onslaught of thoughts, of an impetuous combustion. The insomnia returned several weeks ago. At night, when I start to go to sleep, whole "systems" run through my mind, and I make plans for another dozen books.

As usual, after such periods of spiritual and mental fertility, an interval of spiritual drought and depression will follow, sometimes accompanied by neurasthenia. And what am I doing in this splendid time of mental aggressivity? I'm writing the little book about Romania, and I'm writing it timorously, using a huge documentation, because I'm not a historian and I don't want to seem to be a dilettante. Once again I postpone the several books that have been "exploding" inside me for years. And when I shall become free again, God only knows what new crises will have to be dealt with.

27 October

Herescu has been in Lisbon for a week, invited by the university, at my intervention, for a lecture. (Parenthetically, the lecture is nothing but a French translation of an article from *Universul literar* about the royal destiny of the poet.)

We are together all the time. I stop working on anything.

Herescu has a great virtue: he cultivates friendship very seriously, scrupulously. Some reproach him for not being a "savant." But he has realized, certainly, how useless erudition is. (I engage in it out of passion and not because I consider it a highly valuable endeavor.) A poem, a loved one, a night spent with friends—these are more enduring than all the erudition in the world. Then, too, for his ambition—and he has a boundless, though controlled, ambition—there is no need to kill yourself working. A few foreign university contacts open the doors of all the academies to you. Sometimes scholarly glories come to you through a few invitations abroad, through contributing to an academic periodical, etc. Man of the world, with a head for politics—Herescu, in his profession of Latin scholar, obtains things that an erudite fool would never dare to dream of.

From our many conversations, I retain this detail: Condiescu's[33] memoirs are preserved, hidden. "If they had been found, Carol would have appeared such a scoundrel that both Mihai and the dynasty would have been overthrown."[34]

November, Madrid

Traveling with Herescu and Busuioceanu.[35] Unfortunately, we have to stay at the Ritz.

Why do I enjoy visiting in Madrid so much? This is the fourth time I've seen it, and I'm still not saturated. The Prado and the bookstores, the park and the Castellana—maybe it's these; but also my great love for Spain, for its height and its depth. The lukewarm people of Portugal bore me.

Everything in Spain pleases me, even the smell of olive oil frying. Must write about my first encounter, in May 1941, with *pulpito*.

Herescu's visit entails a fascinating schedule. The great cocktail party at the Ministry, with 350 people. There are also some six or seven *Infantes* [princes]. If the monarchy were restored tomorrow, the Romanian Ministry would have the best diplomatic situation.

Notations and sketches of meditations in the black notebook.

I meet a large number of professors and journalists. I will meet Asin Palacio and Menéndez y Pidal later. I buy a large number of books.

I'm speaking horrible Spanish, as I do any language I've never studied.

Toledo

My second visit to Toledo, after the one made with Cotruş last year, in May.

Superb fall day. Castile is harsher now; last year poppies were blooming all along the roadside. I've brought my notebook, but since I'm in a car with the minister Nicky Demetrescu and Herescu, I have time only to sketch points of departure for later meditations. Each word, each name recorded in my black notebook evokes certain emotions, certain thoughts that I shall amplify when I write my impressions of Spain.

Entrance to Puerta de Sol. (I recall how we saw it last year from the other side of the Tagus.) The houses are grayish-rose and grayish-yellow. It is a distinctive color that saves this city from an extravagant asceticism. Describe again, in detail, all the pleasures you had in May 1941 and October 1942 in the Casa del Greco. The brick floor. The garden, so different now in autumn. And how *different* Toledo is, seen from here. Next door, in the workshop where swords are made, I bought a dagger last year. (Don't forget the visit to the "specific" house—the girls who waited so long for us to come in and to photograph us together.)

Pomegranates. What is the name of that building from beside which we could see, at our feet, the Tagus? Clouds had just then covered the sun. The wind of Castile . . . (I still haven't given up the idea of spending several days in Toledo. There are streets I haven't walked on even yet!)

Special page for the walls, houses, street lamps. Cathedral of St. Juan de Reis; outside are hanging the chains of prisoners who have been released. Inside:

pigeons, rosette window; the royal coat of arms repeated five times on both sides. The cloister, with the saints killed by the Napoleonic armies.

Describe in detail *El Entierro del Conde de Orgaz*. Only this time did I look at it with such close attention. The Minister's opera glasses. The sun's rays that touch, for a moment only, this divine canvas. Frightened by the *space*, the cosmogony, the apocalypse—of El Greco. In each fold, in each cloud, gates open to new universes. And then, the poor Iglesia Santo Tomé, with an interior of the most vulgar baroque style. All this exasperatingly palpable "concreteness," introduced by the Counter-Reformation in order to promote the cult of the Madonna and oppose the temptations of heretical mystics! (How much it cost the Roman Catholic Church to extirpate the Albigensians and the medieval mystical heretics!)

Inside the Cathedral. The strange presence from last year is gone. (I entered once during an organ concert.) The monster: St. Christopher, ten or twelve meters tall. How many things I must say relative to this return to paleontology! The Chapel of Santiago, private; the family of the Infantes; on the walls, many seashells of gold. Follow up on the symbol. The Cathedral, like so many others, is not *one*; it has grown, and it continues to grow. It "becomes." It is an organic thing. Cf. the liturgical year. An attempt to elude architectonic destiny.

The man with the wig. An El Greco in the vestry. The exceptionally beautiful smile of the Madonna on the altar. Oriental.

The visit to Alcazar has filled me with sadness. I remember the film seen last summer. Details learned from Tempori, since it was necessary to put on a mask in order to be able to enter the shaft. It is the Day of the Dead. Wreaths, flowers, and widows in the catacombs and in the garden below Alcazar. On the hill opposite, political detainees are working at another barracks.

It is strange, nevertheless, that the myth of Alcazar has made people forget that there was a fratricidal war.

The Synagogue. It is very beautiful, nevertheless. Noble dereliction.

The plane trees near the walled city, at a restaurant.

The Drive through Castile
The villages are grayish-black, of stone and gravel, at one with the soil. ("Soil," in a manner of speaking; it is mostly rock, flint.) From the right, it looks camouflaged. Everything is black, dark, except for the cemeteries with their white walls and white monuments, all the more strident among the cypress trees.

The villages between Toledo and Aranjuez—destroyed by the war. Big battles in the Aranjuez Valley.

Aranjuez
After the flinty hills, an oasis with a surprising amount of vegetation. We come upon whole forests of poplars and plane trees—with yellow leaves.

Toward the west—the road to Casa del Labrador fills me with love—for Nina, for autumn, for my long-lost youth. The joy of being able to say to someone, ten years from now, that you were together on such a day in the parks of Aranjuez! We see that the house is almost dark. But I keep casting my eyes out the car window, toward the forest. The Palace—red. The magnolias. At the Palace, the groups of marble statues. We can hear the Tagus, cascading. The drive through the palace park: leaves thick on the ground. Fall has come. The nightingales. The miniature labyrinth of shrubs. Round benches. We are the last persons in the park.

4 November, Madrid

Today I was at Eugenio d'Ors's place, rua Sacramento, the building of the Spanish Encyclopedia, where he has a little apartment.

I met him last year in May, and at that time I spoke to him about *Mitul reintegrării*. He was kind enough to tell me that he had "guessed enough" Romanian to be able to read my little work. I met him again, then, day before yesterday, at Busuiceanu's, and I reminded him of my idea of making a translation, with commentary, of his most important texts. He seemed startled and invited me to his place to talk.

D'Ors has long been one of the men who interest me (who "excite" me) in modern Europe. What I like in him is the universal, the paradox, the unevenness. Reading a large part of his Spanish books, I realized what a great journalist and what a genius he is, how close he comes to Goethe, and yet how far from him he has remained. Like Papini, Huxley, Gide, Unamuno—d'Ors interests me more for his defects, for what is frail, fragmentary, or even factitious in his oeuvre.

We spent two hours talking about the "Anthology," each with a notebook in hand, noting texts, making synopses, indexes, etc. Seldom have I met a writer who would be a better manager of his own works than d'Ors. He wants his whole protean oeuvre to appear in Romanian, even when it is a matter of a trifling piece like "The History of the World in 500 Words." He values, with his good sense, minor texts, sometimes ridiculous. Among other things, he has a sense of humor.

Madrid

Christianity, as I hope to demonstrate in detail someday in a special work, has "saved" an immemorial tradition, giving a spiritual (Christian) meaning to an infinite number of pagan practices and doctrines, reintegrating this ocean of fragments into a new spiritual unity. A similar thing, at least in intention if not in scope and validity, has been attempted by modern European culture, which has taken over nineteenth-century historicism and is endeavoring to give ultimate, metaphysical, or (in the worst case) "cultural" meaning to all eras of world history, to all human experiences, from folkloric superstitions to furniture and sports. What was "art" in the time of Winckelmann, and what is it for modern aesthetics? How enormous is the field of artistic investigations! Even the "ugliest" moments in the history of art (rococo, etc.) find their significance and spiritual value today. And from art one passes easily to the history and philosophy of culture, to ethnography and psychology.

Toward Segovia

Departure in a fog that foretokens, as it so happens, a magnificent day.

The place called "The Two Castiles." We stop the car. Buildings for winter sports. El Paul: grayish-white, cheerful. Snow on the mountains. We descend through pine forests. The scenery all along the road from Madrid has been exceptionally varied. Guadarama, beside a cloud. The landscape of Velásquez. Here the plain is not arid, as on the road to Toledo. Meditations noted.

La Granga

Entrance to the city: yellow, very yellow, green, and white. Birch trees. The sky. The church and the cone-shaped pine next to it. The park, about which Carmen reads in the guide book that it surpasses the one at Versailles. Marsyas—nymphs, fauns. The Fountain of the Dragon.

We visit the palace where Franco sometimes holds audiences. Iron bedsteads.

Meditations: groups, leaves, the waterfall, the sky.

Segovia

The first thing, quite improbable: the [Roman] aqueduct. The inn where we eat, Horno de Asar—Mesón de Candido, P. Azoguejo. Here Cervantes, Calderon, and others have dined. On the third floor, with a view of the aqueduct. Roast piglet. We drink the wine of Segovia from ceramic mugs. Herescu and Busuioceanu in high spirits.

The medieval wall that cuts through the aqueduct. We climb the stairs: on the right, the yellow, parched meadow. Praza San Martin, Igreja San Martin—with magnificent capitals. The street where we stroll. The cathedral: massive, Islamic exterior. The interior: purer. The convent with decaying vegetation, a funereal odor; the sky looking very close. The windows in the church.

Calle de Escuderos; in the plaza, beside a Cathedral.

The road on which we start out. Praza at Merced. The willows. Roman apse, twelfth century. The exterior decorations on the houses—*azulejo* [blue glazed ceramic tile], in very low relief.

Toward Alcazar. On the right, the house in which the American painter once lived.

The valley below Alcazar. Water, trees—the village, the wall. The cliffs, the colors. Farther back, on the right—the monastery. Meditations.

The visit to Alcazar. Things seen from the terrace. The bridge. The trip back, below the city wall. The people. The old houses.

El Escorial
Long meditation in a cathedral. The road to the place from which Filip II looked at it.

Madrid
(Notes taken during eight visits to the Prado Museum.)
You can understand Spain from the time of Don Quixote only through El Greco. Spiritual tension; paradox; flirtation with madness.

The baroque—realistic vocation, dramatic intuition of the human concrete. Art of the Counter-Reformation, with the presence of pathos and authenticity. "Flesh and bone"; experientialism. How is it that Unamuno hasn't written more about El Greco, about the statues of the Madonna in the churches of the baroque era: so "hic et nunc," so "undivine," so concrete, proclaiming in their ugliness the thirst for salvation "in the flesh," for the eternity of forms?!

Meditation on Velásquez. I'm just now beginning to like him. *Los borrachos* [The Drunks]—the matte, white light of the naked body—is it not perhaps a sign that the person is Dionysus himself? We must not imagine the Greek gods otherwise than as Velásquez paints this man, a naked youth. His calmness, his perfect lines, the absence of "embarrassment," pertain to the god. Don't forget that Dionysus could be intoxicated without resembling drunken men.

Velásquez's courage in painting dwarfs: everyone can be saved, even the most ugly and most wretched of men must and can be saved, in their flesh.

The calmness of Mars, as though he were a naked warrior in a moment of rest—but not rest after a battle. His power is extraterrestrial; it is not provoked and amplified by heroic experience. No trace of *furor*. How can this be?

A great many meditations on the canvases of El Greco, which it would be pointless to transcribe here. I must write them somewhere else, separately.

The same with Goya. I'm beginning to like better and better his works on tapestry, in the basement of the museum. This man has "rescued" a great number of human types and actions considered prior to him as outside the realm of art, devoid of aesthetic interest and significance, simple gestures and figures from the "profane" world (an unreal world—from the standpoint of art). Exactly like Camões, who introduced into the European mental universe and validated aesthetically a whole exotic oceanography and biology, Goya introduces into painting the "leisure hours" of the nobility and the poor (games, amusements), and peripheral customs, types of work, and events (a marriage in a lower-class neighborhood). Goya brings also a new world of human faces—even before *Caprichos*. These things must be understood in relation to the valorization of the nonaristocratic man and his work, realized at the end of the eighteenth century (the Encyclopedists, Diderot in particular, endeavored to homologize manual labor to spiritual creation). Thus, Goya corresponds to the French Encyclopedia. I don't know if any specialist has observed this.

✳

It must be remarked, however, that it was not Goya who introduced ethnography into painting (as d'Ors says somewhere). Villavicericio (second half of the seventeenth century) has a splendid canvas: *Muchaches jugando à los dados* [Boys Playing Dice]. It is a totally "profane" subject—it pertains to ethnos and not to the canon. Goya, however, generalized and imposed this revolution.

✳

Murillo: *La Concepción Immaculada de la Vierge.* Brought here recently from the Louvre. Madonna in white, with blue velvet. You sense the "becoming" of motherhood: she stands with one foot on the new moon and she is surrounded, assaulted on all planes, by children. You have the impression that she is wrapped in infants. The symbol of maternity (but also of infantile angelism). *Ludus puerorum.* The same symbol in *La Concepción de Aranjuez*: children, moon. One child (angel archetype) is holding stalks of wheat and flowers. Magna Mater. (To be elaborated.)

Lisbon, 10 November

I arrived last night in Lisbon, after spending nine days in Spain. As I usually do, I lived so totally the environment, language, and culture of the country I was visiting, that I felt like a stranger here when I returned. I have to make a new effort to be able to find myself again—the Portuguese self.

✳

The events in North Africa (Rommel's defeat, the landing of the Americans) troubled me enormously between the sixth and eighth of November. Insomnia, nightmares, depression. As usual, I saw everything in relation to my country: I said to myself that the German divisions being withdrawn from Stalingrad and sent to France will be replaced by Romanian divisions; that, in any event, to an intelligent Romanian, the defeat of the Axis cannot be acceptable now, when our army is on the Volga, etc. (Needless to add that our whole Legation at Madrid, as well as the one here in Lisbon, is overjoyed!)

This morning, however, without understanding why, I awoke serene, detached from events, without any anxiety. Once again, my interest in research, in philosophy, has returned. Maybe it's just an anticlimax, a recovery of my spiritual equilibrium, by a process of alternation. Or perhaps this could be a troubling presentiment of mine—that things are not so tragic.

12 November
The problem of the sacred (therefore, the religious problem) is the fundamental problem of knowledge. *The Other, the Other One*—is, in fact, the object.

✳

The relation between the musical scale and the seven planets—in China, India, Greece, the Arab world. Music—Cosmology. An Indian text says that sounds are direct imitations of animals, but actually, as is true in China too, it is a matter of the animals of the zodiac.

Not only is there a correspondence between sounds and planets, but in any melody a cosmic, astral ascension is followed.

For traditional cultures, everything had a cosmic and soteriological significance.—The time is approaching for me to say these things plainly, in a *big* book.

13 November
The pathos, dynamism, and realism of the baroque is explained as the reaction against the rationalism of the Renaissance. The Counter-Reformation is a return to the concrete, to the visceral, and to ritual mysticism. Through the "carnal" statues of the Virgin, the cult of Mary is launched—nourished on a popular devotion that heretics had used through the whole course of the Middle Ages—and in this way Catholicism is saved. It was the penultimate attempt made by Western Catholicism to save itself from an enemy within, by assimilating en masse the elements of a popular mysticism, hitherto kept under supervision if not even under pressure. The last attempt to do it in our days (and Catholicism will do it especially after the war is over): accepting social mystics into its bosom. (The flirtation with the extreme Left has been known for several years in the case of the Holy See.)

I believe that someday the 1920–40 era will be understood as a reaction full of pathos, "authenticity," and "experience" against the pseudorationalism of the nineteenth century.

14 November
Ambivalence and polarity are verified not only in any culture and on any plane (for example, in art: the tendency toward the ideal archetype—and realism), but also in the life of the individual. The impulse toward the archetype, toward the clear and creative personality, alternates with the opposite tendency toward degradation, larval state, orgy, drunkenness, etc.

I've arrived at this theory by observing myself very closely. Seldom is the polarity verified more sensationally than in my life: asceticism and orgy, the individual and the craving for the collective, creation and degradation in erudition. Multilateralism is now an outreach toward the universal, now a falling into fragments.

15 November
Never have I had any passion, not even in the least, for old and rare books, deluxe editions, and such. In my library, outside of two volumes from the seventeenth century and a first edition (1914) of *À la recherche du temps perdu*, there are nothing but modern books. My obsession is for the critical edition, the definitive text, the erudite monograph, complete information. I never buy an old edition unless a new one is not available. Neither at London nor at Madrid, nor here in Lisbon where I work, have I rummaged through used-book shops for antique books—but only for serious, learned publications that are no longer available in bookstores.

I've begun to read *Orígenes de la novela* by Menéndez y Pelayo, my old idol from youth (Rome). With all his enormous learning, Menéndez nevertheless wrote about things he did not know. An abundance of titles, copied from notes or bibliographies.

There's one thing, however, that never ceases to impress me about Menéndez y Pelayo: the courage of his gigantic works. One of the few men of the nineteenth century who succeeded in preserving his passion for the universal in spite of historicism. If Hasdeu[36] had not started so many different works, and had not exaggerated to the smallest detail, he would have surpassed him.

16 November
Concert with Hans von Benda at San Carlos. Handel, Mozart, Max Bruch, Haydn. "Andante Cantabile" from Mozart's Concerto in B-flat Major made me imagine the final scene in *Faust*—the angels scattering flowers on him.

In general, the concerto brought another personage close to me: Petru Anicet;[37] there are things about him I don't understand very well, and sometimes I suspect him of snobbishness and insincerity. But the angelic grace of "Andante Cantabile" revealed to me not only *Faust*, but also my dear Anicet.

Yet how is the "Concerto grosso" of Handel to be understood? The exacerbated repetition of the motif—is it not a kind of intuition of the infinite?

17 November

Dinu Cantemir[38] finds something irritating and in bad taste in *Nunta în Cer*: the main characters gape looking at travel bureau posters, and when they travel, they do so with the air of the *parveneux*.

I replied to him that nomadism was the spiritual climate of the 1920–30 era. People traveled—superficially, indeed—to Paris or to Italy because they lacked roots.—But there's something else: I wrote *Nunta în Cer* at Ciuc; all my melancholy at being behind the barbed wire, my suppressed freedom, were avenged in writing that book.

✳

Too often we judge history on the basis of certain elements to which a restricted social group has given an exaggerated importance, leaving it to be understood that it dominated the whole era and all strata of society. The popularity of the ideals and arts of the Renaissance makes us believe that they were shared by the whole world of that time. The Renaissance man was the creation of an elite, and his ideals were imposed "by fashion" on all other cultural regions: France, the Low Countries, Germany, to a lesser extent on Spain, still less on Portugal. The world contemporary with the Renaissance was, however, different from the one that the humanists suggest to us.

Another example: The success and popularity of rococo makes the seventeenth century seem to be one dominated completely by the royal mystique, by the monarchical apotheosis, by erotics, mannerism, etc. This is true only to a degree. Not all of France created in the framework of rococoism. The baroque was still alive in the Provinces. And eighteenth-century France was not entirely "enlightened." There existed also numerous phenomena of degraded mysticism, the pious Fronde, etc.

✳

How falsified is the vision of history, whereby we understand it as validated exclusively on the basis of documents! A medieval city, because it had a dozen literate men who left a few hundred documents, "participates" in history—whereas the deep dramas of the Eurasiatic Middle Ages, the tensions in the Ponto-Baltic Isthmus, are "unimportant," and historians summarize them in a few sentences!

This is why a world history cannot be constituted on the basis of written documents—but only on spiritual documents: that is, on myths and beliefs. Europe—Western Europe especially—must be compared with the East and the Steppes of the nomads not through its written documents, but through its myths.

For example, Romanian history must be homologized with Western European history on the basis of our myths: "Miorița," "Meșterul Manole," heroic ballads, "Făt Frumos" [Prince Charming], etc.

9 November

The thing that exasperates me in discussions with Anglophiles who are happy about a possible defeat of Germany is that their political passion makes them forget the decisive fact of the current war: the active entrance of Russia into world history. Just as, earlier, the Latins and the Greeks were beaten at Constantinople, allowing the Turks to gain a foothold in Europe. Then, for three hundred years, we Romanians had to shed our blood to prevent the Turks from reaching the heart of Europe. But this time I don't know if history will repeat itself.

20 November

Writing the article, "Dor—A saudade romena" [*Dor*—the Romanian *saudade* (Longing)] for *Acção*,[39] I read again Eminescu's "Mai am un singur dor" [I Have Yet One More Longing]. Heretofore I believed that it had to do with his desire for reintegration in the Cosmos. Now I'm beginning to think it's something else: the desire to find again, through death, his true cosmic family (rivers, mountains, stars, forests). Not reintegration—but the return home, to his own place.

22 November

For years now I've been working without the stimulus of the presence of exceptional beings. I have some very good friends; but my relationships with them don't enhance me intellectually. There is no one around to stimulate me, to confirm me or congratulate me for all I'm doing. I'm sure I'd have had a more abundant output if I'd conversed more with Noica and Cioran. But our get-togethers were taken up with political discussions, anecdotes, or bantering.

Now, I've been living for almost three years in the milieu of legations, where, at best, I meet men who can understand what I'm saying. Then, add to that, my infinite modesty, which makes me bring the discussions down to trifling matters, to keep from giving others inferiority complexes.

27 November

I'm so frightened about the future of my nation that my whole autonomous life and all my power of creation are suspended. I make daily efforts to rid myself of this obsession (what will happen to Romania if the problem of Russia is not resolved militarily?!), in order to be able to work, to think, to live even. Because my life itself has become an agony—all the more so in that I feel that here in Lisbon I'm the only one who holds this view. The others, all good fellows, clink their glasses to honor Anglo-American victories, forgetting that our divisions are on the Volga.

28 November

I've written some thirty pages of the little book about Romania. I write for about an hour; then I go and listen to the radio for the latest news. Sometimes the news is so grave (the scuttling of the French fleet, etc.) that I have to expend a considerable effort to maintain my composure and take up the work again.

I don't know if I'll be able to publish this little book requested last summer by João Ameal, and in preparation for which I've read a shelf of books (thereby discovering the history of the Romanians—of which I found nothing to be ashamed). But I must write it. Because, speaking frankly, I can't be sure of anything. If the Reds win, then I and my oeuvre and my nation—will disappear, actually or figuratively speaking. This doesn't mean I should renounce my vocation or the duty that I've imposed on myself: to work till the end, no matter what happens and no matter how convinced I may become that my labor is in vain. If I hadn't imposed this upon myself, I'd have had to enter a monastery.

1 December

Nothing harder than to fight against the sentiment of the futility of any work whatsoever. Each week the problem besets me—and what an effort I must exert to resolve it and go on with my labor! If it were a literary or philosophical book, I'd find the spiritual impetus and moral sustenance in the very act of creation, because such a work justifies itself simply by its production. But unfortunately it's not a matter of such a work. I'm writing, still, the same little book about Romania—and the sentiment of uselessness is overwhelming me. It seems to me that there won't be time for this book to be published (do we not expect an invasion—British or German—from one month to the next?), or, even if it does appear, who will read it? Whom will it convince? The Jews, the English, the Americans are having great luck with the Russians—the only ones who are holding up. If this resistance brings about the military defeat of Germany, not one of the three great nations cited in the previous sentence will take any account of our historical rights or historical necessity. Or even if the

English were to try to take account of them, it would be too late—and the Russians too strong.

What a pleasure it would be if I could let myself be caught up in writing a book on art, religion, or metaphysics! The act of thinking and creating liberates me from all these nightmares. If I could stop feeling so Romanian, maybe I could detach myself without difficulty even while performing tasks imposed by circumstances. But Corneliu Codreanu[40] made of me a fanatic Romanian. So long as I'm dealing with history—and not with the Absolute—I can't think about anything without taking my nation into account.

4 December

2:00 a.m. I've finished the little book about Romania (48 large pages—circa 120 pages printed). I'm rather well satisfied with the way it turned out. A large number of thoughts have been provoked by the readings and questions imposed by this work.

6 December

Nina's name day. All our guests are Romanians, and after dinner we start playing a parlor game, "Academia"; then another: someone goes out of the room and when he returns we read him a list of adjectives or opinions formulated about so-and-so, and he has to guess the author thus characterized.

I remember we used to play this game in 1932–33 at Floria Capsali's, Mircea Vulcănescu's, and Misu Polihroniade's. There's one amusing scene I recall, when Petru Comarnescu was the "guesser." It's been ten years since then, and I can still have fun playing such games. The terrible thing is that everyone—all of us over thirty—tries to appear as intellectual as possible, to "distinguish" himself or herself, even here.

9 December

This evening, for dinner: João Ameal with his wife, plus Leontin with Zoe, and Cantemir. A discussion concerning the "black market" in Germany leads me to speak about the collective, statistics, and the modern way of understanding history. What Nae Ionescu said in his courses nine or ten years ago. No one understood exactly what I meant, and I felt terribly sad. I'll have to sterilize myself if I continue to live abroad much longer.

10 December

For the *Cluj Tribuna* I have extracted a fragment from the novel and have copied several pages (about Vizeu—especially meditations at the Museum of Grão Vasco) from my Portuguese notes.[41] I've begun an article too, but I'm writing with difficulty and badly, oppressed by the sentiment that the censor won't let it be published. It's the first article I've written in Romanian since leaving for England. I've refused to contribute to periodicals in the homeland. That's why I want what I publish at Cluj to be good. I want to mark this exception I'm making for the ceded Transylvanian area.[42]

Transcribing my notes from the fall of 1941 at Vizeu, I'm impressed by an observation I make rather emphatically concerning Portuguese painting: the ugliness of the personages, which I explain by the realism of the painter's choosing his subjects from the world around him—men hardened by their struggle with the sea, with diseases, fatigue: the men of the maritime discoveries. I believe there is much truth in this observation. The Renaissance was made by men of the Mediterranean who had the time and the wisdom to contemplate classical canons. The maritime cultures—Holland, Portugal—discovered realism in art through the struggle of men with the sea. The great Dutch painters of the sixteenth century, as well as the Portuguese, painted from nature—ugly men, exhausted by their efforts or gorged on the satisfactions and ambitions the sea had created.

12 December

I spent the afternoon thinking, in the main lines, about a novel I would call *Apocalips* (although it has nothing to do with the novel with the same title of a few years ago, contracted for Cugetarea, and abandoned definitively). The final chapter takes place in London during the blitz. My first novel in which a crime occurs. And the first in which no woman plays any part.

13 December

I've written four pages the size of those in this journal. But I'm happy to say I've begun well, not as I thought I'd begun last night.

14 December

I've written six and a half pages. Too bad that this week is taken up with other things.

16 December

The novel is abandoned. I have to write an article, a talk about "Colinde" [Romanian carols] for Emissora Nacional [National Radio], etc.

18 December

Yesterday evening I had dinner at X's place. Among other very exciting things that I don't have the courage to record in the notebook (God only knows into whose hands it could fall before I can hide it away in the homeland!), he told me how, last year, he was arrested three times by gangs of insurgents in Serbia. And despite this, he succeeded in meeting with Mihailović,[43] whom he had met before; he showed me photographs of himself with the famous guerrilla leader. The latter even gave him a handwritten letter to keep him from being arrested again by the insurgents. Mihailović told him he has nothing against the Germans, but only the Croatians (who have assassinated 250,000 Serbs) and the Italians. If X obtains a letter from Hitler that no Serb will be assassinated, the rebellion will end today. "Unfortunately," he says, "we know that the Fuehrer can't do anything. The Italians wanted Tunisia, Corsica, and Southern France. They couldn't have them. They had to preserve at least a trace of influence. Croatia was to give them this satisfaction."

X lost his father and a brother in the other war. Two brothers lost in this war, and a third gravely wounded. And still he is calm, sure, even serene.

He tells me that his brother was wounded the first time last year, in November, in the suburbs of Moscow. How near victory seemed!

He says that the war was supposed to begin on 6 April 1941, but Donovan,[44] knowing this, staged a coup d'état in Yugoslavia. The Russians had ten weeks to prepare. "And those weeks were decisive!" A whole first-rank army was massed at the border.

He believes that the Anglo-Americans have sent around 10,000 tanks into Russia.

19 December

I went to bed near 4:00 a.m., because it was not till after midnight that I started work on the novel. In three hours I wrote four pages. But that isn't the reason I'm writing these lines. Last night I woke up several times with a terrible melancholy, a state of cosmic sadness—in the midst of which my despair brought me, nevertheless, a throbbing of life. Because otherwise everything seemed void of substance, sense, and soul.

I remember several scenes that appeared to me in that definitive melancholy: a reunion with the Perris family somewhere in India, and my despair that I can't relive my life of 1929–31, that time has passed, that we all have grown older.

When I was an adolescent and, later, at the university, I never suspected that my bouts of melancholy had a metaphysical function. I considered them a late manifestation of sentimentalism, linked to childhood and to memories of childhood. Not until several years later, after I had observed such attacks better and had followed their inner resonance, did I become convinced that they pertain to a plane other than that of "sentimentalism" (as I supposed in 1922–28), that they have their source in an intuition of a mystical or metaphysical nature. I'm beginning to believe that such attacks of melancholy constitute my own particular kind of religious experience.

20 December

I can affirm that there is no personal sorrow that I cannot absorb in a few hours, and no tragedy concerning myself that I can't get over in a few days.

But what I cannot accept, and what I cannot assimilate, is the tragedy of my nation. The fact that the Romanian state and people could perish because of the Russians and the ferocious imbecilities of a Churchill or a Roosevelt—exasperates me. My despair finds its source mainly in this Romanian destiny.

22 December

For several days I've been reading *Del sentimento trágico* by Unamuno, happy that I can understand him so well in the original. For the first time, I'm reading this book straight through and to the end. Previously, I knew only the first three chapters and parts of the others. Unamuno's courage is amazing—to raise the questions of immortality, irrationalism, and despair. I have the impression that in this book the contemporary existentialist philosophy is treated in anticipation.

23 December

Among my "big" books will be that *Introducere în istoria religiilor* which I've been thinking about for two years and which I began at Oxford. The exceptional importance of this book lies in my completely personal way—"personal" by modern criteria, but archaic and valid from a multimillennial history of religions—of judging the mystical event and religious experience. I am not a man with normal religious experiences; neither am I an agnostic or an antireligious person. For me, as for an Indian, a primitive, a Greek, a medieval man—religion *is*. I know the divine presence only in my moments of great despair—but at all other times I ascertain this presence in any human act. More clearly, religion for me is the thirst for and intuition of the *real*, the Absolute. I identify this thirst in any significant human act in all times.

That is why the introduction to the history of religions that I shall write will have a revolutionary value—because I will show the permanence of "metaphysics" so-called in ancient gestures and rites; I identify Socrates or Plato at least ten times on the religious plane.

25 December

"These splendid times!" said Churchill in his last speech, speaking about our era, the war, the tragedy the world has known for the past several years and that threatens to become permanent and aggravated. If I weren't a Romanian, perhaps I'd say he was right. Because, compared to the number dead in 1870–1910, undoubtedly our era is grandiose. Out of all these tragedies there will be born a new world, and it is an invigorating spectacle, one that very few have had the good fortune to know.

I am, however, a Romanian. I can't dissociate myself from that fact now. And as I see things, Churchill's "splendid times"—if things turn out according to the desires of his heart—will entail the destruction of the Romanian nation and state. If I were Portuguese or Swedish or Brazilian, perhaps these events would seem insignificant compared to the grandeur of the world that will be organized after the Anglo-Bolshevik victory. (Although I do not believe that such a world *can be* "grand," from whatever angle you judge it.) I only agonize at the thought that Churchill could be right. Because, so far as I'm concerned, I could not accept history without Romania as I've known it. To me there would remain open the path of mysticism, of withdrawal from the world, or of anarchy, of total detachment from it. Never has the struggle between hope and despair been more fierce in my mind, my flesh, than now. That's why my production is paralyzed. Any new creation is suspended for the duration of operations on the Russian front.

26 December

In the same edition of Unamuno's *Ensayos* that I'm reading now (Aguilar, two compact volumes) I find extensive extracts from his correspondence. There would be many things to underscore and transcribe. But in addition to a great many interesting observations, I'm struck by the leitmotif of Unamuno's correspondence: Spanish literati read nothing but literature, and that is why their production is so mediocre. Unamuno recommends anything other than literature: science, philosophy, life. He prefers to return to "his Hegel," "his Schleiermacher," rather than read fashionable French novels. "Literature's purpose must be to unify" is his expression.

It's the same position I've always taken in Romanian culture: against readings limited to literature; for vital experience or exacting cultural effort (science, erudition, philosophy). Unamuno speaks, as do I, about the example of Goethe. He is the figure who has obsessed me from the age of twenty. "Science has not spoiled poetic inspiration," says Unamuno. "On the contrary, it has deepened it and purified it."

27 December

Goruneanu writes me from Berlin that Ernst Jünger,[45] en route to the Russian front, stopped two days at Carl Schmitt's place, and there he read *Zalmoxis*, "deeply impressed," making numerous notes. Schmitt sends me his little book *Land und Meer* [Land and Sea], about which he spoke to me last summer, with the following dedication: "Mircea Eliade, als kleine Gegengabe für seinen grossen *Zalmoxis*" [To M. E., as a little gift in return for his great *Zalmoxis*].

I have recorded this because, once again, I have verification of my opinions about "Romanian propaganda." Never have I believed in journalistic propaganda. If our cultural reviews and our works of value were appearing directly in a foreign language, published in major university centers, I believe we would stand today alongside Finland, Norway, and Denmark.

28 December

After almost twenty years, I reread *La rôtisserie de la Reine Pidanque*. I believed it was the only book of Anatole France that would stand the test of time. I was wrong. The only tasty portions are the erotic ones. I was forced to skip over many pages in order to get to the end of it.

And yet I believe I've read *Le Père Goriot* twelve times, and I don't know how many times the other books of Balzac, and still I haven't become satiated with him. Just as I would not be satiated with Tolstoy, with Stendhal, or Gide, not to mention Unamuno and Kierkegaard (with their "literature," I mean).

29 December

Working on the novel begun two weeks ago (I don't know if I'll keep the title *Apocalips*, used for an old novel in the fantastic genre, which I abandoned for a thousand and one reasons), I observe that I have present in my mind an increasingly smaller number of Romanian words. In it, I display a vocabulary of only mediocre proportions. The separation from the homeland is harder for me to bear than for others. The lack of Romanian readings is impoverishing my vocabulary.

30 December

The most serious obstacle I encounter in the writing of this novel is the "presence" of the war in Russia. No matter how hard I try to detach myself, to forget about the terrible struggle that the Romanians there are undergoing, in order to concentrate on my writing—I can succeed in doing so for no more than two or three hours. If I undertake to write at 4:00 p.m., by 6:00 I begin to hear the evening newspapers being hawked on the streets: *Diário de Lisboa, Diário Popular, República*, the continental editions of the *Daily Mail* and *Izvestia*, as I call them (and I'm not far off the mark). The shouting lasts three hours, because the Portuguese are rather slow, especially here, in my poor neighborhood. I haven't read these newspapers for a year now, but I know what they say, and it scares me. What if something's happened?! . . . My work is compromised until 9:30, when I listen to the radio, and again I twist and turn until 10:00 or 11:00, in order to eliminate "the present" from my consciousness. During this time, all I can do at best is read. But how can you *create* in this atmosphere of panic and terror, how can you write when you're wondering if your country will continue to exist, if you'll survive?

Sometimes I envy people who don't believe in God or a future life. What a serene and cynical existence I'd live today; with what sarcasm I'd ridicule the imbecility and dementia of humankind.

The Journal, 1943

3 January, Lisbon

Can it be that the year of my death has begun? A great lust for work; an unexpected facility for writing. And especially: a desire to write much and quickly, to finish as many as possible of the books I have in my head. No longer do I feel any difficulties; no longer am I beset with obstacles.

I had a very strange dream about N. Iorga and Nae Ionescu. I've written about the dream in a letter to Picky Pogoneanu.[1]

I'm beginning to be tempted again by the thought that the end of our continent is near. But this thought gives me peace.

4 January

The despair from last year returns. But it's not related to a personal experience, it's not an effect of my condition in the universe—but a result of meditations on the course of the war. It all seems useless and absurd, if a new world is going to be made at the price of the disappearance of Romania as a state and a nation. I'm not interested in some kind of terrestrial paradise (in which I don't believe anyway) if it's obtained at the sacrifice of my people.

I never would have believed that I'd arrive at metaphysical despair by starting from politics and nationalism!

5 January

When I'm working on a novel, I waste a considerable amount of time, not because I write and meditate, but because I try, by all sorts of devices, to "set the stage" beforehand. I leaf through books, reread pages already written, lie down, sit with my feet propped up on the desk—and the day passes with only a few pages finished—all written in less than an hour's time. For that reason, I hate periods of literary work. When I'm writing a scientific treatise, at least I don't waste the time while I'm not writing. That is a time when I reread note slips, examine the problem more deeply, and think—not a time I kill.

✳

I can write almost nothing on a day when I know I have something to do. Even if it's only an evening engagement, I'm incapable of creating. I can't work without being certain that I can stay at my desk for an indefinite period of time.

6 January

Sometimes it frightens me—how much and how deeply I understand postmortem realities. I hardly have the courage or the vocabulary to communicate them. I see things that very few lucid moderns can grasp. What happens after death is, in some sense, known to me. In particular, I'm obsessed with an image, beyond my powers to describe, through which I have discerned how the souls of those who died long ago are "resting," being fused again into ancestors, into archetypes.

7 January

I believe that, some fine day, I ought to abandon all my literary and philosophical plans and devote myself entirely to this journal. At least until the end of the war. Because, what else is there any sense in writing until then? The novel I'm working on now is small and not timely. I've abandoned *Viață Nouă* because I'm paralyzed by the thought that it might be a posthumous novel. The philosophical and scientific works would be only a small challenge. And because I can't live without wrestling with my thoughts, I ought to go out and buy a large copybook in which to record, with more love than I've done up till now, each day's harvest. It would make it more interesting, too, since I've never noted in this journal any philosophical reflections, scientific observations, erudite anecdotes, etc.

8 January

I'm having a hard time getting used to the idea that basically I'm a melancholic person subject to attacks of despair—yet one who detests both melancholy and despair. This is what gives me my famous "verve" and good disposition in "society."

I've not yet learned to conduct myself in conformity with my mental capacity. In those moments when I believe that the person I'm with feels overwhelmed by my personality, I make desperate efforts to seem like an "ordinary fellow." I'm embarrassed by my "proportions," my singularity, only because I'm afraid that others will suffer on that account.

I believe the same timidity lies at the base of my literature in which "nobodies" predominate. It embarrasses me to have my skills and genius intrude.

9 January

Today, classifying the papers from the top of my desk and the drawers, I find these two sentences copied from Unamuno:

"Gracias al amor sentimos todo lo que de carne tiene el spíritu."[2] (*Sentimiento trágico*, Ch. VIII, in *Ensayos*, vol. II, p. 778.)

"La pasión y la sensualidad son incompatibles: la pasión es arbitraria, la sensualidad es lógica."[3] ("Sobra la europeizacion," in *Ensayos*, vol. I, p. 895.)

I've copied them here in order to rescue them from a possible drowning in the mass of papers and notes that inundate the drawers. Then too, how well I understand the difference between sensuality and passion!

✳

In his *Journal* (I, pp. 28f.) Julien Green speaks about the "menaces de guerre" and about the imminence of war ("two months, a year at the most"). Dated 19 October 1930. I was in the Himalayas then. I had no idea that a war was impending. How good to be sheltered from the rumors of the press, from politics! While Julien Green was wondering (in 1930!) if it was still worthwhile beginning anything, given the fact that a catastrophe was approaching—I was suffering from my separation from Maitreyi and studying Indian metaphysics. I didn't lose anything by being absent from history.—Now, I'm endeavoring to gain as much spiritual freedom as I can. I don't read the newspapers or discuss politics anymore.

—Something else, too. In 1930, Germany was democratic. It didn't have Hitler. Then, how did this business of Fascism come about, which led inevitably to war? Is it not more natural to say that *any* Germany had to lead to war, because it had been mutilated? . . .

10 January

In Julien Green's *Journal* I read that he requires three to four hours to write 25–30 lines of a novel, while Gide tells him he becomes suspicious when he notices that his writing of a novel is progressing without difficulty. And I complain about sterility because I can't write eight or ten pages a day!

It's true, this honest labor, the corrections and recorrections, make an *Adrienne Mesurat* in two years and a *Les Faux-monnayeurs* in five. When I think that *The Idiot* was dictated in two months, that *Le Cousine Bette* was written in just a few months, and *Maitreyi* in six weeks, I find that any effort, if the work doesn't call for it, is not only useless but also noxious. In art there are no fixed rules. No one can say that the writer has to write slowly. He writes in conformity with his genius, taking account of the "resistance of the materials" of the particular book on which he is working.

✳

The importance acquired by things that last, that abide: for example, a love, a marriage, a friendship, an institution, a newspaper, etc. As if, in this universe which is in a state of eternal becoming, of continuous decomposition and reintegration—the real would begin to mean only that which remains itself, which preserves its form, which lasts. I believe more in a thing that was and continues to be. Not only do I believe in it, but I'm thrilled to approach it. Is it not perhaps an ontic thrill, an emotion I feel especially in the presence of objects that don't belong to the human condition?

13 January

I receive a letter today from the German Ambassador, Baron Hoyningen-Huene, by which he invites me, in the name of the Rector of the University of Munich, to participate in the inauguration of the Sven Hedin Central Asiatic Institute, which will take place in Munich, 14–20 January. Sven Hedin will be named Doctor Honoris Causa by the university on 20 January, at which time he will deliver an address that will be followed by various festivities. The German government is bearing all travel expenses.

Von Bredow[4] telephones me in the evening, saying that I would leave on 18 January by plane. On the 19th I'll be at Stuttgart, where someone will be waiting at the airport to accompany me by train to Munich.

What I'd like would be to pass through Paris, but I believe that would be hard to arrange.

I must go, even though the weather is infernal and an airplane trip in winter is rather risky. Last month, Cantemir tells me, two Lufthansa planes crashed. I think of myself as on military duty, and I'm going.

14 January

Just how "Oriental" and antimystical I am structurally, I realize from the revulsion I have toward any suffering, any pathos. I am, par excellence, a contemplative and rationalist. I like to pursue the dialectics of ideas or the meaning of the symbol. The vocation of metaphysician. A horror of living in a passional tension. It pleases me to be in love, but the pathos of lovers, the agony of separations, makes me shudder. Antilyrical. I adore stable things, broad horizons. My inclination toward "adventure" is not by nature "pathetic": I like play, detachment, surprise—but nothing that sighs, bleeds, attaches itself. My despair is fed always by impersonal causes.

15 January

One of my great melancholies is nourished by the thought that I didn't have the luck to live, while still a young man, in Paris. I don't regret studying in India, but I'm in despair when I think that I might have lived in Paris in 1932–38. Now, it's getting too late. What would I still be able to assimilate of the Paris of my dreams at the age of forty?—Because I'm sure I won't be able to live there sooner than four or five years from now. And, too, who knows what kind of France, disfigured by Communism, I would find?

When my despair reaches its point of culmination—despair arising from the fear that Europe will be destroyed and a new world, uninteresting from my point of view, will arise—my whole being takes refuge in erotic desire. As if it were avenging itself by threatening the permanence under which it lives. The desire to love, to embrace, to perpetuate yourself in sons.

And there's something else: the impulse toward "totalization." My being, without my rational or even conscious intervention, seeks a new equilibrium, even in this tragedy assimilating the tragedy, reintegrating contrary elements in a new and higher unity.

I find myself, sometimes, meditating calmly on the new Slavo-Communist world that Stalin would organize. Romania become Soviet will lose its bourgeoisie and its intelligentsia, but the mass, if it is not deported, will gain a better education and proper health care. After 500 years the Russians will withdraw. But what will my country look like then?

16 January

I don't know why, but on days when the sun doesn't shine, I like to remember the park at Aranjuez. A sweet melancholy floods my soul. The woods with the yellow leaves, with so much beauty that you can't bear it except in the company of the woman you've loved for so many years, beside whom you have lived, whose life is irremediably interwoven with your own . . .

17 January

Burilianu[5] telephones me that he has received a coded telegram from Ică Antonescu giving me permission to go to Münich, asking me to come afterward to Bucharest. I don't understand. What if Ică proposes to me, as he did last summer, some political or administrative post?

And I still don't know if I'll leave tomorrow morning. For two days it's been stormy and no planes have come.

I have a certain anxiety I can't explain. Last night I dreamed of my aunts, Viorica and Vița, who died twenty years ago—something I've never done before. They looked very beautiful and they spoke to me.

Could all these things be obscure premonitions—or just the creation of my indolence, annoyed at being disturbed in the middle of winter?! . . .

18 January

A case of the flu—and the fear that Ică will offer me some post or other in his government—makes me cancel the trip. I consult with Brutus Coste[6] and Busuioceanu, and we all agree that it's better for me to stay here. If Ică is dead set on having me in his government, he'll give me a special summons, and I'll see then what pretext I can concoct not to go.

19 January

I can scarcely contain the emotion I feel reading Book I of Herodotus, in Le Grand's translation (Les Belles Lettres). I'd never read Herodotus, except selections from Book IV for my research in the history of religions and Book II for Egypt in lycée. I remember that compact volume I still have in my library in Bucharest, bought from a used-book store in 1923–24, which I devoured in less than a week of long nights of reading. I remember too that a little after Herodotus, I began to read the five volumes of Plutarch's *Moral Dialogues*, from which I learned a lot of trifles. I read Plutarch in the summer, immediately after the close of the school year. At midnight, I would slip down from the attic and go walking on the streets, almost as far as Cișmigiu [Park]. Once, neurasthenized by the reading, intoxicated by the mythological and archaeological particulars, I asked myself, "What's the use? What's the use of all this larvalike labor?" And I remember the answer I gave myself: "Now, when the others are doing nothing, and when you can't do anything either (because we were still in lycée)—learn, assimilate, read to the point of saturation. Soon, times of freedom and other activities will come. Then, you won't have any more time to read."

Another time I answered, "Precisely because it makes no sense, I must keep on reading Plutarch. What else would make sense anymore?"

✳

Since the appearance of my last works—*Honigberger, Iphigenia* [sic: *Ifigenia*],[7] *Salazar, Mitul reintegrării*—I haven't read a single review. With very little effort, last summer at Bucharest, I could have taken some interest and collected at least the more significant ones; because I was told about certain reviews that were worth reading.[8] But, I must confess, it interests me almost not at all what people write about me. I am, perhaps, the most indifferent writer—toward the critics and toward the public. When someone starts talking about my books, especially about the literary ones, I conclude the discussion as summarily as I can. Only when I have an urge to talk about my passions—something that happens rather seldom—do I deign to discuss my literary oeuvre. Actually, what has always interested me was my own idea about my books. I realize perfectly well what is worthless and what is permanent in my production. No one can judge it better or more objectively than I myself. If I ever get the time, I'll write a book about my whole oeuvre—literary and philosophical—and I'm sure it will be better than one any contemporary could write.

20 January

The extraordinary impression left on the reader of any Dostoyevsky novel is due in large measure to the fact that time is dilated in it, to a considerable extent, and to the fact that his characters, whom he follows closely to keep them from repeating their gestures and words to the point of satiation, explode or contradict themselves out of exasperation, making you think they're possessed or are acting from "profundity." Anyone who has written a novel in which he proposes to follow a character closely, day by day, even hour by hour, knows how hard it is to hold him in check so that he doesn't go mad, saying or doing something really insane. You cannot impose your will on a character except by holding him at a distance, that is, by speaking about him in somewhat general terms, summarizing his life and ideas in a global way. If you get too close to him, if for example you try to write a scene that takes place in a specific span of time (a certain afternoon, etc.), you feel a kind of neurosis that ends up controlling you, and then you write under the dictation of that character. It's a sort of magic, provoked by the fact that you are trying to give concrete life (hour by hour, with dialogues, etc.) to a creation of yours, that in a certain sense you are a *creator* of people. I don't think a writer exists who hasn't sensed this magic, this exasperation that your character provokes and that forces you to let him have his way—a demonic way, because the first thing the character does is to contradict himself, to annihilate himself (as you *created* him). I'm sure that if ever I write a novel that takes place in a twenty-four-hour period, and if I write it with invented characters (not with my "microscopized" memories, like Proust), I'll write something that people will say was copied after Dostoyevsky.

Someday, I ought to say all these things clearly, because people see Dostoyevsky as doing something different from what he really did: actually, Dostoyevsky's genius is that he let himself be possessed by his own characters, and this act of demonic magic in itself made him venture into places where other novelists hesitated to tread.

21 January

Have been working steadily at the novel for the past several days, taking advantage of my cold that keeps me in the house. Adding up the days on which I've worked effectively (because, since *Huliganii*, I always record the date and number of pages written), I observe that I've progressed at an average of five pages per day. The novel, begun with the thought of returning to literature after an absence of four years (because *Viață Nouă*—God only knows when it will be finished—or when published!) was to comprise the life of an ambitious but luckless young man in a maximum of 300 pages. Working on it, I realize it will be much longer. And it won't be about only the one man (Spiridon, as I called him), because the secondary characters crowd and shove, trying to obtain more important roles.

All these things would still be endurable if, as it always happens, the enthusiasm for the novel didn't leave me only a few weeks after I've begun it. My thoughts are stolen by other things, other readings. How passionately I could work now on the history of religions or even philosophy! A good part of the day I spend reading, anyway. Only at 5:00 or 6:00 do I start to write. And with what efforts, with what spiritual macerations! At 7:00 I begin to hear the cries of the newsboys, and that brings my mind back to reality, to the Russian front. After the evening meal, I read till 11:00, when I return to the novel until 2:00 or 3:00. I take a sleeping pill and struggle with insomnia for about an hour. This is my life.

22 January

In *Studi e materiali di storia delle religioni*, XVII, 1941, pp. 82–83, I read a review signed by Ernesto De Martino of the book by E. Bozzano, *Popoli primitivi e manifestazioni supernormali* (Rome, 1941). The reviewer writes, inter alia, that "it would be opportune to put in relief the connections between cryptesthesia pragmatica (or psychometria) and sympathetic magic, something that neither Carrington (*The Psychic World*, London: 1937) nor Bozzano have done."

I did this very thing in 1926 in a column in *Cuvântul*, and again in 1937 in the study "Folclorul ca instrument de cunoaștere" [Folklore as an Instrument for Obtaining Knowledge].[9] And I didn't stop at the connections between psychometria and sympathetic magic, but I went even further. How many of my Romanian readers I convinced, I have no way of knowing. But, lo, after so many years, foreign scholars are beginning to verify my hypotheses. However, it will be several decades more before the conclusions of my study will be accepted.

And no one will know about these things outside the country, because I made the mistake of publishing the study in Romanian.

24 January

From a postcard from Giza of 29 December received today, I learn that Gicu[10] was arrested and interned in a prison camp. Haig[11] was released and is completing military training in preparation for being sent to the front. In the first rank, of course, as is the order for all Legionaries.

I wonder with horror what has become of my journal that I gave to Gicu to keep for me. And was it for that he was arrested? Could it be that Ică is calling me back to the country in connection with these events?! . . .

25 January

Was it, perhaps, that I left Himalaya in 1931 because I didn't yet know the world, I hadn't yet been convinced of its great illusion?! What if, nevertheless, my whole life since then is nothing but a series of trials intended to persuade me of the uselessness and absurdity of any "modern life"?! Maybe the true poles of my life are not birth and death, but the year I left Himalaya and the year that I will return, definitively, penitent and prepared.

26 January

I read *Domnișoara Christina* [Mademoiselle Christina] today, for a new edition. Am surprised by its value. This book, which I haven't looked at since 1936 when I wrote and published it, seemed to me a failure, as was suggested also by a chorus of critics and some friends who considered it either perverse and erotic, or artificially fantastic. Today I realize I was mistaken, and I'm sure that in twenty or fifty years this book will be rediscovered.

Some readers don't understand why Simina is only nine; her erotic precocity disgusts them. But it was precisely to show that Simina is possessed, is a demoniac, that I made her a nine-year-old. At fourteen or fifteen she would have had the air of a sick precociousness, but in the natural order of things—precisely what I wanted to avoid.

I remember G. Călinescu's bad opinion of this book. It seemed to him "artificial" and influenced by foreign novels. The detail that in Mme. Moscu's house dessert is served and the guests are given milk in the morning with butter and honey—in a "poverty-stricken household," although the estate is large, rich, and Mme. Moscu gives 1,000 lei to the doctor for his visit. In the second place, he speaks about the smell of blood in Sanda's room as something atrocious ("menstrual blood"!), although everyone realizes that blood had been sucked from Sanda a few hours before. Doesn't he understand what vampirism is?

26 January

"Rozanov, le seul penseur peut-être qui, durant deux mille ans de cristianisme, ait soulevé la question religieuse du sexe . . ." [Rozanov, the only thinker, perhaps, who, during two thousand years of Christianity, has solved the religious question of sex . . .]" writes Merejkovski in *Les mystères de l'Orient* (p. 181), a less absurd book than I'd expected, but rather uneven, incoherent, and basically insignificant.

But the whole chapter about Christianity and sexuality is interesting. I believe that he and I are among the few, very few, Europeans who have known, attacked, and confessed (so far only fragments of) this mystery. The reader of my novels, if he's not completely hypnotized by prejudice against my literary "erotics," also has something to say in the matter.

27 January

A whole afternoon spent reading periodicals received from home (*Vremea* and *Gândirea*). As usual, the mediocrity of our contemporary culture depresses me. But, inter alia, I observe one thing: although I published two books last fall, my name does not appear once, even among the advertisements. Again I confirm that in Romania as in any other place, you are not present in culture unless you are living there—unless you are writing articles, lecturing, giving interviews, etc. In a certain sense, the experience gained in these three years of absence is invaluable. I'm beginning to realize what I will be, in Romanian periodicals, after I die. I realize how transient all things are. I judge more serenely, and therefore I judge myself better. It is not in this provisional, journalistic "presence" that I will realize myself. My detachment from glory and wealth will allow me to write works of incontestable worth. And I ought to start writing them one of these days.

28 January

If there's anything that worries me about this novel I'm writing now, it is that here, as in the case of *Huliganii*, the action unfolds too rapidly, it's too "agitated." My greatest misfortune—on account of which I haven't yet written the brilliant novels I'm capable of writing—is that I hurry: not that I write things down too fast, but that I narrate events too quickly, because I have the feeling all the while that the reader might get bored, and so I try not to exasperate him. My fear of exasperating the reader with long descriptions, interminable dialogues, tedious analyses, contradictions and incoherencies—in a word, with the "filler" inherent and indispensable to any masterpiece—has prevented me thus far from writing a book equal to one by Tolstoy or Dostoyevsky or even Balzac. I'm increasingly convinced that you can't create a great work without doing violence to the reader, without tiring him, exhausting him—forcing him to lay the book down sometimes, but obsessing him enough that he returns to it after an hour or a day. Obviously, not just anyone can accomplish this miracle. Ionel Teodorescu and Cezar Petrescu have plenty of length and pseudoanalyses in their novels, but neither has yet written a masterpiece. I, however, could write one. Two hundred pages of ballast, little details, impassioned discussions and dialogues—two hundred pages additional—and I'd have made of *Huliganii* something resembling *The Possessed*. But I was always feeling sorry for the reader. I didn't want to bore him—or exasperate him. The action, often, is *too rapid*. No matter how slowly I write, I still hurry. The pages gambol. And when I find myself in a scene full of pathos, I don't carry through with it, I don't dilate it to the point of delirium. I noticed this again last evening when I was writing the scene with Spiridon and Arethia—an excellent scene, in which Spiridon confesses his dream of having discovered the North Pole.

29 January

I am deeply distressed by the agony of the men at Stalingrad, the agony of Europe. And in order to be able to endure this tragedy, I take refuge in myself, in the book I'm writing, and in my long-standing thoughts concerning the end of our continent. I have banished the war from this notebook, in order to keep from becoming neurasthenic. I can no longer work without taking vitamins and Neurasthenin, and I can't sleep without Pasiflorina and Adolina.

And from out of this hell, I hear Aeschylus turning over in his grave. He who sang the heroic resistance of the Greeks against Asia witnesses now the surrender of Europe to the Asiatic hordes. Churchill and Roosevelt have met again at Casablanca. And none of their men sees how Stalin is playing with them, how they are the victims of the most tragic farce in the history of the world: the Red assassins—who, in comparison with other political assassins, have the merit of operating on a large scale, in the millions—the Red assassins are awaited as the liberators of Europe . . .

29 January

How can I explain this absurd coincidence—that whenever my right hand itches, soon afterward I hear disastrous news from the front or from the homeland?! It's happened not once or ten times, but regularly—and *never* have I found out any grave news and never have I had any trouble, without having anticipated it through an exasperating itching of the right palm. So it is that on days when my right palm doesn't itch, I'm at ease, I work in peace, almost certain that nothing serious has happened.

Can this solidarity be the result of the state of anxiety in which I live? Can it be that I'm so prepared by all my thoughts about the Russian or African fronts that any change is communicated through a kind of "sympathy"? Maybe I've become so sensitive as a result of my uninterrupted meditation on the fate of European culture that I constitute an excellent reception post, and all that is happening to this Europe that obsesses me I receive before the newspapers or radio report it.

Or maybe I've simply become capable of anticipating certain emotions, provoked by certain events of a historical or cosmic order.

30 January

When I went to Bucharest last summer, I took along a copy of Shelley's *Poetical Works* in E. Dowdant's edition, published by Macmillan, a volume I purchased in Calcutta, which has accompanied me on many of my travels. I took it even to Ciuc, where I lent it to Nae Ionescu, after having read to him once my favorite passages from "Epipsychidion." Nae took it with him to the hospital at Braşov, and when he was sent back the second summer to Ciuc, he had it with him again. A week after his death, Cella Delavrancea returned it to me.

On the flyleaf, in Cella's handwriting: "Me, you—you, me, 1937–40." And "Epipsychidion" was annotated: January 1939: "I am not thine: I am a part of thee"; July 1939, March 1940: "Spouse! Sister! Angel!" etc.; "The last reading with him, Thursday, 7 March 1940."

Often, when I think of Nae, I recall his wonderful passion for Cella. Only a young genius such as he could realize this total passion—which consumed him and perhaps killed him. His favorite book then was *Tristan and Isolde*. "Epipsychidion" complemented wonderfully that spiritual fire.

1 February

From the Marchesa Della Rosa[12]—ardent Legionary, who is working on a novel in English (because she is an American) about the tragedy of the Legion—I learn that Vojen[13] has been interned in a camp.

I see Baron Huene [German ambassador] today. He tells me he is optimistic concerning the campaign in Russia. A great army is being readied in Germany today that will liquidate the Soviets.

May God grant that he is right! In any event, I believe that Stalingrad will have an effect on morale in Germany. There will be the same sudden change that we observed in England after Dunkirk and the London blitz.

For me, Stalingrad has an additional significance: it makes me understand how Germany will defend itself when it is attacked from all sides.

Last night, when I was trying to fall asleep after working many hours on *Apocalips*, I realized that from now on I will be able to write only big novels. I have promised myself that, under no circumstances, not even the direst poverty, will I write any novels of under 400 pages, or even under 800–1000 pages. Otherwise, the novel can't be "finished"—at least, the novel as I see it now. For the rest—many short stories and novellas; and I'll write enough of these to be able to take it easy and pay, if need be, the rent.

3 February

Again, a terrible attack of nerves. The disaster of the Russian front could turn into a catastrophe. Here there is talk of a possible fall of Germany in the course of this winter. The irresponsible and the Anglophiles are happy. I am thinking that 1943 could be the year of tragedy for Romanian history.

I can defend myself only by thinking as often as possible about death. If *afterward* there will be nothing—then all our exertions today are useless. While if there will be something—it will be of enough interest to [make you forget][14] the agony of Europe.

5 February

Magnificent day. A liquid sky of an intense blue, such as Lisbon does not have after the coming of spring; a blazing sun, a fresh breeze, still ascetic, without too strong a vegetal sharpness. The first shrubs in the Edward VII Park are in bloom.

Spring is beginning. I can't work, but I'm more reconciled—to my fate and to that of the Continent. Under one form or another, life always triumphs, reintegrates. The millions of dead now rotting in Russia, the tens of millions who will inseminate the whole of Europe in the years to come—perhaps they are nothing but the sacrifices necessary to a cosmic equilibrium of which we, the victims, are unaware. Perhaps human beings have multiplied too much, and any catastrophe is good that reduces their number. Just as in the jungles of Ceylon billions of sprouts, crushed by their own number, decay, so that the "totality," the forest, will endure.

Never have I been more pessimistic than I am now. But I don't want to lose my reason. And this phenomenon of spring, like any cosmic rhythm, must be judged as it is in reality. It is enough to carry this judgment to its conclusion in order to understand how indifferent—viewed from above—is our fate and that of our cultures, our continents. How ephemeral are those forms that are being born continually to occupy a certain space, to animate it, to color it! What a tremendous lucidity the people of India have in this regard, as in so many others!

And is there no meaning, no ultimate value, in all these historical existences?! This I cannot believe, not even in my attacks of nihilism. Poetry, metaphysics, mysticism—these are universal, eternal, and of value. But they must be purified of their historical contingencies if they are to be indeed helpful to you. They must be objective, self-contained experiences—something hardly possible for me now. How happy I was in India! . . .

6 February

In these pages I do not rationalize, I do not recollect; I record here only cries of despair.

My vital trajectory—what a beautiful expression! What can it mean, what value can it still have in the universal becoming?! . . .

✳

The attempt of moderns to think impersonally has led to the discovery of species and to its opposite, the individual. How far we are from the impersonal thought of the ancients, from myth and folklore! We have succeeded in projecting everything vital, everything "becoming," onto the level of the "impersonal."

✳

I've not yet written a masterwork because I've never had the sentiment that what I'm writing might be my ultimate book—"ultimate" not in the chronological sense, but the existential: that I have said all that I am, know, and sense. Always, while writing, I have the impression that I'm practicing for something else, something greater. I have been quite reticent, sometimes mocking my genius, my potentialities.

When I was about twenty or twenty-two, I compared myself to Goethe. I said then that it would be only by accident that I would write a great book—but that my oeuvre in its entirety would be great, important. As a matter of fact, what everyone reads by Goethe are *Werther* and *Faust I*. Exactly as people will read, so long as the Romanian language exists, *Maitreyi*. But this is not what matters; rather, my work considered as a whole. This sentiment, that I cannot reveal myself entirely in a single book, has kept me from writing a masterpiece.

7 February
The only pleasures of which I'm capable are of a wholly peripheral nature. I can feel happy when I receive some ethnographical books, when I find something that interests me in the bookstore. But the feeling doesn't last long. A few hours of reading dissipate it.

Sometimes, when I'm with friends, I start talking about something, anything, with enthusiasm. If my friends judge me according to the way I seem to be in such moments of narcosis, they're mistaken. These are my little escapades in life and society. The rest of the time, I'm a misanthrope, struggling between despair and metaphysics.

✳

Terrible sadness. I write in order to survive, to keep from thinking, to keep from being conscious of myself. Poor Spiridon, he's still helping me with something!

9 February
Two years ago at this hour (3:00 p.m.) I said good-bye to friends at the railway station in London. I was leaving for Bristol, in order to take the plane

for Lisbon. I was full of hopes and apprehensions. My great desire was to escape from England, which was destroying me (the press, public opinion) and to return to the homeland, to see what was happening there. It never occurred to me that I'd spend two years in Portugal.

10 February

Two years ago today we left Bristol by plane and arrived in the evening at Lisbon. I remember our being searched to the skin, both myself and Nina, a process that lasted three hours. I remember the confiscation of the diplomatic bag, the photographs, etc., my refusal to leave "under such conditions" (I had the nerve to complain to the English officer who had ordered the body search), the violent examination of the luggage (all our clothes trampled on, the suitcases torn, etc.)—and all that followed.

In the evening we arrived at Lisbon: light, food, release from the hell of the airplane. Bristol had depressed me with its sinister ruins. The rain that fell on us in the half-ruined station, etc., etc.

✳

Seeing that I can't work on *Apocalips*, I've begun *Comentarii la legenda Meşterului Manole.*

11 February

My great passion for erudition, my obsession to gather and bring together as many facts and documents as possible before sketching the most modest theoretical explanation—is nothing but my tendency toward the concrete and experience, that which has been called my "experientialism." The fury with which, in literature, I throw myself into the vital and the erotic—is found again in my hunger for erudition, my pursuit of "facts," real, historical events. This is the source of my hesitations about "theoreticians" of the history of religions and ethnography. I don't want theories—these I make myself; what I want are facts, as many as possible, so that I never lose contact with reality.

12 February

The fact that I am mortal is not something that impresses me. Starting from this certainty, my death doesn't seem "interesting," worth being "accepted," etc. But death seems completely otherwise when I think of its imminence. I need only realize this imminence, and I see the whole of existence—from the Cosmos to the last foolish deed—changed, transfigured. Only with this experience do I understand life and death.

Too tired to continue.

14 February

My passion for symbol, structures, traditions: a more universal way of reliving the human drama, of remaining at the center of disappointments, metaphysics, and salvation.

15 February

On 10 February I broke off work on the novel at page 134 and began writing *Comentarii la legenda Meșterului Manole*. I'd observed that in the last days I was writing very little and poorly on the novel. My mind was captivated by "something else." It was then I decided to begin *Comentarii* and come back to the novel when I feel the desire for literature again.

What made me abandon the novel was the realization that I was spending a whole day and night writing at best five pages—pages I actually composed in two hours, while the rest of the time I wasted, leafing through books, sighing, chain-smoking cigarettes, and yearning for "something else." In order to escape into "something else," I began the insipid—and yet inspired—work on *Comentarii*.

17 February

At the German Press Counselor Klein's place, I met a very interesting man: Dr. Mário, correspondent at Paris for the *Kölnische Zeitung*. He was correspondent for *Cuvântul* in 1938, and I remember that I even translated an article of his once. Of course, I no longer remember its title. He tells me that Nae Ionescu and he were good friends. He had forewarned him, in Paris in January 1938, of all that was going to happen, because he, being Austrian, knew how serious governmental repression could be. (He had lost his best friends—shot. By whom?) Correía Márquez from *A Voz* was present also, and I was happy to hear this Dr. Mário say that Nae Ionescu had been one of the most intelligent men in Europe.

We talked a long time. He has just come from Paris. He doesn't seem to be much of a fan of Hitler. He believes René Guénon is the most interesting person of our time. (I don't believe this *always*, but often I do. Although I consider Aurobindo Ghose more "perfected.")[15] Very well read, speaking perfect French. He asks me for news about Nae's works. I tell him that the first two volumes of his philosophical works have been published. He seems excited. I mention my conversation with Carl Schmitt of last summer. He is surprised that Schmitt esteems Guénon. What impresses me is that he finds the era in which we are living "thrilling," although he is well aware of the fact that we could sink into an apocalyptic cataclysm. I speak to him about the "Pre-Nicopolean Era"; we are on the threshold of Nicopolis, when Europe could still have been saved from the Turks. But I don't see any sign anywhere that this time it will be saved.

I don't know if he said it just because Correía Márquez was there, but he declared that Salazar is the only truly popular leader the world has today.

8 March

It's been some time since I opened this notebook. I've succeeded in breaking away from the despair that threatened me, by starting on *Comentarii la legenda Meşterului Manole* (so far I've written about sixty pages, small-sized). For several days I worked a great deal preparing a diplomatic report, and I've written a considerable number of letters to people at home. Since Stalingrad fell, I've refused all invitations to places where I knew people would be having a good time—plus the cinema, the theater, etc. I've renounced also the ten days in Algarve that I had promised myself long ago.

A few days ago I received the first proofs of the little book *Os Romenos, latinos do Oriente* [The Romanians, Latins of the East]. In addition, I've collected the articles published to date in Portuguese and corrected them, in order to publish them in a volume of around 120 pages.[16]

Tomorrow, 9 March, I'll be thirty-six. To me, it seems I'm waking up from a dream. I've always had the impression not only that I was a young man (even now I feel very young), but that I have the right to feel this way, since my years do not confer any maturity on me. I awaken to the fact that I'm thirty-six. In four more years I'll begin getting old. If I were to try then to make a woman love me, I'd succeed only by means of my intelligence, and not by my youth. The thought is rather melancholic . . .

But apart from this tragedy, I ask myself what I've accomplished in the past year. A series of catastrophes began in the fall of 1937. I haven't been able to enjoy life since then. From the arrest of the boys until Stalingrad—in a continual state of mourning. During this time I've written some eight books, but no masterpiece. The three books I'm working on now will hardly advance me or reflect the man of thirty-six years. I've got to hurry . . .

18 March

Yesterday, at Bolasco's, I met Professor Camillo Pellizzi, president of the Institute of Culture in Italy, here to deliver a lecture on the occasion of the opening of the Italian Book Exposition. He was, for twenty years, professor of Italian literature at the University of London. After dinner, a discussion with him and the director of *Diario Popular* (a conceited young man who believes he's a great political thinker because he's discovered the "gigantic possibilities of America"), L. Sima (Hungarian press attaché), etc. We talk about the "destiny of Europe." I'm proud that I make everyone recognize the relativity of all those "great" problems; for the Portuguese, for example, it seems regrettable but natural that a new Europe is being made by sacrificing fifty to sixty million men from Helsinki to Bucharest; my furious outburst on hearing this:

why do you still talk, then, about a just and Christian peace, about "man" as such whom the democracies will restore, etc.? They had to admit that 4,000 kilometers' distance changes a great many things—beginning with morality and ending with freedom.

I have been elected an active member of the Portuguese Archaeological Institute. The amusing thing is that I didn't know it, and Buescu[17] telephoned me after he happened to read about it in *Diario de Noticias*.

28 March

My first address at the Institute of Ethnography and Archaeology: "Ethnobotanique roumaine comparée. La cueillette des plantes magiques." A study from the mandrake cycle that has been sleeping in my drawer for some six years! But how boring—the session at the Institute! And it was at Belém, next door to the magnificent wonder of the Church of Jeronimos, under a sky with a sun, on a melancholic Sunday afternoon!

This isn't the first time I've seen what a farce science is. Every little man knows a great deal about something the others don't know. Papers are read to which people listen without understanding anything said. All my theories about ethnobotany, mythology, and ritual—who could understand them? Luckily, such papers are published in *Ethnos*, and can circulate.

1 April

Have finished reading and correcting *Întoarcerea din rai* for a new edition. As usual, I'm crushed by the massive sadness of that book. But what a great book it is! How many like it can you count in Romanian literature? Almost everything I've written since then is found, *in nuce*, in that "insipid" novel, as Nae Ionescu called it.

What a great mistake I made in not reprinting it, even though it was sold out in 1934, the year it appeared! It is a document without equal and admirably written, with the exception of the sexual passages, or rather the rhetorical ones that I sexualized.

April

Working hard to finish *Comentarii*. As usual, after two months, a book begins to cease to interest me, and I ought to lay it aside and come back to it after an interval. But with this system, I've lost five or six years, and today I'm obliged to finish books conceived or begun in 1936–37. So, come what may, I've decided to carry it to the end—even summarizing, condensing, sketching.

Os Romenos, latinos do Oriente has appeared, the first book about us [Romanians] in the Portuguese language, and one of which I'm very proud. How amusing it was when I did press service at Livraria Classica Editora, writing dedications following a list supplied by the publisher.

The weather has turned bad, after three weeks of no rain—and the most beautiful sky I have ever seen in the springtime. My melancholic moods are starting again. On the one hand, Nina is leaving on a trip, and it's strange how tightly bound a person can be to you. On the other hand, I'm thinking more and more about death, about old age and my lost youth. Where have the years gone? It seems like only yesterday that I returned from India, overlearned, with a heart in mourning, but with fiery blood and a lust for life.

14 April
I awoke from a sound sleep at 3:00 a.m., and in the hour of insomnia that followed, I "saw" a wonderful play. Unfortunately, I haven't finished my useless volume of philosophy, *Comentarii*, yet, so I can't start writing it.

Then, too, Nina's about to leave and a week later I'll be going to Spain, for Easter.

*

More and more melancholic.
Rumors of a troop landing. Everyone admires Nina for her courage in traveling alone across Europe, on the eve of decisive events.

16 April
Nina left today, [looking] rather sad and worried.

I return home and start working quickly, trying to finish the book. A diplomatic bag is coming in two or three days, and I have to send the last chapter in it, so that *Comentarii* can be published by summer.

Why so much haste? Because I don't know how much longer I'll be allowed to live, and I want to say at least a part of what I have thought and discovered. Because I'm "in arrears" with my thinking formulated over the past five or six years. Because I don't know how to dissociate myself categorically from the dementia around me. Because I want to have my hands free if, God forbid, I am granted to be a witness to the cataclysm of Europe. I'd want to be "at liberty" then, in order to die mocking the imbecility of the white race.

18 April

Via the diplomatic bag I receive today a copy of *Insula lui Euthanasius* [Euthanasius's Island],[18] and I leaf through it excitedly. It was supposed to have appeared in 1939. Who will still be interested in it today?

I receive also a copy of *Maitreyi*, fifth edition. A blue cover, which amuses me. It's been ten years since the book was first published.

But thirteen years have passed since I separated from Maitreyi. I stopped thinking about her a long time ago. My life has taken a different path, and I must follow it to the end.

Rumors persist about the imminent occupation of the Azores by the Brazilians, etc., etc.

In the past few days, a rumor has been circulating of a separate Russo-German peace. Everyone's talking about these things as if they were gossiping at the café about the imminent divorce of the Popescus or a practical joke of Ionescu.

A total and blissful irresponsibility.

19 April

I receive a considerable number of books that I had ordered from Helsinki and Berlin. There are so many of them, and they're so interesting, that I am seized with a hearty disgust for culture, scholarship, and philosophy. If I were to lose them now, I almost wouldn't be sorry.

Melancholia and vacuity.

22 April

I finished *Comentarii* the day before yesterday.

Dinu Noica writes me, after reading the first part of it (sent via the previous diplomatic bag), that he is a little disappointed by the fact that I haven't eschewed footnotes. I reply to him at length, trying to explain. The truth is, that in the areas where I'm working, the honest thing to do is to cite your sources. Only Lucian Blaga had the courage to steal ideas and suggestions from all over without citations. That may be why he refused to use notes in his books. That may be why, also, his books are published only in Romanian. The last book of his I read, *Despre gândirea magică* [About Magical Thought], I found deplorable, with an alarming self-importance. Nevertheless, I have admiration for Blaga's genius. I believe, however, that his obsession with his system and his megalomania will end up discrediting him.

✳

Tomorrow I leave for Madrid and beyond, perhaps to Ávila, perhaps to Seville. I'm not making any plans. I am living, as I once did, "in adventure."

In these nights of work, I have reinstated the voluptuousness of chastity, and I have been reminded of its great power.

✳

Because of the rumors of an invasion, I've taken the "Journal" and part of my manuscripts to the Legation. In case of an evacuation, at least that much will be saved. The rest—as God wills.

(All that follows, up to 13 May, copied from the black notebook.)

Madrid, 24 April
  I left yesterday morning from Lisbon, without benefit of a sleeping car. The French consul from Argentina—and his daughter. How I almost lost the briefcase with the money and the diplomatic bag. The girls from Valencia-Alcántara: how they arranged meetings in their compartments (with one of the officers of the border police, and one from our group) without the others observing.

✳

San Antonio de la Florida, the church painted by Goya. I see it for the first time, although this is my fifth trip to Spain. Blue, gray, white. *The Dead Man Resurrected.* The two windows through which the ceiling can be seen. The angels look like women en déshabillé and froufrous. Madrilenian figures. And an astonishing error: the huge hands of those supporting the resurrected man.

✳

San Francisco el Grande. Cathedral, Sevillian red. Magnificent Life of St. Francis in the vestry, by Velásquez. Admirable frescoes in the lateral altars. *The Sermon on the Mount.* The battle against the Moors. The Arab who is literally coming out of the painting. The cupola—looking as if it were a decor for *A Midsummer's Night's Dream.* Meditation on modern religious art.

Ávila, 25 April
  Easter. Superb day. In the minister's car, together with the Grigores and Aron Cotruş.
  The walled city, seen from beyond the river, from the place where St. Theresa, as a child, a runaway from home, stopped, not knowing which way to go. The towers. A shame it's too hot and the sky too blue. Ávila must be seen in a state of fatigue and under a rainy sky, in order to understand its spirit. The visit in the private residence with that magnificent patio.

I keep having the impression that I'm in Braga. The same air of an episcopal city, the same light colors. The unforgettable *Annunciation* by Juan de Bourbon in the retable. The stone out of which the cathedral was built has red veins; a singular effect, as though it had been painted (and badly, in dubious taste).

The Santo Thomás Church (15th century), with the tomb of the son of the Catholic king, age 19. It is situated outside the fortress. The only church in which I have seen the altar where services are conducted elevated—almost to the height of the choir. The tomb of Don Juan's tutor. Also that of Torquemada. The cloister: "Day of silence," because some monks are being buried. The great Cloister de los Reyes. And the groups of seminarians who watch us, with troubled looks. (Women can't visit this church, because of the seminarians who are in training to become missionaries.)

From the garden of Santo Thomás, the Sierra de Gredos, capped with snow, can be seen.

The hermitage of San Segundo, beside the Adaja River: pure Romanesque, incomparably beautiful, profiled against the blue sky, with the walls of the fortress in the background. Lizards. The sun beating down.

We climb the defense tower of the citadel. Then, the visit to the most beautiful cathedral of all, San Vicente. Romanesque.

Following the itinerary of St. Theresa. The place she was born, which today is an altar. Relics (uninteresting). The convent where she lived for nearly thirty years. All I thought and felt then. There are only twenty-one nuns—buried alive. The matron who explains things to us.

En route to Seville, 26 April.

El Cesarde la Guardia (90 km.): houses dug into the clay hillside.

Tembleque: village with white houses.

We enter La Mancha. Plateau, with mountains on the horizon in all directions. Windmills. Rather monotonous.

Madridejos: white village with gray tiles and much greenery.

Manzanares. Delightful house of the tourist service. Breakfast. The library above the road, in which I find two copies of Codreanu's *La Guardia de Hierro* [The Iron Guard]. Flowers. Am reminded of Oxford.

Sierra Morena. Mountains of slate and granite. The ravine through which we see the train passing. Another mountain range, and then—Andalusia. The landscape changes abruptly. Rich green fields with orchards of olives and oranges with beds of poppies. Then, all the way to Córdoba: fields—rich, but without personality. The thrill of crossing the Guadalquivir. Entrance into Córdoba. Hotel Regina. Evening: cf. Córdoba as it appears to you from the way you enter. At dinner: Franco's sister. All I was reminded of.

Córdoba

Notes: the Mosque, with orange trees in the courtyard. The streets: Averroes, Moses Maimónides. Maimónides' house. The heat—and only one meter between the houses. Narrow, Arabic streets. Visit to a museum of modern art (deplorable) at La Vila Viana.

We wander around. Where I look, what I see, what I feel.

The bridge over the Guadalquivir, from where one can see Córdoba in the twilight.

To be completed.

Seville

Calle de Bailén, no. 12, where the minister was able to find us a room for fifteen days for 1500 pesetas. My bed in the entryway.

In the evening I go alone into the city. Stroll along Calle Sierpes. How I got lost. The café. The couple: she, old and coy; he, proud, dressed in Andalusian style, twisting and crushing his cigarette. He orders coffee. His lordly look. He refuses the necktie peddler. The other couple. The blonde girl at the bar.

At 11:00 I arrive by taxi at the neighborhood of Santa Cruz. The brightly lighted square, where the young girls are practicing with castanets for *la feria*. Las Cadenas. I enter. In the rear, with the girls, von Breisky. Andalusian dances. The place fills up toward midnight with guests of the Duke of Alba. At my table, a young man with two older women. The flirting of the young man at the next table. How he starts a conversation. The Gypsies. Jealousy.

I leave at 1:30. The road below the wall of the Alcazar, to Guardia del Murillo. The park at 2:00 a.m. The fragrances. And the many Sevillians still on the streets.

Seville, 27 April

I slept only a few hours, with the light on, because I found the walls covered with bedbugs. It was no surprise; the hosts are all intellectuals, or at least the youngest one is—an individual some fifty years of age, who has written a book about the education of children (he doesn't have any), the proceeds from which are for the aid of orphans of the Civil War.

Visits: the Cathedral (chapel where Columbus prayed before leaving for India, with a superb painting of the Lord's Mother); La Giralda; Casa de Pilatos; la Caridad. Meditations: Don Juan, Valdéz Leal. The bridge over the Guadalquivir. The Tower of Gold. The neighborhood of Triana.

Night. The revue at 10:00. Lola Flores. Again at Santa Cruz. Maruja.

28 April

The Alcázar in Seville. Enormous magnolias, resembling trees. Orange trees, trained like vines, growing on the wall. Primitive garden. The pond. White pigeons. The baths. The prison. Cypress and eucalyptus trees.—The modern part. Yellow sand. Nightingales. Roses. Lanes lined with lemon trees. A wild pepper with little yellow flowers. The Guadalquivir passes below the garden. Formerly a swamp.

The fish in the pool that come when called. Arabic gateway, of stone. In front, the old wall, with blue and red bougainvilleas.

Patio de las Doncellas. The Sultan's throne. The bedroom of the kings. The glazed tiles (*azulejos*): green, white, maroon (restored). Roman columns. Patio de los muñecos. Jewelry, embroidery. Overhead—the sky.

The kitchen. The salon of the ambassadors: gold with pale blue. The secret door that leads outside the citadel.

Preparations for a visit of Franco. He will stay in the Alcázar.

✳

The highway to Granada, lined with eucalyptus trees.

Alcalá. Castle wall in the river. Arabic houses, white. The wine cellar.

Aguadulce. White village.

Estepa. The city can be seen from a distance, on a hilltop. Here, all the inhabitants perished in a battle with the Romans—as happened also at Sarmizegetuza.

The village of Fuente de Piedra. Yellow houses beginning here.

Antequera. Park with poplars. Mountains. The castle to the right of the cathedral. From the Tourist Service rest house the valley can be seen, with the city on the right; in the background, the Sierra Nevada. Locust trees.

Peña de los Enamorados. Gray, with a steep slope. Reverie. Love song.

Archidona. White. The rain.

Loja. The panorama.

Granada

The former Arab square, beside the cathedral.

My first visit to the Alhambra. A. Linares's old bookshop. Meditation on the photographs of people in Arab costumes, the horse in the corner, etc.

The Albaicín quarter. Beautiful girls who come up to the automobile. The descent into San Pedro. The River Darro, swift. How the Alhambra looks from here. The woods, the houses.

Evening. Sevilla Bar. The man with the ball in his nose. Apéritifs. Manzanilla, not perfumed.

Night. Flamengo in a grotto, in Albaicur. Carmen, who looks very much like M. Antoñita. "Casada, pasada!" Josefa. The dance: Sevillana de Sacromonte (three times). Manolita in a fandango gitano; obscene movements of the hips. She sings "La Gazpacha."

Then, the Ballet of Soledad. Describe the grotto; discussion, etc. The parting: Carmen and Antoñita, with flowers in their mouths.

Granada, 29 April

A few hours of sleep. Then alone, to the Alhambra. Useless to write. I'm recording here only fragments, rich in resonances for me. I loved the Alhambra too much not to write about it, to unburden myself. Will do it as soon as I arrive in Lisbon.

Patio da Linda Maja. Cypresses, laurels, orange trees.

The view from the tower with Queen Isabel's boudoir. Italian frescoes.

The garden. Paradise. Waterlilies. Flowers. To the Tower of the Captive: a lane of cypresses. Nightingales. Gardin de los Adarves; view of the Sierra Nevada. Hotel in the woods. Wide promenade. The walls in the rear, covered with roses and orange trees. La Vega.

Alcazaba. Military garrison. Towers. The Generalife Gardens. Entrance through an ivy-covered arch. Flowers. Perspective from between white lilacs, wisteria, and roses. Terraces. The Cypress of the Sultana (Abencerraje). Enclosed garden, archways of ivy.

Patio de los Cipreses. Enormous magnolias. The rain on the balconies above does not reach us. Melancholy, melancholy.

When you come to Grenada, you must come always with the woman you love.

And return ten years later.

All that passed through my mind. Mythical geography.

30 April

Toward Málaga. Sospiro del Moro, with Grenada in the valley. Rightly did Boabdil weep here, as if he were being banished from Paradise. Where would he find another Alhambra?[19]

Mountain roads. Bridges. Then . . . suddenly, the sea. Almond trees, cactus, sugarcane. African atmosphere.

Salobreña: the castle, high up. White houses on the hill. Carts with reeds. Children.

Almuñécar: in a valley, quite colorful. The remains of the Alcázar on the hill. The river. The sky.

Mirador: the cliffs extending into the sea. The Mediterranean, with its weary mountains.

Curbele: houses. Red trees, *mandroños*, growing right on the beach. Remnants of castles standing guard.

Málaga. The entrance into the city, beneath palm trees in the park. The castle gardens. Ruins, and flowers. Twilight in the castle. We descend. Visit to the cathedral. Partially burnt by the communists. The buildings beside our hotel—also burned.

Night: hours spent wandering around the port (deserted), cafés, the park. A great cosmopolitan port, now become a provincial town. Poverty and gardens.

And in spite of everything, how melancholic and restful! The Mediterranean. Once more, among the ruins of castles, I see how the flowers heal and cover everything.

1 May

Toward Cádiz. Beach with grayish sand, then forests of pine and eucalyptus. Red soil.

San Roque. In the full sunlight, facing Gibraltar. Plaza de los Amores. Soldiers. The appearance of the officers. Antiaircraft batteries.

Algeciras. Dinner at Hotel Christina. The ships in the Gibraltar harbor. Germans who are watching with binoculars.

Chiclana de Frontera. Superb village with white buildings.

San Francisco. White. Iron bars at the windows. The salt, the sunshine.

Visit to Cádiz. The museum with Murillo. The chapel with Goya. Ascent of the tower. The port. The gardens. The inn: La Posada del Trasni. The children who are playing in a procession. Calle Duque de Tetuan. Four-hour stroll, at night, alone. The blonde. The café. Again, to the port. The accosting. The adventure. The dream.

The second day.

2 May

Cádiz. Murillo, *The Virgin* in the Colegio San Felipe de Neri. *The Head of St. John the Baptist*, with the veins cut (terra cotta, Pedro Roldán). At the entrance to the college, a list of students and teachers killed in the war. *The Last Supper*, by Goya, in the private chapel: Madrilenian style, reclining on their sides. Popular.

En route to Seville. Jerez, with a visit to the wine cellars of Pedro Domecq. Two hours. Evening, at Seville—on the third day of the *feria*. Description. The walk. The adventure.

Seville, 3 May

Names of the cantinas in the *feria*: La Revoltosa, Peña el Maestro Currito, La Gitana, El Baratillo, Centro Cultural la Armistad, Peña Trianero, P. Jerez, P. Campero, Maestranza aérea de Sevilla, P. Puerta Triana.

The bullfight. The bull that wanted to die of its own accord. Notes in the other notebook.

Visit to Itálica. The sunshine. Poppies. Mosaics. The arena.

Evening: with N. D.[20] at Las Cadenas. Night: at *la feria*.

4 May
    On the way back to Madrid. At 4:00, Aranjuez. Less beautiful in the summer. Too monotonous; too green.

5 May
    Agustina. I've decided to write my impressions of Andalusía according to the same system I used in 1938:[21] that is, to relive all the moods I've experienced in these two weeks in Spain. Proust on the road. Only in this way will I preserve all my memories.

Lisbon, 13 May
    Since returning to Lisbon, I could have written every day the same word: "melancholy." I haven't done anything. And the nights I waste until 3:00 or 4:00, in order to accelerate my equilibrium.
    It's too hot. Suddenly—summer. Only after midnight does it cool down.
    I keep thinking about the same thing: that I might die—and for the first time I doubt the reality of a postmortem existence. What if there is nothing, only annihilation?! To what good, then, is all that's happened?! Nothing in this world has meaning anymore, if there's nothing *beyond*.
    Once again, melancholy over the life I've led. Where has it gone? I can't believe that in 1947 I'll be forty. Until a few years ago I thought of myself as so young that I'd say to myself sometimes, "When I grow up, I'll do such and such a thing." And then, too, I'd say that at age forty a man begins to cease being young . . . Another, more serious thing: self-reproach over the thought that I don't have any children. In 1933, I forced Nina to have a curettage. For years after that, she kept asking me to let her have a baby, and I refused. I would tell myself, "When I grow up . . . I'm barely an adolescent now."

14 May
    Reading *Ciuleandra* in a Portuguese translation.[22]
    . . . When did all those years pass?!
    I say to myself that this is *Le démon du Midi*.[23] Or, perhaps, it's a poison that will end up killing me. Because, the neurasthenia that threatens me can't be cured in any way. I don't see anything that can satisfy me. Only if I could accomplish a total reintegration—youth, Nina, all pleasures, genius, with time arrested—would I be happy again.

15 May
    To discover—as does modern thought from Dilthey on—that man is, and remains always, in history is more serious, more tragic, than it would seem at

first glance. The response to this discovery is despair—as is verified in every circumstance: for example, the consciousness that I've lived with Nina for ten years is a source of despair. No matter how hard I try, I can't return to the time when we hadn't begun our life together. It is a *history* from which I cannot separate myself, which I cannot annul, and which continues to make me, to influence me. The same sentiment is verified in any area. Man apart from history does not exist. And when he begins to love a history, he is destined to despair.

28 May

I've gone back to the novel again, after trying in vain to redact my Andalusian impressions and meditations. On the night of 21 May I began writing my play, *Tinereţe fără de bătrineţe*. The next day I gave that up too. I don't yet have the dramatic spirit necessary for this play.

But it wasn't work on the novel that has been the dominant thing in these weeks, but, as usual, melancholy, and, what's worse, neurasthenia. There are days when five or six "neurotic storms" assail me. And each is triggered by a different cause or pretext. The most frequent are metaphysical melancholies. For the first time, I doubt—during such attacks—the postmortem existence of the human personality. If, indeed (to take one example), Heidegger is right, then nothing in the world seems significant any longer, nothing has any reason to be. If we came from nothing and return to nothing, then death has no meaning, nor does creation or effort. If this is the truth, then there's nothing left for me to do but to kill, rape, and lounge around sunning myself. Without a spiritual unity destined to continue its experiences after death—when the great verification and valorization of deeds begins—everything seems useless to me.

But I have another kind of attack too: of jealousy. Sometimes I imagine Nina is being unfaithful, which is absolutely absurd, because Nina lives only through me and the love she bears for me. But this fantasy is created and fed by my neurasthenia.

30 May

Gide bases the ethics and philosophy of his epic novels (especially *L'Immoraliste* and *Les Faux-monnayeurs*) on the lesson of the natural sciences. Recall his pages about suboceanic fauna, the "ethics" of fish that withstand desalinated water, etc. They are the ultimate consequences of Darwin and Nietzsche, purified of incongruities, made accessible to the "elite members of the general public." Actually, despite the fact that he has avoided falling into the clichés of "contemporary truths," Gide is a man of his era. His works reflect perfectly the effort of the average sciences of his time. This does not diminish his importance but, on the contrary, heightens it, because, while succeeding in creating points of contact with later eras, Gide's oeuvre remains at the same time a document representative of the era 1880–1930, and yet a document of brilliant authenticity.

I think, however, that the ethics and philosophy of a great modern novelist, one who wishes to reflect in his work a striving for knowledge of contemporaneity, can no longer be content with the lessons of the natural sciences in vogue at the time of Gide's youth. He will have to take account of all that has been revealed by a Heisenberg, a Ueskull, a Heidegger, a Froebenius—and especially all that I could reveal.[24]

June

No one, knowing me well and even reading this journal, can possibly imagine the intensity of my drama. Several times a day I have to struggle with an attack—of despair or of neurasthenia—so grave that I believe it would overwhelm even the stoutest of men. No one can suspect the quantity of genius, willpower, and sheer physical energy expended day after day in this combat with myself and my demon.

7 June

In the apocalyptic struggle of today, my country has very little chance of surviving: this is my daily obsession, which, if it does not overwhelm me utterly, in any event exhausts me down to the marrow. Why can't I save myself, as I did ten years ago, by adopting other principles and joining myself to another destiny, more grand, more universal?!

Romania and even the Romanian people (in their elements of historical and cultural continuity) are passing through the greatest crisis in their existence. We are neighbor to an empire six times larger than all of Europe, with two hundred million inhabitants, and which by the year 2000 will have circa four hundred to five hundred million, with a formidable economic and geopolitical space, with an ecumenical social mystique that will be popular especially at the end of this war (hunger, poverty, ruins, revolts, despair, etc.). In the face of this colossus, soon to be victorious—a sick Romania, optimistic and credulous. A dominant class that expects everything in reward for its hatred of the Germans. In this decisive storm, our "pilots" are blind. Our army was decimated in Russia, we lost all our weaponry at Stalingrad, while Hungary preserved its military strength intact. Our sacrifice of blood is compromised by the idiotic acts of our political leaders who are attempting to play a double game with the Anglo-Saxons, losing what we've gained from the Germans, obtaining nothing from the Anglo-Americans. The great Ică has played politics 100 percent with the Germans, and now he wants to play politics with the Anglo-Americans, sending imbecilic emissaries who are caught by the Gestapo and cost us more divisions at the front. Ică doesn't understand what the Hungarians have always understood: that the same man cannot take two different political positions, that his duty is to get as much as possible from the Germans on the basis of our sacrifices, leaving *someone else*, if need be, to engage in a *different* policy.

From Nina's letters and those of others in the country, I understand that almost all is lost. The fall of Tunisia was celebrated with champagne by the same Romanians who toasted no German victory against Russia. They all have the illusion that an arrangement will be made with the Anglo-Americans. The same tragic illusion is held by our Legation in Lisbon, and probably all the others. No one can see the simple fact that if Russia can't be defeated, the fall of Germany will bring with it the occupation of Romania by the Soviets, with all that will follow: the execution of 100,000 men who, despite their faults, constitute the Romanian phenomenon.

10 June

Man is a creator only in the biological order: he can bring babies to birth. An impersonal kind of creation, having to do with the species. But the act of creation, Eros, can unleash primordial powers and visions of a force that far surpasses the contemporary mental horizon: cf. the mystique of archaic origins, Dionysus, etc. The sentiment that he *can create*, the certainty that he is *life* and can *give birth to life*, transforms man into a vast, cosmic being. The being in whom Eros dominates as a metaphysical element and instrument of insertion into reality lives a completely different life, much more grandiose and significant than ours. If there are certain archaic secrets, accessible to man as such, to the uncorrupted animal-man, then these secrets are revealed only to the individual who embodies Eros totally, cosmically, without problematics, without neurasthenia. It is interesting to observe how these Dionysian structures survive in modern civilizations, and how many problems they give savants, doctors, and moralists in trying to decipher them! The Christian Church has fought against these erotic structures. God cannot withdraw from Eros, even in its frightening, fecundating form. Only *sterility* is demonic. The fertilizing Eros cannot be opposed to God.

11 June

Because Adolf Hitler was not a seafarer, the history of Europe will have a different course. In the summer of 1940, when England could have been conquered with a few divisions and a hundred tanks, Hitler hesitated to launch the invasion—all the preparations had been made—because he thought of the losses—*the men drowned*. A continental mental structure: he had a fear of water, a horror of shipwrecks. For a sailor, the men drowned have no importance. Shipwrecks happen even when there is no war. That is why the Anglo-Americans will attempt the invasion of Europe. Hitler, hesitating in the face of those thousands of men drowned *without having fought* does not quaver in the face of the millions who are dying in Russia, on dry land. It seems to him that at least there, their deaths are positive. But a thousand times more positive would have been their perishing in the waves as part of an invasion army.

And, lo, this is the way world history is made: owing mainly to mental structures, to an individual destiny, and very little to the pressure of economics or the class struggle. Everything is determined, certainly, but not by the belly or sex—rather by *spirit*, by heredity, by existential style.

15 June

Tantzi Coste[25] has finished reading *Întoarcerea din Rai* and *Huliganii*, which she did not know. We talk about them at length, and the conversation serves to remind me of those novels I had almost forgotten by 1941, but which I've reread twice since then: once to be able to resume work on *Viață Nouă*, and the second time to make corrections. The latter time I became aware of the total absence of moral problems in them. The heroes do what they want, without any self-restraint; the girls surrender readily, no one gets married, and no one gets pregnant. A metaphysical problem exists, and perhaps a social one, but a sexual ethic does not yet appear. Why? The critic G. Călinescu is content to cite my aversion to marriage—but he does not ask himself why?! Actually, this ought to be the business of the critic: to explain. Especially in the case of a writer of my type, obsessed by "problems." The truth is that with me the obsession with metaphysics and biology leaves me no room for another problematics. Eros, for me (the man of eight or ten years ago), had a metaphysical function. Love obliged and entailed penalties—without any necessity for the presence of society, institutions, accidents (out of all the "adventures" of my characters—only one accident, and not a single "love child").

Something else: I had been much impressed by the vocabulary and symbolism of Indian Vaishnava mysticism, which expresses mystical love in terms of adultery rather than marriage, precisely in order to mark the transcendence, the essential "otherness" of the mystical experience. I remember that I gave a lecture at the university once in which I said that it seemed to me that the saying of St. Silvester that "God is like an onion—because he is good and he makes you cry" is more consistent with mystical experience than a rational definition of God that attempts to limit him through attributes.

Why have I mentioned these things? In order to say, confusedly and preliminary, that love, for me, is primarily an experience with metaphysical meaning. What interests me is the reaction people have to it as such, as a destiny—and only secondly its moral, social, and gynecological implications or consequences. My characters make love at any time and with anyone because I am interested exclusively in this experience, which reveals to them a destiny.

The great critic, Călinescu, never asked himself such questions of course.

17 June
    Tomorrow Nina and Giza are coming by airplane, on a direct flight from Berlin to Lisbon. At least, so a telegram received a few days ago informed me. The two months of my being alone have passed, in which time I've suffered terrible attacks of melancholy. Nina's presence would have attenuated them or, in any event, would have transferred them into other, less serious spells of nerves.
    And yet, I have a strange uneasiness.

20 June
    Nina arrived yesterday by plane. Unrecognizable as a result of her illness. I knew nothing about it, because she was afraid to write me lest she alarm me. At Bucharest she spent some ten days in Doctor Ioviu's sanatorium. At Berlin she saw Dr. Wagner, and only four weeks from now—after she has been examined by a student of the latter, a German doctor in Madrid—will she know whether or not she'll need an operation.
    She is very weak and her nerves are worn out. Her "Oltenian"[26] spirit has disappeared. This fact has a calming effect on me. All my neurasthenias and other attacks are muted, living beside another suffering human being. I observe that my insomnia has ceased. I go to sleep at midnight instead of 5:00 or 6:00 a.m., because I know that if I sleep well, her sleep will be better too.
    I know why I wanted to go to the front: in order to escape from myself, from egotism, from neurasthenia. Because neurasthenia is the most terrible form of egotism.
    But may there not exist a subconscious symmetry between Nina's illness and my own sufferings of May and June?

24 June
    I interrupted the novel a week ago, after working productively for almost a whole month.
    Have begun reading *Un port la răsărit* (A Port in the East) by Radu Tudoran.[27] Great narrative talent. I believe that in twenty to thirty years Romania will be the country of novelists. When I think that twenty years ago we boasted only of *Ion*, and that today a novice can debut with *Un port la răsărit* . . . !

    My German translator, [Günther] Spaltmann, sends me a long letter (15 May, received a few days ago through the diplomatic bag). He tells me, inter alia, that I am a "European" and that his mission is to "launch" me beyond the borders of Romania.

I think, once again, that I would be represented in the world today, if I wrote in a major European language—English, for example.

28 June

I unwrap a copy of the third edition of *Huliganii* sent to me some two months ago by Delafras, and I shudder at the large number of typographical errors. Alarmed, I close the book and put it back on the shelf. I wonder what the new generation of readers—those who have heard that I'm an "intelligent" writer—will say about this meaningless prose. "Tema ei era" [Her theme was] is printed as "Teama ei era" [Her fear was], etc., etc.!

If I were to die tomorrow, before I've had time to revise my entire oeuvre published in Romania, I'd be known only approximately.

10 July

An Iberian grippe has kept me in bed for a week, incapable of working, allowing myself only after three days of a high fever had passed to reread Cargaiale's plays and Book II of Herodotus. Have interrupted work on the novel again. This means it won't be done by fall. Therefore, it won't appear this year as I had promised myself.

12 July

I receive a copy of *Comentarii la legenda Meşterului Manole*, admirably printed at a new publishing house, Publicon. Too bad there are so many typographical errors. Horrible errors have crept in, even on the page next to the flyleaf where "Books by the Same Author" are listed.

I'd start working on the novel again, but I'm depressed by the course of the war. The Anglo-Americans have landed in Sicily, and it seems things are going well for them. Their aerial superiority allows them to move anywhere in the Mediterranean. Nothing more to write . . .

15 July

Manole is the twenty-fifth work I've published. With the two translations, the Nae Ionescu edition (*Roza vânturilor*), *Iphigenia* [sic: *Ifigenia*], the unpublished volume of political articles and another, also unpublished, of ethnographic studies, with *La Mandragore* (nearly finished), the first volume of *Viaţă Nouă*, the travel notes already published, as well as some twenty studies in print—to which can be added *Ensayos luso-romenos*, in the press[28]—my bibliography is raised to circa 55 books and booklets. Not to mention *Romanul adolescentului miop* and *Gaudeamus*, which will be left to appear posthumously—as will also my private journal. I'm thirty-six. I ought to consider myself satisfied. In a certain sense, I haven't wasted my time.

Yet in spite of all this, I have the sentiment that I've given almost nothing, that I've said nothing essential, that I haven't declared a tenth part of the truths for which I was sent into the world. The majority of my production is haphazard. It was written under the pressure of publishers, magazines, or events. I haven't had the chance yet to fructify my past labors with a masterwork. I am a Goethe who has not even written *Werther*, although he has already thought through *Faust II*. It's not that I lack the power of concentration. Nor faith in my genius, nor in the enduring quality of my creations. I realize that since Eminescu, the Romanian race has never seen a personality so complex, so powerful, and so gifted. But what kills me is the sentiment of the perishability of Romanian culture, and of Europe. We were born next to Soviet Russia. That says it all.

26 July

Last night, at the moment we were preparing to leave the Costes' house in Estoril, Della Rosa comes up in a car, agitated, to ask if I've been listening to any radio station. I—the radio! But I ask him, "Has something happened?" He takes me aside. He can hardly speak. He tells me that someone telephoned the Italian Ministry, where he was dining, to say that [Pietro] Badoglio has been named head of the Italian government and Mussolini has been overthrown. But he asks me not to say anything, because it's not confirmed.

I understood from his emotion that these things really had happened. And, curiously, I who until then had trembled at any bad news from Sicily, became suddenly calm on hearing about the departure of Mussolini—who is signing a separate peace treaty in a few days or weeks. *Fatum*. Nothing to say, nothing to regret. Now I wait for history to be fulfilled. My nation may perish because of this event, but I look to the road ahead. That same, strange peace has stayed with me all day today.

The ambassador in audience with Salazar, who tells him (and he conveys this to me in a confidential way) that the Anglo-Americans, despite their Russophile appearance, are fully conscious of the Bolshevik peril. But did Salazar say this, perhaps, to prepare the way for abandoning his neutrality?! Because, the main reason that has kept him from doing so has been the pro-Soviet policy of the Allies.

29 July

After fifteen years, I'm rereading *The Brothers Karamazov* in an unabridged translation. Amazed by Dostoyevsky's "tricks." No character is coherent with himself, with what the author has said about him beforehand, but he contradicts himself, he abases himself (when you aren't expecting it), he hates, etc., leaving you with the terrifying impression of a "deep life," of "power," of Slavic genius, of subconscious analysis, etc. Not for a moment do I doubt that Dostoyevsky has genius. But, to me, he applies his "manner" to the saturation point. There does not exist, in all his books, a single normal person. I don't believe this is accidental. (It's amusing that the German doctor, who is summoned by several characters, always declares, "I don't know anything!" Is it Dostoyevskian irony—or the European point of view?) The poem of the Grand Inquisitor, admirable as imagination and conception, is prolix, mediocre, and sometimes unreadable precisely in its essential episodes (the problem of freedom). I have read it twice, and you have to extract the meaning (of these episodes) with forceps.

But the courage of Dostoyevsky—to heap up facts and words, and to describe, and to let the main characters speak for dozens of pages!

August

A long time ago I bought a copy of *Le démon du midi* by Bourget. I wanted to see if, indeed, it contains anything of my "drama." I read the first chapter. Impossible to continue. I haven't read anything more contrived, more pretentious, more artificial in years.

3 August

My attacks of despair are starting again. This time, without a personal reason, but provoked by the danger that threatens my nation. The Allies continue to demand the unconditional surrender of Italy, even after the deposing of Mussolini! Thus, it is no longer a war against Fascism, but one against Italy. What can Badoglio do? We are approaching a "Kerensky moment" in Italy.[29] It is said that Eden[30] prefers an anarchical and Sovietized Italy to an Italy honorably withdrawn from the war.

And after that? We won't be able to pull out of the war, because we'll be occupied immediately by the Germans. The Russians are still very strong. The Allies don't dare land in the Balkans, for fear that Russia will make peace with Hitler. We are, therefore, destined to be "liberated" by the Bolsheviks. And after that? Will we survive?! When I hear that in Romania people are going about their business, carousing, talking, writing, and publishing—I envy them. I myself have no peace anymore.

4 August

On Sunday the letter of the [Cardinal] Patriarch [Manuel Gonçalves Ceregenira] appeared, forbidding Catholics to read the writings of the historian, theologian, and polemist Alfredo Pimenta.[31] The conflict was an old one, and of a political nature. While the Archbishop sees red when he hears about Hitler, flirting at the same time with the Soviets and the Jews (in his New Year's Pastoral Letter he said that Maripsa Maritain[32] is of the "race of the Virgin Mary"), Pimenta is a monarchist, anti-Communist, and anti-Mason.

But it is amusing to notice that the Patriarch published his decree exactly at the time of the Communist-Democratic strikes, which the government has strangled energetically (moreover, the strikes broke out in 185 enterprises exactly two days after the overthrow of Mussolini!), that is, at a moment when the whole press has become anti-Communist again, and public opinion is beginning to come to life. The Archbishop's letter attempts to create a diversion: Nazism persecutes Catholicism.

I'm curious to see how Pimenta will defend himself. I've learned that the Jesuits some time ago threw a girl into his arms, to whom the old writer penned verses and wrote fifteen impassioned love letters. The Jesuits photographed these letters and now are waiting. Pimenta, it is said, published some two months ago a pamphlet in which he hints that two pro-Soviet priests have apartments in the city.

10 August

Where is my wisdom, my power to detach myself from the world and from pain, which I once possessed and of which I was so proud? Today I live pathetically, possessed and violated by any disastrous "news," the tragedy of my nation and of Europe. No longer can I "detach" myself, nor can I find equilibrium except while working. But I'm not in control of my work any longer.

I've started reading philosophy again, a pursuit I had abandoned a long time ago. I've read Max Scheler (*Das Ewige in Menschen*) and Edward Spranger. Now I'm reading *Die Götter Griechenlands* by Walter Otto. I content myself with what I can find here. As usual, a philosophical reading—or, better said, the meditations it facilitates for me—calm me. But only for the time being, for the blessed interval of the reading. After I close the book, the "drama" begins again. "*What if we perish?!*"—this cry I hear continually in my mind. For a while I suspected that my fear of the disaster of my people was a form of egotism: I would lose my library, my fame, my public, etc. But I don't believe it's that. In America, after three or four years, I'd acquire fame, a public, and a considerable amount of money, if I were hard-hearted enough to renounce Romanianism for another culture. But I can't do that. Without my nation, nothing in history matters to me any more.

15 August

What a shame that I'm not trying to make this journal an "instrument of knowledge"![33] I'd have to give up the system of noting only events or melancholic moods, and transform it into a "jacket" containing papers of all sorts—even notes and quotations from the books I'm reading, plans for works, etc. In my desk drawers there are always such jackets containing "fragments," the majority of them infinitely more important than the pages of this journal.

In order to give more substance to these pages, I'd have to record not only what I've thought or suffered on a given day, but also recollections. Many events and conversations have not been noted here. And they do not remain inert, but often I relive them, telling them to friends, pondering them, validating them.

And how many amusing facts about important people from the homeland have I happened to hear! What Pangal told me about Nichifor Crainic, when he himself approved the request of "Ion Dobre" to continue his theological studies in Jerusalem, annotating his petition thus: "Inasmuch as the law does not allow the sum of 500,000 lei, the amount Ion Dobre requests, it approves 330,000, the maximum permitted by law."[34]

20 August

If I wrote in my moments of boredom, I'd succeed in making even the most healthy bourgeois man neurasthenic. However, in such moments I'm incapable of making any effort. What's the use? The "blues" are quite enough.

21 August

I am sad—very, very sad. My heart is "closed up," as Mother says. Is it only a sign of my melancholy, or is something grave in the making again—for me, for my country?

✳

There's nothing I hate more in this Portugal than the shouts of the newsboys in the afternoons. What new catastrophe are they announcing?!—I wonder. There's no escape from those hucksters who cry out the three different dailies with the same melody (in fact, all kinds of goods are peddled this way, melodically, in Portugal). They come onto the trams, into the train to Estoril, into the cafés, onto the beaches. I believe if there were services at these hours, they'd go into the churches . . .

23 August

Mackenzie King,[35] after an Allied conference at Quebec, announces that the Allies will bomb Rome until Italy surrenders. So this is what the military genius has come to in 1943! And Stalin didn't even send a representative to the meeting in Canada. No one sees anything.

✳

Solitude, for me, is an open invitation to vice, folly, adventure. As soon as I'm left all alone—that is, when I learn that Nina and Giza[36] have gone into the city—I feel tempted to stop my work, whatever it may be, and do something foolish, make some absurd and senseless gesture (yell, leave the house, leaf through an uninteresting book, etc.).

✳

Nauseated all day, from the moment Mihăileanu showed me the worms on the walls of the office of Georgescu-Olenin, our Counselor of Economics. Who knows what putrid things are shut up in his desk drawers—things Olenin does not find appropriate to throw away, even today? The walls were washed twice, and the worms are back again.

✳

Marius Cișmigiu, age twenty-five, doctoral candidate in law, son-in-law of Șeicaru, has been appointed Press Counselor. He came here two months ago. Prior to this he was agent for Rador at Lisbon.

✳

Cotruș tells me a painful detail concerning Mussolini's downfall. Many Spanish newspapers have written beautiful things about Il Duce—and the Italian Minister at Madrid has gone to the Ministry of Foreign Affairs and has protested vehemently against this.

26 August
In the past few days I've spent several hours reading Antero de Quental, Camões, and Keats. As I've often said, my unfortunate memory does not allow me to retain poems. While I'm glad that I *forget* a great many things from all the books I read, I cannot take comfort in having a horrible memory for poetry. There are sonnets of Camões that I've read ten or twelve times, and still I can't recite them.

28 August
I enjoy reading the second page of the newspaper *Timpul*,[37] following especially the lively, intelligent, and sometimes impertinent prose of Miron Parachivescu.[38] (I seem to remember that this young man insulted me earlier in *Stânga*,[39] but I didn't read the article, because I have the good habit of not reading what people write about me, especially if I've been warned that it's insulting.) I take notice of one thing: that M. P. is free to make Marxist-Leninist theory in the press. That's his business, but it amuses me to remember that in Romania today a totalitarian, antidemocratic, military dictatorship exists. This man of the Left will boast someday about the martyrdom he suffered "under the dictatorship." I think about what happened with the Legionaries in 1937–39, and how even my apologia of Eminescu was censored then . . .[40]

8 September
The surrender of Italy—which everyone was expecting, but not in this wretched state of perfidy (the armistice signed 3 September!)—has made me lose

the shred of hope I still had left. Probably the Germans will pull our divisions
from the Russian front in order to delay the occupation of Italy by the Allies.
And since the only thing that interests me—as a Romanian—is the Eastern
front, I see nothing ahead. The only salvation would be for the Allies to make
a landing in the Balkans. But I doubt that Stalin would allow this.

The last sympathizer with Italy in Lisbon—I'm that one now—turns his
head and spits. I never thought the Italians could be lackeys. But now I'm
convinced. Their withdrawal from the war is just as shameful as their entrance
into it.

I hope to live long enough to see the diaspora of the Italians—transformed
into waiters and singers—and to see Italy leased to tourist agencies.

25 September
    A tremendous number of readings, all in connection with the history of
Thracian and Hellenistic religions.
    Noted: the progress of the books I'm thinking about writing.

29 September
    To defend myself from despair, I go out walking on the streets frequently.
Autumn. Of my thirty-sixth year. And I've begun to see more clearly, to be
reconciled. Am approaching equilibrium. The only thing that matters is not to
surrender definitively to despair. There must be some way out for my nation.

2 October
    In the car with the Grigores and the Costes to Alcobaça, Obisos, Batalha,
and Coimbra.
    Notes for a possible book of memories and comments about Portugal—in
the black notebook.
    Obidos, for the first time. The most impressive medieval city I've seen in Iberia.
Plane trees from the ramparts of the castle. The wall. The entrance—the courtyard
with the *azulejos*. Fig bushes, plane trees. The meal at the S. P. N. Bar.
    At Alcobaça we meet Mme. Storek and the Botez couple.[41] We take tea
at Bau. Sunset at Batalha. My daydreams at the monastery.
    We enter Coimbra in the evening. Stroll around the city. Few lights, in
preparation for the camouflaging on Sunday. The promenade of lovers, with
poems carved in the stones. The pale light of the streetlamps.

3 October
    In the morning, at the university and the cathedral again. Through Luso.
We eat at Buçaco. After lunch, to Cluinta das Lagrimas. Seemingly more beautiful this time. But, for some unknown reason, Portugal seems even sadder to
me as time passes. It is dying.
    A past without glory.

8 October

I don't know if I've ever written in this journal about Colonel Bianchi, with whom I became friends soon after his coming to Portugal in February 1942 as aeronautical attaché. At that time, this tall, handsome man—a hero, because at age 35-36 he was a colonel, had fought in Spain and Libya, had shot down fifteen planes, and had survived several crashes—was one of the most sought-after members of the diplomatic corps—by the women as well as the men. His last accident in Africa had left him unfit for combat. His left eye was bloodshot and he had a slight palsy. He didn't drink and didn't smoke, except for an occasional cigarette. I liked him because he wasn't boastful or rhetorical and because he was a young man with a clear mind and not impulsive. We have remained very good friends. During periods Nina was away, we were often together. Especially last summer, when we had some good times at the beach, at Guincho, etc. Politically a Fascist sympathizer, but he did not underestimate the difficulties of Mussolinian Italy during the current war. Friends with Mutti, who, after having visited him here last summer, found out the next day in Madrid about Mussolini's fall and flew directly to Rome. What happened after that is well known. We were dining at Atanasoff's when Bianchi appeared, very somber, and told us that Radio Rome had announced the shooting of Mutti. As we later learned, it was he who had arranged for Mussolini's escape.

I hadn't seen Bianchi since that evening. Today he ate at our place, and he told me several things that I record here "for history," as they say. Moreover, he asked me not to pass them on to others, and I will keep my promise.

Bianchi is amazed at the ineffectiveness of the German espionage service at Lisbon. The ambassador Hoyningen-Huene left on vacation for Buçaco saying, sarcastically, "Call me when you hear Mussolini's returned to Rome." The spies of the Gestapo took to drinking. On the arrival of the planes from Italy, no one was at the airport. Likewise, when Granoli arrived, no German was there to meet her—just our Jew, Kirschen—who knew her and handed her over to the Romanian Legation the next day. But, as was evident later, Granoli had no role in arranging for the armistice. Bianchi tells me that he had dispositions to greet certain fellows. What their mission was, he didn't know, but he had his suspicions. They walked around the city, and they amused themselves on the beach at Guincho with two German "secretaries" from the Secret Service. These two messengers went by taxi to the English Legation every day. No one followed them. When, after the armistice was signed, the English press published their photographs, Bianchi showed them to the "girls" and asked them, "Do you still remember these men?"

More: the Italian airplane usually brought two or three passengers. When the messengers came, there were thirteen. No German was at the airport; no one suspected anything. Among the arrivals was the English general, C., missing one hand and one eye, who had an Italian passport, although he couldn't speak a word of Italian. General Castellano, who came daily to the English Embassy, could be recognized from a distance as an officer by the way he saluted. Everything was done in broad daylight. The Germans, suspecting nothing, could not avoid the armistice. Because, if the messengers had been arrested and the secret found out, they could have arrested Badoglio, and the whole drama of the surrender could have been avoided.

12 October

Last evening it was announced that the Americans have occupied the naval bases in the Azores.

Yesterday I was told by the German Legation that my request for permission for Nina and me to go to Paris for seven days has not been approved. I am furious.

15 October

This morning I receive a call from Baron Huene informing me that, as a result of a two-page telegram he sent, he has received a visa for us directly from the Headquarters of the German Forces in France. We have a whole month to stay in Paris. Nina and I have decided to go first, leaving Giza to come a few days later along with the diplomatic courier.[42] Everyone is surprised that we are letting Giza go, precisely when the Russian offensive is in full swing. Giza, who has nothing of importance to do in Lisbon, replies that whatever is going to happen to all of Romania could happen to her as well; that if all our professors, writers, and persons of importance are living in Bucharest, what sense would it make for us to save ourselves individually?

Nevertheless, things are going so badly on the Russian front that I'm leaving with an anxious heart.

16 November

We spent fifteen days in Paris and returned with two hundred books, but heartsick. To have to stay in Portugal—when such a place as Paris exists! Surprised at the good situation of the Parisians. We didn't see anybody starving! The famous dinners in which I participated. I met Jean Cocteau, Paul Morand (just back from several days at Bucharest),[43] Georges Dumézil, René Grousset. Grousset tells me that he has written a review article for *Journal asiatique* in which he states that my *Yoga* is "*Le livre sur Yoga.*" He gives me to understand at the same time that I have somethng new to say to these Europeans.

With Cioran[44] all the time. An orgy of paradox and lyricism. I meet Marica.

The situation on the front grows worse and worse. I don't know why, but I'm not afraid anymore. I have the sentiment that nothing catastrophic is going to happen. Or, more precisely, that the danger is pan-European, that no longer can I judge things locally, with reference only to my own country.

25 November

After receiving telegrams from Dinu [Noica][45] and Herescu[46] summoning me to present myself in Bucharest on 12 December to compete for a lectureship in the History of Culture, I receive today a telegram that Giza sent in the code of the Ministry of Foreign Affairs: "Please come, without fail, on 12 December to Bucharest, for competition. The committee: Blaga, Gusti, Oprescu, Ralea, Bagdasar. I inform you confidentially, Gusti for Zamfirescu; Oprescu, Bagdasar against. Signed Giza Camil Demetrescu."[47]

I haven't replied definitely as yet. The day before yesterday I telegraphed Giza, Dinu, and Herescu my doubts with regard to the appropriateness of this lectureship at this time. Today, however, I'm more determined than ever not to present myself. And if Herescu keeps insisting, I will telegraph him: "At 37, after six years of university teaching, and with forty scientific works in print, the majority of them published in foreign languages and journals, I do not believe it is an honor for me to compete against a journalist."[48] The truth is, no one ever intended to call me to the chair, since it was a matter of establishing it for Zamfirescu, that upstart protégé of Petrovici. The truth is, likewise, that I'm no longer interested in speaking and writing for a public that, even if it understood me, could not create a worldwide resonance for my ideas. At Paris I learned a decisive thing: that one cannot bear fruit on the universal plane of the sciences by acting within the limited framework of a minor culture. I believe I have something major to say. I believe I am something more than a simple savant. My ideas and methods could spark a reform and have consequences for European thought as a whole. But only provided that my ideas and methods are made accessible.

I've decided to "penetrate" Europe more deeply and more persistently than I have done up till now with *Yoga* and *Zalmoxis*. I want to express my ideas more precisely in short studies and monographs that will appear in European journals of specialization and general culture. I have concluded—on the plane of science and essay writing—my Romanian phase. It's risky, but the results will be considerable.

December

We dine at Dr. Mariaux's, at Estoril, with Ortega y Gasset. From his long and stimulating conversation, I record these statements: "The philosopher must have, politically, an equivocal position: he must live equivocally, so that after his death his commentators will have to wrack their brains to explain it." In reference to his current situation: he's been living for two years in Portugal, but he has taken refuge in Lisbon in order to return later to Spain, to his university chair. Although his son is a Falangist, he himself is on good terms with the Spanish ambassador, [Nicolás] Franco,[49] here.

An amusing thing about Don Juan: Frenchmen are incapable of "don-juanism," of getting rid of a woman; on this account, the French women have created in the past two centuries a type of conquering male who does not correspond to their men.

Ortega is working on a metaphysics. While investigating the beginnings of metaphysical thought in Europe, he was struck by Orphism, and just now he is in the midst of reading about it (Rohde, Burnet). He asks me for some clarifications and books.

Leaving him, my melancholy returned, recalling that I've been obliged to express myself in a noncirculating language. And not only I, but also Nae, Blaga, Eminescu.

December

Nothing matters except that which can "fertilize" us. No person, no environment, no book interests me if it doesn't enhance me, *uniting* with me, helping me become more fecund, more powerful. Every man, in relation to the Cosmos, behaves like a woman: he waits to be fecundated, so that his self may be revealed, so that he may accomplish his mission. You only become yourself in the moment you sense that your being is increased. The erotic symbolism of all religions and mysticisms has its point of departure in this destiny of man: that he only becomes himself and feels he is living (participating in events, "concerning himself" with others) to the extent that he unites and is fecundated.

I don't know where I read that what makes a genius is *attention* to genius. A Leonardo is a genius because he was attentive to his genius. My tragedy consists precisely in the fact that I am not attentive to my genius. If you knew the visions that I contemplate in my solitary perambulations, you'd take my books and burn them. When the day comes that I have the courage to proclaim the exceptional element I have within me (and not merely the "normal" as I've done so far), I'll become what I truly am.

In Labat's study about the religious character of kingship among the Assyro-Babylonians,[50] I read this quotation from Böhl (p. 8): "Chez la Sémites, la force était le signe de la sphère divine" [Among the Semites, power was the token of the divine sphere]. This explains the political revolution of Sargon, the first man in history to envision a world empire. The Semites see the world dynamically, that is, politically. Even the Semitic religious life is centered around the idea of *power*. Compared to Indo-European religious concepts, for example, or to Far Eastern ones, Semitic religion is revolutionary, both in its intensity of devotion and in its character of total dependence upon the divinity known through religious experience.

The more seriously I study "what has happened," the more convinced I become that history, the event, that which might or might not have occurred, has a decisive importance. The Vedic Soma, for example, is a recent invention. Before, there were animal and human sacrifices. The drink Soma is introduced late, and its introduction was not "obligatory." It happened to appear among the Indo-Europeans. And yet Soma creates the Vedic literature that we know. It modifies a whole culture. The immensity of presomic theology has disappeared. Nothing has remained except the Vedic document, and we can judge only by means of it.

Those who do not believe *perish* by virtue of the simple fact that they are convinced that a postmortem fate does not exist, that there is nothing but a cosmic void, nothingness. You find after death that which you believe you will find. Hence the expression, "they will perish of themselves": because, not believing in immortality, they die definitively in the moment of decease.

I read in [Gomez Eanes de] Zurara about the separation of members of families fallen into slavery. Compare with families in territories occupied by the USSR. The attitude of the master toward the slave is always the same.

4

The Journal, 1944

1 January

We had a very modest New Year's Eve celebration at our house, with the Costes and the Constantinescus. Unlike other years, there was no music, no dancing, no alcohol. Three hours of conversation, dinner, and a glass of champagne. In order to make it a party, we played a sleepy game of cards (*bacara*), which lasted half an hour. At 2:00, the guests left. I've written all this in order to verify later to what extent our modest observance of the New Year did or did not anticipate the events that we expect, and consider decisive, in 1944.

This morning I continued reading Waelhens's book about Heidegger.

In 1943 I wrote 233 pages of *Apocalips*, [plus] *Comentarii la Meşterului Manole*, and almost 40 large pages (equivalent to 70 the size of these) of *Prolegomene la istoria religiilor.*[1] Considering that I made two trips—to Spain and to Paris—that I suffered (May–June) from terrible bouts of melancholy, and that in September, after I abandoned the novel, I read enormously (especially in philosophy and the history of religions), I don't believe I've concluded a sterile year. I lost at least five hundred hours in 1943 in "historical" fears and depressions over military catastrophes in which, directly or indirectly, the fate of Romania was involved.

Speaking about the rhetorical dilettantism of the romantics, Tieck is revolted by their "detestable mania" of presenting world history "in pizzicato."

The intervention of the plebeians into the militia, the liquidation of feudalism in Greece (Aristotle, *Politics* VI [IV] 13, p. 1297), has decisive consequences, the departure from the custom of the State's maintaining warriors.

January

I remember the sickish melancholy I felt looking at the old book stalls along the quays of the Seine. I didn't dare get too close to those dead books, yellowed by the sun, whipped by the wind. From a few glances I understood: sad, dead leaves—waste paper, too ephemeral even for ridicule. That mass depressed me. My love for books was transformed, in that instant, into a total revulsion for the written letter and the printed page. In such moments I cease to believe in "culture"; I cease to believe in anything but death. I have the impression of being in a cemetery.

And, actually, it's the truth. Nothing lasts, no oeuvre is spared. The antiquaries on the banks of the Seine represent the destiny of every cultural effort, of every creation. They receive the ephemeras of our century. In the libraries, the ephemeras of other centuries repose. In ten thousand years, even Dante, even Homer, may be just as insignificant as a novel of 1900 yellowing today in an antiquary's stall. And if ten thousand years seems too little time, make it a hundred or five hundred thousand. It amounts to the same thing. Only Ecclesiastes had the courage to speak the truth—and the luck to have people listen.

✳

Working on *Prolegomene*, I sometimes have the impression that I'm taking a *fausse route*. These things need to be said either in a hundred pages or in a library, the way Frazer did it. A thousand pages, as I thought at first, are either too few or too many.

✳

My disgust for history has grown so much that almost nothing that's happening in the world interests me any longer. Since the first of January I haven't touched a newspaper, haven't read a single communiqué from the war. Not even in my saddest hours in Himalaya did I believe that man could be so imbecilic and historical life so dominated by futilities and fixed ideas. I have witnessed the disappearance of France as a major power. Will I witness the transformation of England into another Albania? Anything is possible.

At first I believed I was living through an unparalleled tragedy, an apocalypse. There are days when it strikes me that we are living rather in a great, terrible illusion. When I think that I came down from the Himalayas because I believed in life, in humanity, in creativity, in the help one can give his neighbor! . . . It's idiotic.

15 January

In Spain, en route to Paris, I lost the black notebook where I was in the habit of recording all sorts of things, especially my incipient thoughts. Fortunately, I had left many of the written pages at home.

17 January
    Last night I dreamed of my paradisal island in the Atlantic. I was approaching it by night in a small boat; the liner that had brought me had stopped well out to sea.
    Readings having to do with the island. Nostalgias. In dreams, sometimes, I'm happy to find it again.

    Actually, I have every reason to believe that Soviet Russia will win and that a new historical cycle will begin. The "man" I discover in all archaic societies was superseded long ago in Europe. From the Renaissance and the Industrial Revolution on, we witness another anthropology. Only the Soviet man can achieve it completely. Modern man is a hybrid. He no longer thinks like the traditional one, no longer valorizes life as he did, but he lacks the courage to become a machine for the production of economic values, as in Soviet Russia. Should we try new "syntheses," new "adjustments," new "compromises"?! . . .

22 January
    Bambi, the new film by Disney, which I enjoyed, and which I'm convinced is a work of art that shames human beings more powerfully than any example or theory. When the doe tells Bambi to watch out because "man" is nearby—the whole audience held its breath, petrified with emotion but also with shame. No one, in that moment, had the courage to look at the person next to him.
    The same shame, certainly, made the manager of the cinema decide, suddenly, and in a completely exceptional way, not show the newsreel of the Anglo-American war. I believe that the audience would have left the theater with such a sad and guilty shame that the English Legation would have protested!

25 January
    Am writing an article about Iorga[2] for *Acçaō*. I scour the bibliography in L. Predescu's encyclopedia. And, as usual, the same reaction: not only admiration but also stimulation. It's prodigious—that reserve of energy hidden in Iorga's works! I remember that as a lycée student I would banish my fatigue late at night, after midnight, just by looking at my shelves of Iorga's books. The mania is still effective today.

27 January
    In the *Journal* of Miguel Torga, the medical doctor and intelligent writer from Coimbra, I discover a discussion of the problem of the validation and ecumenicizing of creations in Portugal and in the Portuguese language, which is the

same problem we (Cioran and I, especially) raised concerning the "chances" for creation on a worldwide scale in Romania and in the Romanian language.

29 January

I'd like to be able to write someday a book about this horrible thing: the terror of history, the terror of man vis-à-vis man. It is not true that man is afraid of nature, of gods; that fear is minimal compared to the horror he has suffered for millennia in the midst of history.[3]

Our era is, par excellence, a terrorized epoch. The future masterpieces of world literature will be created with this terrifying experience as their starting point.

2 February

Mariaux tells me that Ortega y Gasset, speaking about me, declared that only a Romanian could be a philosopher, a mystic, and a man of science all at the same time, because we are located near Orpheus, but we can also look toward the West. The way he put it: "Eliade is an Orpheanized scientist." I responded that I consider myself a Trojan Horse in the scientific camp, and that my mission is to put an end once and for all to the "Trojan War" that has lasted too long between science and philosophy. I want to validate scientifically the metaphysical meaning of archaic life, that is, to convince sociologists, comparativists, ethnographers, and folklorists that their studies find their purpose in valorizing rightly, in understanding properly, the man of traditional cultures. I believe that only in such a way can the ethnohistorical sciences emerge from the awkward impasse in which they find themselves today.

10 February

Three years since our arrival in Portugal. As usual, I make an accounting of this time period. I'm better satisfied than I was last year. I've worked very well on *Prolegomene*. The neglect of the journal is explained primarily by the enthusiasm and continuity with which (knock on wood!) I've been working steadily for almost three months on that book. I have passed one hundred pages, written in a small hand. I estimate one thousand pages more, therefore 1200 printed in octavo, plus sketches and photographs. Through this book I wish to validate and make fruitful all my labor in the history of religions for the past fifteen years.

18 February

I make corrections of the Hasdeu edition for Cugetarea.[4] I'm reminded of 1934–36 when Nina and I both were working at the Academy, transcribing texts and checking variants. What a horrendous task! And, above all, how useless! Three years of exhausting research in order to "reactualize" a great pioneer—and then to be rewarded with the brochure by that gentleman (I've forgotten the name)![5] Almost no one realized the meaning of the *sacrifice*—a sacrifice pure and simple—of my labor.

25 February

I continue to make good progress with the writing of *Prolegomene*, interrupted only by the hours of service at the Legation, frantic days of preparation for the courier, and the few invitations I still accept in "the world." I've been a terrible recluse this winter, and I don't regret it. Since the first of January I've ceased reading the newspapers. I don't talk about politics anymore, I don't listen to commentaries. I want to write the book, to say something, and that's all. For the whole world, mad and imbecilic, I have a sentiment of pity mixed with disgust.

Monday, 6 March

On Tuesday, 29 February, I began writing a play that I had "seen" that same afternoon. Although I had a heavy schedule (Thursday, dinner party at our place until 1:00 a.m.; Friday, the Luso-Romanian Circle until 2:00 a.m.; Sunday, dinner at the Costes'), I wrote it as if I were in a kind of trance, as I've never written before in my life. Yesterday I found a title: "Oameni și pietre" [Men and Stones].[6] Now, tonight, I finished it, including the stage directions. All that's left is to transcribe it—that is, better said, to decipher it.

I believe it's one of the most powerful dramas ever written in Romanian. I'm happy that I created it, and I don't care if it's performed or not, or whether or not it's successful.

I wrote Scene 1 of Act I first, then the last; next Act III, and then Act II. Yesterday and today, I finished Act III, Scene 2, which seemed the hardest one for me. It's amusing that I'm so enthusiastic about drama. You can say things briefly and directly. And, especially, without straining your brain![7]

9 March

Thirty-seven years old today. I don't know if it's due to the anticlimax provoked by conceiving and writing the play in something of a trance, but for the past two days I've been terribly sad, depressed. I'm struggling hard against despair. Several plays are echoing in my head, and I'm sure if I were to sit down at my desk, I could write them in a few weeks. But I don't do it, because the world as I see it now, in these unwritten plays, seems too tragic and pessimistic (one is entitled "Joc de societate" [Party Game]). I'd like to get back to *Prolegomene*. This evening, however, I've promised to read "Men and Stones" to a few Romanian friends from the Legation.

The depression comes from a long way off. I'm beginning to understand life, its lies, its lack of absolute values. I've learned that Minister Cădere[8] has been "plotting" against me at Bucharest. He wants by any means to get rid of me, although he realizes that if Romania exists today in Portugal as a reality and not as a diplomatic relationship, it is due primarily to my work and my presence. Talk about the persecutions of Eminescu!

10 March

The discouragement, the sentiment of nothingness, and the absurd illusion of every existence that engulfed me yesterday, my birthday, has continued today, despite my efforts to fight it by reading from volume II of Eminescu's works (Perpessicius's edition). How many times has Eminescu helped me to bear my condition of having been born a Romanian, that is, a son of a luckless people, destined by geography and history to a deplorable wandering in the Slavic mass! But, today, not even the spirit of "Luceafărul"[9] could bring me peace. Again, the sentiment of imminent, inevitable historical catastrophe. When I imagine how the Romanian elite will perish, how the "personalities" will be suppressed, how hundreds of thousands, perhaps millions, of Romanians will be displaced in order to remove the Romanian thorns from the great Slavic community, I'm seized by a kind of despair. Why, O Lord, were we ever born? Why have we attained a Romanian consciousness of the world, if this tragedy must come to pass?

Last evening I read "Men and Stones" to the dozen Romanians from Lisbon. They didn't like it.

12 March

Yesterday and today I've suffered a horrible case of depression. Couldn't read anything, couldn't even work on *Prolegomene*. Last night I began another play, "1241" (provisional title), and I wrote four large and rather successful pages. This afternoon I wrote six more pages, finishing Scene 1, with which, without having reread them, I feel satisfied. But as soon as I stop work on my play, the awful sadness returns. My soul is desolate. Lord, Lord, have pity on me and deliver me!

15 March

In order to realize how much your life is worth, how well you've succeeded in giving it value, imagine that tomorrow might be the last day. But not the last day of your life—because then you could still find some satisfaction: you've written something, you've helped someone, you will be able to console a reader fifty or sixty years after your death—or, if you've been active in history, you have modified the history of your country, you have contributed to the uplift or the salvation of your people, etc. Such a death is consoling—and yet it does not validate the life you have lived. But imagine that tomorrow could be the last day of the world, that tomorrow the earth will return to its predestined mode: gas. See, then, what remains of your life: just the good deeds you've done, the love you've shared, the comfort you've given others.

6 April

For the past two weeks, ever since we learned that the Russians had crossed the Dniester, our lives—Nina's and mine—have been a nightmare. I don't understand why the catastrophe is harder for me to bear than it is for the other Romanians. Maybe it's because I don't feel right here, I feel I'm out of my place. For that reason, I decided a few days ago to ask to be recalled, and to return to the country. I haven't done anything yet, because the railway connections between Hungary and Romania are interrupted. But, mainly, I haven't done anything because I don't know what to do. I sense that my desire to go back to the homeland is nourished primarily by the desire for extinction. I'd go to the front, not to fight, but to die. A final disgust for history. A craving for suicide. I almost suspect myself of cowardice in this neurasthenic desire to be *there*—where you can die without others' finding out why you wanted to die. At any rate, at this first examination in the face of tragedy, I have failed lamentably. I can't bear the tragedy of the collectivity. I'd rather perish first, before it has been consummated.

The bombing of Bucharest by the American Liberators[10] has made me think of Russia for the first time with less horror and disgust. After the treacherously benign declaration of Molotov,[11] the Americans destroyed our capital. For me to comment further is useless. I believe that the readers of this journal will have seen the judgment of history by the time they read these pages. The Anglo-Saxon imbecility will make it possible for the victorious Russians to leap over the last obstacle that was in their path.

I have walked around the city and have said to all the Portuguese I met: You should know that if Romania falls, then all of Southeastern Europe falls. The Russians will be in the Adriatic and the Mediterranean. And when they take Germany, they will be on the banks of the Tagus.[12] No one will stop them.

And yet, in spite of everything, I can't believe it will happen that way. If it does, then nothing in history will make sense anymore. Who will justify the deaths and tragedies we have suffered for hundreds of years?

I'm thinking of writing a book, *Teroarea Istoriei* [The Terror of History], on this theme: that until a little while ago, any personal tragedy, any ethnic catastrophe had its justification in a cosmology or soteriology of some sort: cosmic rhythms, reabsorption into water, ekpyrosis or purification by fire, historical cycles, "our sins," etc. Now, history simply terrorizes, because the tragedies provoked by it no longer find justification and absolution.[13]

24 May

I discontinued this notebook again, disgusted with recording over and over the same melancholy thoughts and the same disgust with history. The month of April I spent terrorized by the Anglo-American bombings that have begun the scientific destruction of Bucharest. I'm not thinking now of my city itself, but of the smattering of cultural institutions it had, which the Liberators have destroyed. Once again I see verified the imbecility with which the Anglo-Americans are conducting the war—and the cleverness of the Soviets who are forcing the Allies to bomb open cities[14] while they content themselves with strictly military victories.

✳

Giza arrived 7 May.

✳

The past three days have been spent with Carl Schmitt, invited to Portugal to give several lectures. Sunday morning we go together to Janelas Verdas Museum, where we spend more than an hour gazing at Bosch's *The Temptation of St. Anthony*. He tells me that interpretating the symbolism of Bosch is the latest fashion in Germany, that everyone is interested in him, although very few speak and even fewer publish. The air raids and the insecurity help the Germans to understand Bosch and to rediscover themselves in him. His work is not so "fantastic" as is believed, but it is full of biographical details and contemporary history. (For example, Schmitt tells me about the secret societies that enjoyed the Emperor's protection, and that executed corrupt magistrates after a preliminary trial and a sentencing to death according to all the legal formalities. In *The Temptation of St. Anthony*, at the bottom, to the left, the bird—symbol of justice—is carrying in its beak a sealed envelope, probably containing the death sentence.) A friend of Schmitt, Wilhelm Fraenger, has been working for some ten years on the decipherment of Bosch and has written a huge monograph of over a thousand pages—as yet unpublished.

I dine several times with Schmitt. I believe I saw him more than anyone else in Lisbon did. He tells me he regrets that he didn't meet Blaga[15] at Bucharest; he is sure that in the Blagan conception of space there are some interesting things to be found. We both comment on his *Land und Meer*. For the book that he is creating about the nomos of the earth, I offer him several historical-ethnographical parallels.

He tells me he is an optimist about the fate of Europe. Nationalism as well as internationalism are outmoded forms.

26 May

The characteristic trait of my personality is a total lack of ambition. This explains the meagerness of my oeuvre, the fact that today I am not a European author. All that is more significant, more original, more profound in my thought—I communicate in certain conversations or I keep to myself. I've never written a book with the idea of bringing out my full value, or *giving all*; it's been either forced by necessity or else to teach others something of what I knew or thought. I've never concerned myself with the translation of my books. I have not responded to invitations to write for foreign journals or give lectures at foreign universities. At Oxford, at Coimbra, earlier at Calcutta, at Rome—I could have held a series of lectures at any time. That I did not do so was due to laziness, to modesty—but especially to the lack of any grain of ambition. I've always been happy to be free, to leave the world in peace, to mind my own business. If Freud had had the same structure, psychoanalysis today would not exist beyond a small circle of specialists. I am inhumanly detached from my genius, my works. If I had been rich, probably I'd have written two or three books but wouldn't have published them. I'm happy only when I feel I'm my own boss, not dominated by an "oeuvre" to which I have to give form. Perhaps my indifference and lack of ambition constitute my way of being religious.

3 June

Horia Stanca,[16] just arrived from Berlin, makes me regret again the mediocrity of the Portuguese milieu. Speaking with Stanca, I had the impression I was coming home from a resort city. The conversations I have with my Romanian and Portuguese friends never rise above the level of psychology.

✳

The sentiment that I'm becoming sterilized in Portugal. The tremendous effort I'm making not to sink into a mere cultural counselor.

6 June

The invasion—at last! I remember about 1940, in London. Who would have believed then, after Dunkirk, that four years later the English would attack—and with success!

The great futility of this war. Actually, if this had to happen—why those four years of victories, tragedies, ruins, and bluffs? Never will I be able to forgive the Germans for weakening the Russian front in order to defend themselves in the West—if their defenses turn out to be ineffectual.

9 June

Ortega, with Mariaux and Antoniade, at my place for dinner. To keep from annoying Ortega, we let him talk, let him shine. He is in high spirits. Excellent observations about the "muteness" of South American peoples: they write in Spanish but they don't "speak" it, since they have nothing to say; because, as Hegel saw already, the South American continent has a weak fauna; because there one cannot get beyond prehistory.

Antoniade makes a gaffe at the table; turning to Mariaux, he says, "Mais sont les boches qui . . ." (But it's the Huns who . . .). This, after a life spent in diplomatic service!

13 June

 For four days Nina has been very ill. The sciatica again, etc., etc.

 Through the diplomatic pouch we are informed that I will receive a salary of 62,000 lei instead of 85,000, the amount I've been getting and the amount Leontin Constantinescu will continue to get. This is due, probably, to the classification of "counselor" that the Foreign Ministry has made. That's how much I deserve—and how much Leontin.

June

 I read again—how many times does this make?—Balzac's *La fille aux yeux d'or*. Exasperated by the long and inert introduction that, undoubtedly, has made this masterpiece fail to become popular. But how brilliant, and how strange, to bring together Paquita, Marsay, and his sister! I reread also the rest of the volume, *Histoire des Treize*. Balzac's preface is obviously inspired by the fashion of the time. It amuses me to count how many times he uses the word "splendid" or "superb" in one short story. In *La duchesse de Laneais*, Montriveau's African guide is "that giant of intelligence and courage." Who is not a giant, who does not have genius, who is not doing a splendid thing in Balzac? These weaknesses, belonging to his era but also to him, make him even closer to me than he was before.

 At Belem, taking Stanca to see *The Tower*, I realized that the Manueline style is only a plastic manifestation of the madness, the delusions of grandeur, and the intoxications of power provoked by the maritime discoveries. The men who had conquered continents and discovered new lands simply lost their heads. There's nothing demiurgic about it—just the drunkenness of riches and newfound power.

 I must collect someday the notes and meditations on Portugal, transcribe them, clarifying and completing them—in order to make a book that will be, above all, a book that is mine.

 I interrupted work on *Prolegomene* two weeks ago. For the past three months I've worked very little on that book.

 The sentiment that I can't finish the things now that I've begun. That I lack the strength to carry them to conclusion. Over 600 pages of *Viață Nouă* and *Apocalips*—and how many others? . . .

✳

I find in Ortega the following sentence: "No creo que haya imagen mas adecuada de la vida que esta del naufrágio" [I don't believe there is a more adequate image of life than that of a shipwreck] (*Ideas y creencias*, 1942, p. 90). I remember that the same image obsessed Nae Ionescu in his latter years and his last courses. And not in the sense of a catastrophic event, but of the general human condition: man is, from the beginning, a fallen creature; he struggles to stay alive, to endure, and above all to save himself spiritually.

It is significant that both Nae and Ortega are preoccupied with history, trying to accord an absolute value to it.

My own principal preoccupation is precisely the salvation *from* history: symbol, myth, ritual—the archetypes.

✳

June

Back to the big problems.

To retake the road of 1928: to seek new instruments for the problems and techniques of that time. Magic, heroism, chastity, etc.—inadequate. The attempt to give coherence to recent discoveries: every individuated existence considered a paradox; salvation through integration; symbol, the only means of contact with all ontic regions, nevertheless remaining in the concrete, not rejecting experience. *Omul ca simbol* [Man as Symbol]—the title of my future book, my first philosophical book.

I can be consoled over the degeneration of Europe, to which I am witness, only by telling myself that the seeds of all these destructions and suicides were sown long ago, and that I can't do anything now but accommodate myself to the history that is being consumed—as I said in 1934. And to interest myself in the history that is being made. Therefore, by any means, a cosmic conscious-ness of man must be recovered. I see no other way out.

21 June

Although we are in the middle of "great events" (the invasion of France), I am very detached, very indifferent to all that will follow. My only concerns for the past week have been theoretical. I'm planning new chapters for *Cosmos și istorie* (Cosmos and History).[17] I'm not working on *Prolegomene*. Have been reading Ortega a great deal and a few recent works of philosophy: Hessen's book, *The Philosophy of Values*, and one by Heimsoeth, both in Portuguese translations, because I can't find anything in Lisbon in any other language.

✳

"Quel ennui d'avoir à répondre à cet idiot" [What a bore to have to reply to that idiot]. Leon Bloy, *Le mendiant ingrat*, 4 April 1892.

This is why I gave up, as early as 1934, defending myself against criticisms brought against me—especially those signed by imbeciles and referring to my theoretical writings.

✳

The adoration of the Holy Spirit, according to Bloy (*Le mendiant ingrat*, I, 13), has as its only fault—luxury. As I recognize!

24 June

I read *d'un jet*, the second volume of Bloy's *Le mendiant ingrat*. Depressed by the terrible poverty in which he lived. Depressed, especially, by the letters he was forced to write, humiliating himself, asking for money.

Extraordinary mythical-hermeneutical glosses by the author's wife.

To be retained: the transfiguration of organic functions into mysteries; the cross-anchor symbol; the cross—shadow of man.

"Mais chaque instant doit être arraché au désespoir"[18] (*Le mendiant*, II, 106).

✳

"Pourquoi, à des certaines heurs, sommes-nous assaillis d'une tristesse noire et mauvaise, toute semblable à celle que determinerait en nous le remords de quelque crime?"[19] (II, 211).

✳

The eagerness of Bloy—"un homme de l'Absolu"—to quarrel with everybody, to be alone, as terrible as that solitude must have been for him, to repeat *ad satietas* that between authentic Catholicism and the modern world no point of crossing exists. The same obsession in the case of Kierkegaard, the same loneliness. Bloy's wife was Danish. She was, no doubt, the wife Kierkegaard needed.

✳

Mau tempo no canal, the novel Vittorino Nemesio sent me with a nice dedication ("The nuncio of Eastern Latinity"), has almost 500 pages in octavo, closely printed. I read it with interest (because the action is set in the Azores), but disappointed, especially toward the end, that it is not the Portuguese novel I had envisioned and expected.

✳

In *Prolegomene* it will be necessary for me to establish the religious and metaphysical nature of all the obscure life-experiences: eating, sex, anger, etc.

✳

In my continual ascent along the edge of precipices, I must not be frightened or discouraged by falls. Such falls are a part of my destiny. Periods of stability and of inaction are due to the superabundance and frenzy of the creative periods. Falls into vice and "outer darkness" are the compensations anticipated by the creative impulses that cause them.

June
The overwhelming importance of these observations: that man has not only potentialities but also *possibilities*. The problem of freedom can be raised again.

✳

To be retained: the observation made by Carl Schmitt when we were dining together: Mommsen played a baleful role in European culture: he "did away with" [Johann Jakob] Bachoven, pursuing him ruthlessly even after death. Historicism progressed under a merciless star, because all that was transcendent and symbolic in history was disregarded, suspected, or systematically ignored.

✳

Looking out my window, observing the beauty of the night—I was suddenly reconciled to the war, to the catastrophe, to the end of the Europe I have known and loved. The destructions of war have a meaning, they fulfill a role in the universal equilibrium. War—like death in the individual case—corresponds to the other cosmic act that man ignores or else fears: regression into the primordial amorphic state, where everything is lost in everything else, merging into unity. War fulfills the same role—on another plane, of course—as does orgy. I have written about the function of orgy in *Mitul reintegrării* and in *Prolegomene*. I'll not repeat it here. But I believe that I number among the few moderns who understand the value and necessity of orgy. War resembles it. But war also resembles a periodic submersion in the Waters, an Atlantis, a *mahāprālāya*, the re-creation process of primitive initiation, chaos. That is why the oriental gods of fecundity are also, at the same time, the gods of death and especially of war. That is why . . . etc., etc. (How I'd like to reformulate here my old theory, fragmentarily set out in *Mitul reintegrării!*)

June

Back in Heidegger again (*Vom Wesen des Grundes*), whom I decipher with considerable difficulty. I can't help but admire Heidegger's philosophical genius. But oftentimes I feel like crying out: where do all these analyses, so stunningly precise and exhaustive, lead?! You have set out on a hard road, which is blocked. Man can reveal to himself more deeply and more fully the mysteries—even the meaning of his own temporal existence—if he looks in a *different place*. Examine, for instance, the Symbol . . .

27 June

Thrilled by the greatness of *Prolegomene* and frightened at the thought that circumstances may prevent me from carrying it to completion. This book, planned to be a thousand pages, cannot reveal its secrets until the final page is written. And the unfortunate thing is that I didn't begin with the beginning, but—on account of the scarcity of material I have available here—I've written groups of chapters for the middle of it. As the manuscript now stands, it gives the impression of small, separate monographs rather than a unity. I will require at least two hundred more pages just to tie together the two parts on which I've worked thus far.

28 June

I begin working on *Prolegomene* again. I write three and a half pages.

29 June

I try to reread *Lumina ce se stinge* [The Light that Is Failing][20] for a new edition. Discouraged, I give up after forty pages. The style is so pretentious and dull that I don't know what I could do to transform *Lumina* into a readable book. I wonder if it merits a reprinting. Maybe so. Without modifications. A document of my narrative experiments of 1930.

2 July

I begin reading *Isabel și apele diavolului* [Isabel and the Devil's Waters],[21] to make corrections in preparation for a new edition. I had never reread this book, and I was apprehensive. But, after the first chapters, I feel attracted to it, as if I were reading a new book. I finished reading it so enthusiastic that I forgot all about correcting it. Never would I have suspected that, at twenty-two, I could have written a book so compact, so full of pathos, and so original at the same time. The doctor—in whom I do not recognize myself completely—is a simply amazing character. All the other characters live with a strange intensity—something I hadn't hoped for. I had the impression while writing it that *Isabel* was a book of dream and dialectics. I was wrong. The theology saves the intrigue, and the human authenticity compensates for the absence of decor, the poverty of the surroundings. Even the stridency of the style, even the un-Romanian rhythm of the sentences, has a charm. It's plain to see that I don't know how to write. A well-written *Isabel* would have seemed artificial. I shall correct some anomalies of vocabulary.

The only exasperating thing is Tom's "fall." Whatever made me introduce a homosexual episode? And even more seriously, the hero's detached attitude sometimes leaves the impression that he isn't interested in women, that he is even impotent. From where could all these absurdities have come to me?!

July

I'm rereading *Anatole France en pantoufles* on a very hot day. The only truly intelligent line: "Il n'est honnête femme qui ne soit lasse de son métier" [There is no honest woman who is not tired of her profession]. I show this to several female friends: all agree that it is so.

Delfín Santos tells me that X[avier] Zubiri, the philosopher who has interested me so much for some time, was a priest who left his order, with the pope's permission, because he had fallen in love with the daughter of a great Spanish poet (whose name I forget) and wanted to get married. He was a man of some forty years, short, nervous, etc. He studied philosophy then with Heidegger. He has published little, but his influence already is overwhelming (he is cited in Laín Entralgo's *Medicina y historia*, in Conde's *Formos politicas*). An extraordinary resemblance to Nae Ionescu's destiny.

8 July

Virginia della Rosa came to our house last night to say good-bye. She is one of the very few Italians (women or men) who have not respected the order of the Buglezi Legation, but consents to greet us, talk with us, and even visit us. (What can I say about my good friend Colonel Bianchi, and the even better one, Bolasco, both of whom have dined at our house and the homes of others of us tens of times—who have not even turned their heads when they met Romanians on the street but, looking them in the eyes, have not spoken?!) Virginia, left here by herself (because Rolando was called to southern Italy), has obtained an American visa, and after 15 August hopes to leave on the Clipper. She's returning to America after an absence of nine years. She is very excited: what will she find? She'll have to begin a new life ("Life begins at forty!"), learn to work, etc. For the time being, she will administer her mother's estate. And, perhaps, she will return to the theater, to dancing. She will be involved with the education of little Roly, who is, undoubtedly, an artist, etc. One thing she is sure about: she will not return to Europe as the wife of a diplomat. The ten years of diplomatic life seem to her a crime against herself: time wasted, neurasthenia. (How well I understand her!) And so—a new life.

She is anxious. But I'm excited only by the thought that she will be flying for four days (Algiers to Natal, to Rio de Janeiro, etc.) in order to begin a new life, starting over from the beginning. When will we meet again?!

12 July
    Today I wrote the two-hundredth page of *Prolegomene.*

13 July
    Asked by a Portuguese friend if she still sees Italians, Tantzi Coste replied, "Depuis qu'ils sont vainqueures, ils ne nous saluent même plus!" [Since they are victors, they don't greet us anymore!] In less than a week, this response has made the rounds of Lisbon. I record it here in order to remind myself later of the cravenly behavior of the Italians.

July
    A newspaper publishes the information that Enzo Bolasco, former Italian press attaché and friend of mine, is reported to have been shot by the French Committee in Algiers, accused of being a "Fascist spy." Bolasco was an old and ardent Fascist. But immediately after the Badoglio coup, he became a monarchist, anti-German, pro-British, etc. In this regard, he circulated a series of ridiculous manifestos. Then he left for Badoglian Italy. He dreamed of keeping his post under the anti-Fascists. And now it seems he has been shot.
    It is an example of what could happen to all opportunists in Europe.
    [25 July: the rumor has not been confirmed.]

20 July
    I haven't wept in a long time. The last time since the Vienna Diktat, was in March, when the Russians crossed the Dniester and I was working on the play "1241" (left unfinished). But today, alone, I came to tears thinking of my life over these last ten years, of my love for Nina, of the times we were happy because we were both in good health. Nina is very ill, and I don't know how she will get well. What do all my despair and melancholy mean, compared to the pain I see her suffering here beside me?

✳

Am working hard, persistently, on *Prolegomene*, despite all the annoyances. I don't know what keeps me going, after four months of sorry results (March–June, forty pages!). It's not even a clearly theoretical work in which I could take pride among philosophers. But I fear I won't be granted to finish a big book, and for that reason I'm in despair over *Prolegomene*. That's why I sometimes let myself be drawn into considerations that go beyond my subject; perhaps I won't have time to write the other books I'm thinking about, and I can at least suggest here some new ideas. Actually, I'm always some five or six years behind in the writing of the books I have in mind. *Prolegomene* was conceived in 1939 (following the courses of 1934 and 1936) and begun at Oxford in 1940. Not until 20 November 1943, did I begin to write it in earnest. When will I ever get around to writing *Cosmos și Istorie* (or *Teroarea Istoriei* [The Terror of History]) and *Om ca simbol* [Man as Symbol]?

23 July
     For the past several nights I've been going to bed between 3:00 and 4:00 a.m. Awful insomnia. Nina hasn't slept in a week. She is terribly weak and in a toxic condition from all the medicines and sleeping pills. And nothing can be done! Her illness has persisted since February, changing only in its phenomenology. There have been sciatic pains, then stomachaches, then more general pains, then her foot became completely numb. Now there are pains as sensation returns to it.
     I'm depressed by man's inability to help his suffering comrade. It is my old obsession: isolation through suffering.

25 July
     Nina's terrible weakness frightens me. I must save her by any means possible, taking her out of Lisbon.

✳

     Heloise to Abelard: "Make of me anything you wish, only don't forget me."
     "La fatiga noble de los omóplatos"[22] (E. d'Ors).
     "Sé que voy a mori, porque non amo ya, nada . . ."[23] (Manuel Machado).

✳

     Maria de C.—twenty-one and almost a virgin . . .

Lousã, 28 July
     Today I brought Nina to "Casa de Saude e de Repouso" [House of Longing and Rest] in Lousã. She climbed the two flights of stairs with difficulty, leaning on her cane. (I told her at Lisbon that the greatest gift she can make me is to give me that cane.) From the window of our room we can see the village—white buildings with red roofs—and the ridge of the hill. A few

clumps of anemic pines back of the sanatorium, and others in the valley that separates us from Lousã. The highway to Montachique is shaded by enormous and vigorous eucalyptus trees.

In the afternoon I climbed to the ridge of the hills. Alone. I remembered the last "ascent" made with Nina, in the summer of 1939, when we were at Bran, and from there we crossed the mountains opposite the sanatorium at Moroeni.

An abandoned windmill. In front of it, a ditch with grass dried up from the wind and drought. That poor little flower! The same coarse, spiny grass everywhere. There's nowhere to sit, because the grass doesn't like you, and if you rest on it, it prickles you.

And where is the "fauna" of our hills in midsummer? Here I find nothing but ants and small butterflies. I catch sight of a vanessa. I look everywhere for *cetonia aurata* beetles, which I remember always from adolescence. None. The view alone is superb. On the left, the estuary of the Tagus, the crest of the hills, the Castle at Sintra—situated on the steepest height.

It's been years since I've done any mountain climbing. The wind is blowing so hard that I have to turn up the collar of my shirt.

Nina has been watching me all the time from the window.

Lousã, 29 July

The image that obsessed me before I fell asleep last night: a young man with gigantism. He grows to a height of twelve meters. No longer does he hear the sounds of human beings. I see him take his sweetheart in the palm of his hand, and when he whispers to her about his tragedy, she trembles (she sees his monstrous mouth, etc.). His final isolation in a cabin in the mountains, built by himself.

Gigantism—a concrete and picturesque formula for the genius and his ultimate isolation. It might be amusing to write a story with this theme.

✳

On the hill back of the sanatorium I read *Smoke* by Turgenev. Somewhat disappointed by the novel, as such. And how obsessing is the social problem in Russian literature! There is not a book in which it is not present actively, even exclusively.

Lousã, 30 July

In primitive poetry, love is never "natural," but the consequence of magic or divine caprice. For a primitive, the love passion is a pathological state, an enchantment. How many consequences derive from this negative valorization of love! Primitive man does not want to lose himself. All he does, thinks, and desires is centered on ontology. He wants to be real, to be whole. If ritual sometimes demands that he abandon his humanity, it is only in order to make him one with absolute reality. In no event does he abandon himself for a fellow human being, for another living, ridiculous fragment.

The tremendous revolution accomplished by Christianity—which promotes on every level the loss of self.

11 September
 . . . I seem to be waking up from a bad dream. It's as though I'm beginning to live a new life. What has happened to me in the past six weeks?

I have the impression that the month of August 1944, especially the second half of it, was the most horrible month of my life that I can remember. There were whole days when I didn't know what month it was, when I suffered two or three attacks of neurasthenia in succession. Nina is still at Lousã, and for the last fifteen days she's been worse than when she came. The edema of the left foot, which began to improve only a few days ago, had frightened me and had frightened her too. She can't get out of bed now. She's so weak she can't move the affected foot by herself. For two weeks she suffered from an eating disorder that prevented her from keeping anything down, even iced tea. She was able to eat a very little wearing a blindfold. She became toxic from injections of Encodal, etc. And in spite of all these things, Dr. Wagner sent her this treatment from Berlin, so we have hope. But her general condition is alarming.

Since she has been unable to get out of bed to come to the phone, one of us, Giza or I, goes to Lousã every day. Every time I make the trip on the bus, I remember other moments in my life with Nina. Indeed, this is the wonderful thing about a successful marriage: that you have a witness to your past life, especially to your great moments, to the various tensions and revelations of that life. Your wife is the bearer of the same secret as you: a certain light on an August evening, on a certain beach—other than you, only she witnessed it; only her memory validates and gives spiritual meaning to the millions of details, images, and happenings. No one but Nina and I know how Titisee looked on a certain afternoon when we saw it. None but we two have seen our Ulm. Nina and I are bound together by more than our love and friendship; we are bound also by the *history* we have lived or made together.

I thought about all these things, and sometimes I was overwhelmed by sadness and emptiness. In those days, spending as much as 36 hours at a time with Nina, I couldn't approach her without crying. I wept for all the happiness and love that were gathered up in our past.

In the first days of August I worked stubbornly on *Prolegomene*. The chapter on vegetation I finished two days before N. I. Herescu arrived by plane. Herescu's luggage and money were burned up in a raid on the airport at Stuttgart. It was a miracle that he himself escaped. From 18 August he and his wife and daughter have been living at my place.

At night we stay close to the radio and telephone, waiting for the news from Romania. Since the surrender,[24] we've been unable to do anything except listen to the radio, read the papers, and telephone friends for news. We experience a variety of tensions: at different times each day we are resigned, happy, or depressed.

With Herescu I have spoken very little about the serious things that concern us, or scholarly matters. Politics and man-to-man confidences—plenty of them.

The month of August was hell for me. There were days when I had neither the strength nor the desire to open a book or look at the sky or even to dream. I existed like a larva, out of my mind with a fever. My whole system poisoned. I don't have the courage to write here all that's wrong with me. I hope I can save myself. It's not just a case of neurasthenia, and not exhaustion from work, as I believed. It's purely and simply a darkness of the mind.

I haven't kept up the journal. *Prolegomene* was interrupted on 18 August. I'm writing a commentary on Córdoba.

14 September

For three days, in bed with a terrible attack of vagotonia. I never would have believed a man could cry from nausea. But I did. To me it seemed to be a simple toxic condition; however, here I am with a sick vagus, defending myself with a strict regimen from a possible case of jaundice. I lie all day with a hot water bottle on my stomach. I eat a little cooked macaroni without butter, or I take some porridge every two hours. The regimen of a sickly baby.

But, at least, I don't feel like a monster morally any longer.

I think: as bad as my spiritual state has been—what if it has succeeded in undermining my physical constitution?! At thirty-seven, I who have never suffered from stomach trouble, to cry over nausea!

I have terrible urges to do things. It has come into my head to write novellas. I promise myself I'll do it as soon as I'm well.

18 September (transcribed from appointment books, Lousã)

Fourteen years ago I saw Maitreyi for the last time.

I am at Lousã. Nina has passed the great crisis, but she is extremely weak. She tells me her dreams from the time of her acute pains that were followed by fainting spells: the dead who surrounded and called her, waiting for her. Her grandmother is waiting for her in the street and sends her word to come. Nina is ready to go, but a torrential rain keeps her from leaving the house. At the last moment, in all the dreams, something always happens.

And the sensation of the night before last: of a fiery teardrop falling on the scar. Whose tear was it? Mine? . . .

I stood at the window a long time, watching two hunters climbing the hill. Superb September sunset. The air—clear and still. Something is happening—inside me, around me.

Look closely! *Never* will this light, these sounds (gunshots from the hill, trucks passing on the highway), this ensemble comprised of nature, life, and history—never will it be repeated. I am the sole witness to a unique cosmic moment. The others around me are inattentive, distracted, confused.

What a terrible summer I've been through! I talk to Nina about Andalusia where I might be going (the Luso-Spanish Congress, 2–9 October, to which I'm invited). We recollect past trips. I keep returning in memory to certain scenes, happenings, adventures in Germany (Ulm, the Rhine Valley, Nürnberg). She likes better going back to Oxford, in the fall of 1940.

Evening in the park. A terrible, overwhelming tranquility! After the hell of the last months, this evening at Lousã is calm, uplifting, divine.

In the past month I have had, at times, as many as ten attacks of nerves a day—unbeknownst to anyone else. Giza finds out about them only when I take them out on her, as happens now and then. Usually, I leave the house as soon as I feel one coming on, even in the night. And, then, there are the other torments, more horrible—which no longer depend exclusively on nerves, but on my whole mental life, and which could end up driving me completely insane.

I'm thinking about writing a life of the Mother of the Lord—*vœux* for the healing of Nina. The Mother of the Lord, who is also Sophia.

19 September
I spend the night with Nina at the sanatorium. Again I realize how sick she is.

Giza comes today, to stay with her. I suffer another attack of nerves, in front of Giza and Nina.

In the evening, with Herescu in the city. I seek therapeutics desperately. Apart from the Mother of the Lord, I believe there is no hope. My sickness is mental. Sophia.

20 September
I leave by taxi this morning for Lousã, and, together with Giza and a nurse, I return with Nina. Along with everything else, she is suffering from a neurasthenia of the sanatorium. Also from a dietary trauma, brought on by the effects of the injections (Encodal and Dolantină).

At home, I carry her upstairs in my arms, without using the elevator. We place her in the living room.

Today, the nurse will stay through the night. Tomorrow, Giza and I will take care of her.

Peace, trust, hope.

21 September

Giza's birthday. Hard night for Nina.

The important thing is—that I stay calm and optimistic. When I feel an attack of nerves coming on, or a darkening of my mind, I say to myself, or I wait for Nina or Giza to say it to me: "The Mother of the Lord!" It's the sign in the shelter of which I hope to regain spiritual serenity. If I don't succeed, I'll remain mentally ill, unbalanced, for the rest of my life. *Sophia* (Wisdom!) defends me.

A telegram from Ticu [Burileanu] informs me that my library on Strada Palade survived the bombing.

22 September

Brutus[25] shows me today the circular telegram of 9 September recalling those of us in the press and cultural services—that is, Leontin, Mica Paraschivescu, and me. These services, says the telegram signed by Buzeşti, are to be reorganized. Until such time as we will be able to return to the country, we will be paid one-third salary. Brutus replied immediately in a long telegram saying that we are necessary and that we have not "compromised" ourselves with the Antonescu regime. On the other hand, he asked Picky to give attention to me, to reinstate me in my post and salary of counselor.

Probably this can't be done now, with the Russians in the country. This leaves me, therefore, the privileged one, the only functionary of Propaganda left who was demoted by Ică and the Foreign Minister.

Today, nevertheless, Buzeşti telegraphs Brutus that, in view of Nina's illness, he is authorized to give me 10,000 escudos monthly (instead of the 5,000 I was expecting). If only Nina will get well . . .

September

The blank spaces in a private diary are also revealing. The month in which I wrote nothing, says much, by the simple fact of its absence from the journal. They are absences that betray.

✳

While correcting the Portuguese translation of *Maitreyi*, I recall certain essential episodes that I'd completely forgotten . . . Do I have so much capacity for forgetting, so much desire to forget? . . . It takes a novel, albeit a completely autobiographical one, to make me remember the most tragic moments I've ever lived! . . .

But will *Maitreyi* ever appear in Portuguese? This book has had exceptionally bad luck: it's been translated into Polish, Italian, Bulgarian, French, English, German, and Swedish—and I don't know if it's been *published* in any of these versions. When the agents of the Prefectura came to arrest me on 14 July 1938, I was with a friend of mine (who?), correcting an excellent Italian translation—of which I've heard nothing since. Another Italian translation was stopped by the censor, because of some law that regulates relations between whites and natives in the African colonies. By telegraph in 1942, I was asked to give permission for Swedish, German, and Bulgarian translations.[26]

✳

I believe that there exist in the world today only a few men from whom you could learn something truly essential about the meaning of life. Men who could be your masters, who could reveal a new quality of life. Think about your days—how ordinary they are, how much alike, how empty! The man I'm dreaming about could change not only your vision, but also the tone of your life—and this not through theories and dialectics, but through the simple exposition of his experiences. I'm not thinking of saints or ascetics (yogis, etc.) who know techniques of salvation or autonomy—but simply of those few individuals who know what it means to live, who know what to do with their lives, what to make of them.

26 September

Jules Sauerwein, who gave us an amusing dinner last evening at Caeilves, across the Tagus, in a restaurant such as I've known only from books (other guests: a female secretary from the English Legation, the young Sein couple—whom S. invited probably in order to forget his "collaborationism"—and several Portuguese newspapermen), asked me for a consultation in my capacity as an "occultist." My friendship with Sauerwein was founded, actually, on the fact that he had known Rudolf Steiner,[27] while I had been to India and had written *Yoga* (which he looked through last year, being especially pleased with the last chapter on tantric yoga and *maithuna*, "yoga à deux," as he calls it).

I agree to hold the "consultation" this afternoon, in Giza's little room, where I have brought my desk since the Herescus have moved in with us, and where with difficulty I do my serious work, because part of my library is in the living room (presently Nina's bedroom) and the rest in my old room (now the Herescus' bedroom). He tells me he is the victim of an occult conspiracy, and he asks my advice: what sort of spiritual exercises should he do in order to conjure it away? Prior to April 1944, when he went to Paris for the last time (where he saved himself in an adventurous way on the eve of the fall), he had relations with the ambassadors of England and America, he could send articles through the diplomatic pouch to the *New York Times*—which were not published, of course, but which fulfilled their purpose, because they were read by the right persons, etc. Since he returned here in August, he has found all doors closed. The ambassadors haven't answered his letters. In some English newspaper or other an odious article appeared—"I Saw Mandel Killed," or something of that sort—an interview invented from *A* to *Z*. His letters to the *New York Times* no longer reach their destination, and checks from America have ceased to come. To his telegrams there are no responses. He is completely isolated. Even here in Lisbon, houses are closed to which he formerly was eagerly invited. English circles have alerted the Portuguese that he is a dangerous character. He is followed by the Intelligence Service. He was threatened with being fired from *Diario Popular* for which he has been writing since August, and even with being expelled from the country.

He explains all this to me in the following way: his name is known in America and it counts in England; on the eve of the Peace Conference he would have been able to write in the Anglo-American press as he had done prior to the outbreak of the war, thereby putting into circulation certain ideas of his, speaking about spirituality, about "Europe," about higher worlds, etc. All these things are unacceptable to the "Luciferism" that directs the war and wants to control the victory.

"For 'them,' " he says, "I am a dangerous man, not by virtue of my degree of spiritual evolution, but through the fact that my articles can be read by tens of millions of persons. 'They' aren't afraid of philosophers, artists, and 'initiates' who have resonances in limited circles, but of someone like me, with access to the masses. I have spoken countless times in America about the tripartite function of the spirit. The powers that are acting against me also rise up against any reaffirmation of the Trinitarian tradition."

I reply that he has chosen a completely unsuitable moment to ask me for an occult consultation. I myself have fallen very low in recent months, precisely from the abandonment of spiritual exercises. I have been living almost entirely in history; the tragedy of Romania and Nina's illness have consumed me to the marrow. I have lost my equilibrium. The latest consequence was vagotonia—which actually did me a service, by waking me up. Sensing myself corrupted even physically, I have been compelled, in order to defend myself, to re-create my spiritual equilibrium. And I show him what he can learn by going to a zoo.

Sunday, 1 October
    The day before yesterday, Nina suddenly began to feel very bad. Between 5:00 and 9:00 p.m. she had five hemorrhages. For a long time I've noticed that

on days she receives shots of Fibrolisină (for healing the incision, to turn the conjunctive tissue into normal tissue), she passes blood. The doctor ascribed no importance to this detail. Nina's hemorrhages worsened, and the whole day we couldn't locate Dr. Moura, either at Lousā or at Lisbon. In the evening Werner came, who, not being able to practice, did not give any prescription. The nurse stayed all night. It was horrible. Only prayer kept me sane.

Yesterday, I consulted with Damas Moura and the gynecologist, Professor Nevo. The blood is not coming from the incision. Therefore, as I suspected, the Fibrolisină has reopened her old gastric ulceration of 1933. In the afternoon, more hemorrhages. In the evening she receives a blood transfusion: 500 grams of Portuguese blood. She takes the blood well. Never have I felt her more closely bound to me than in those hours of terror. I've taught her to repeat mentally, "Lord, Lord," as often as she can. I retain my spiritual serenity by saying the Lord's Prayer as frequently as possible.

The doctor believes the peril has passed and that I can go to the Congress at Córdoba. Nina wants very much for me to go. Up until the last few days, I've been anticipating Córdoba as a time of relaxation. Now, I don't know if I'll go or not. It depends on tonight.

2 October

And nevertheless I go. Without any official order—and yet it seems as though I'm carrying out an assigned duty. I tell myself that Romania *must* be present at the Luso-Spanish Congress today, when no one knows what to think about us.

On the special train that runs nonstop from Lisbon to Santarém, passing all the stations. I meet Gastão de Matos, former General Staff officer under the monarchy, a historian and learned man. From him I learn a great many valuable things about the Portuguese Jews. In Belmonte a Jewish majority exists; in the sixteenth and seventeenth centuries they all became Christians (*Christaôs novos*). They continued to marry among themselves. People suspected them of practicing Jewish rituals. And the fact is that at the proclamation of the Republic in 1910, these *Christaôs novos* abandoned Catholicism publicly, saying that they were Jews. What an admirable example of spiritual endurance. I wonder if the Romanians will be able to remain Orthodox after only a century of intolerant Marxism.

✳

5:30. Birches at the Abrantes station. Between Abrantes and Empola, debarked cork oaks, tomatoes. The sky is a very pale blue.

6:00. Torres dos Varzes. Cork oaks. Enormous nests of storks in the trees at the station.

Evening at Badajoz. The moon appears huge between the willows. As usual, girls are walking in groups in front of the train. And that young invalid man, on the arm of a pale woman.

Córdoba, 3 October

Why does the fact that I know how many days I'll be staying here make Córdoba seem less fascinating?

✳

A Romanian rain. We didn't know at what hotel we would find rooms. We hit upon Cuatro Naciones: bad, but amusing.

✳

How uninteresting savants are! Especially the ones gathered here—nearly all third-rate! And what a farce scientific conferences are, in general—where anyone, if he is brazen or able, can participate.

✳

I walk around the city all afternoon. Again, the Mosque, then through the Jewish quarter.

On the bank of the Guadalquivir. With swift, yellow waters, with its banks green, thick, where reeds mingle with the gardens. Naked children who defecate in broad daylight. Wonderful sight to see.

On the opposite bank, birch trees. Long stroll along the promenade, then through a slum area, unknown from my first visit. An extraordinary house: no. 50, Calleja Consolación.

Waiting for the telephone to Lisbon (after five hours, I gave up on it), I read *San Manuel Bueno, Mártir*, by Miguel de Unamuno. Moved to tears. The consolation of having been born!—what a hard thing it seems to me sometimes!

Córdoba, 4 October

The opening of the meetings. In the section on history and philology, right beside the chairman's seat, there is a horse made of cardboard.

✳

I watch the curious old gentleman, with his glasses slipping down to the end of his nose. A great savant, undoubtedly! He talks only with learned priests. At the Ayuntamiento [town hall], dignified, he does not look at anyone while his wife selects bonbons, wipes them carefully, and hands them to him with a solemn discretion.

I meet the young woman, Hoyos, ethnographer; she will read a paper on Spanish gynecocracy.

My talk was directed to the section on natural sciences because I had the imprudence to mention, in the title, "the origin of plants" ("Quelques mythes sur l'origine des plantes"). With the young woman Sanz, I went to the chairman of the section (the only good savant attending the Congress) in order to have my talk removed from the program. The naturalists were opposed: why shouldn't I read it to them if it has to do with plants?

The large number of papers makes me decide against reading my entire text. I'll summarize it all in a few minutes.

I listen to a paper about some Portuguese fort of the sixteenth century whose location is terribly controversial. Are these people really savants? Who was it that said, "A savant is a man who knows more and more about less and less"?

What's so amusing is the superiority complex of the lecturer. He doesn't read his text, but he improvises, puts on airs, emphasizing the mysteries of the fortress, and then, with false modesty, he acts bewildered over the brilliance of the solutions he has found.

My friend from the dining car is also at the college. In order to take part in a walk that is arranged for today, he explains. He's a smart man. He is not making any presentation, although he claims to know certain things about Brazilian pharmacopoeia.

The Guadalquivir at night, under the moon. An excursion with a driver. The taxi. The garage.

Córdoba, 5 October

In the morning, at the Mosque with members of the Congress. The Patio de las Naranjos invaded by two hundred visitors, plus another hundred local residents, all come to listen to explanations by a scholar-guide—whom, in fact, almost no one can hear.

I notice only now for the first time (and I've been here many times since I arrived) that a paved gutter surrounds the patio, with a thin stream of water running along it timidly, coming from a well. Judging by its appearance, the drain undoubtedly is rather modern. But neither is there any doubt that in the time of the Moors the same fountain existed and there was a channel for the water in the same place. The Moors were obsessed with coolness. I've understood this, especially in Córdoba. Coolness, water, vegetation—making oases everywhere, growing palm trees everywhere, in order to escape from the heat of the desert. The only proper description of the Mosque in Córdoba is this: a forest of palms. And you have the impression that the ceiling is built so low in order to make the Mosque look more like a tent. Even the light here is diffused, indirect. And I don't believe that before it was disfigured by the conquerors—who blocked up nineteen doors—there was much more light. What was lost by walling up the doors has been balanced by the windows.

The Synagogue: I trample some flowers, impiously, walking behind a nervous group.

The house of Maimónides; in the courtyard, the white blossoms of the jasmine; on the ground, little stones.

The Plazuela de Maimónides. In the group of the curious who watch us passing, that wonderfully beautiful girl, with a spot of brown under each eye. Conspicuously Judaic type.

Through Callejuela Thomás Conde, in Campos de los Mártires, full of children. Graceful and calm birch trees.

At the Depósito de Sementales, in order to be shown some horses. The first one presented is a breeding stallion; monstrous but tremendous. Indeed, sex is never beautiful, it has no grace, it has no other quality than monstrous reproductive capacity. I am convinced that the majority of Arabian and Spanish-Arabian horses that are shown to us—superb, nervous, proud—are impotent, or nearly so. The thought that the generative force that I have felt troubling me since adolescence could be the great obstacle standing between me and the pure spirit, that it could be the jinx on my genius—depresses me. What wouldn't I have been able to create if I had been less enslaved to the flesh! . . .

From the names of the horses I retain just one: Unamuno!

✳

I very much doubt that women love rape as an erotic technique or that they have a weakness for brutal men. The woman is sensitive in the first place to intelligence (as she understands it, meaning "quick," "devilish," "witty," etc.): more, even, than to good looks. In the second place, she is sensitive to goodness. All those stories about women obsessed with brutes, etc., are the literary inventions of decadent writers. Statistically, and in small towns especially, that which attracts 90 percent of the women is "cleverness" and "goodness."

It's not the generative power that distinguishes us from women, but intelligence.

Córdoba, 6 October

Last night, *fiesta andaluza y cena fría*[28] in the gardens of the Palace of the Marqués de Viana. I remember the palace very well: I was here last year in May with Nicky Dimitrescu. But how different to enter the gardens at night! And how many gardens are there? The electric lanterns give them an artificial air of *feria* [a fair], which they don't deserve. Fortunately, Louisa appeared rather soon. I must make note, for my enjoyment ten years from now (how easily memories are lost!), of a number of things: the Andalusian faces and costumes (which transform even adolescent girls into lovers—with makeup frankly applied, as is the good custom all over Spain), groups of Gypsies, flamenco dancers with castanets, women I haven't seen before, friends I have made. But I mustn't write too many pages, and I'm tired. I came in at 4:00. I record only what happens to occur to me. If, someday, I write my true Andalusian journal (as I've had in mind to do since May 1943), I'll remember with great pleasure.

First and foremost, Palomitera. Her full name I will add when I come across my book of appointments.[29] Dark complexion, slender, dressed in black; admirable eyes, though a little tired. She is a writer (she promised to give me one of her novels; she has published five, apparently of the Bibliothèque Rose type), and a play that she says will be performed this winter in Madrid. Together all night; now and then she would leave me for a quarter of an hour, disappearing almost without my taking notice, only to reappear, innocent and absentminded. Half an hour after we met, she was addressing me with the familiar pronoun. After an hour, we were sitting side by side on a bench, very close together. Since my Spanish is so bad, all that saved me was the absurd zest that filled me from the moment I entered the gardens. How many interesting things I said to that girl—whom I don't know if I'll ever see again, and whose company, for a few hours, I enjoyed so much!

At 1:00 we were both feeling affectionate—she a little tipsy also—and because I had become insistent, she had the inspiration to suggest that we all—the whole group of us, including an aunt of hers—go to see El Christo de los Faroles [The Christ of the Street Lamps]. It was her wish to show me this marvel of Córdoba (because one is moved to tears by the appearance of the large crucifix amidst the streetlamps in the deserted plaza, after you climb Via Crucis, and you climb slowly, under the light of the moon, not knowing whether or not it would be a sin to put your arm around the waist of a girl you have scarcely met, after praying so hard the week before for the life and health of the woman you have loved for twelve years, to whom your youth is bound indissolubly . . .). Was it, I say, an item on the propaganda program of every Córdoban to show visitors this solitary marvel? Or did she do it to defend herself against the liberties she guessed were coming?—Or as an act of penance, in order to let herself be embraced by the arms of a stranger? As we were climbing the Via Crucis, she told me that she had written a prose poem dedicated to this "Christ of the streetlamps," which ends something like this: "Seeing it in the middle of the night, you can't help being a Catholic!" Maybe she was right.

We returned to the fiesta where almost everyone was a little drunk. I meet and am immediately addressed familiarly by a group of Córdoban youths, who introduce me to all the girls and urge them to sing and dance for me. We finish the last bottle, taking turns drinking from the same glass. Am amused to be introduced by my new and unknown friends to the young woman Hoyos, looking a little chilled in her thin coat.

That girl with the enormous black eyes sang, several times, this sweet song:

> Córdoba, sultana mia,
> Terra donde io nacio,
> Donde tuve mis quereres,
> Donde io te conoscio,
> Donde passi los dolores,
> Del primer amor sentio.

I have written it as I heard it.[30]

How many liberties do the girls take here at the fiesta, and how familiar they are with the men, how quickly they use the familiar pronoun, as if they wanted to avenge their grandmothers and great-grandmothers of all those Moorish and Jewish centuries, shut up, guarded, suspected, and enslaved!

Córdoba, 7 October

Another attack of deep melancholy. I leave the hotel in the middle of the night, and take refuge in this café in order to write on a table of cold marble that shakes every time I move my arm. I tell myself that writing will console me. At the hotel, this exercise is forbidden me. In my miserable little room, I can write no more than a few lines—sitting up in bed, because the suitcase is on the only table. In the lobby, it's impossible, because of the Portuguese. Hotel los Cuatro Naciones is the headquarters of the Portuguese delegation attending the Congress; almost all of them know me, and when they see me sitting at a table they approach for conversation—especially my friend, the "smart" one.

Early this morning the sky was crystal-clear. Now, near lunchtime, it is gradually being covered with white clouds. The cold is something to which I can't adjust: I know I'm in Andalusia and this is just the beginning of fall.

I receive my fourth telegram from Nina; all is well, but the doctor advised her to give up the idea of visiting Fátima. In her days of great suffering, Nina made a vow to go on 13 October to see Fátima, the miracle worker. The hemorrhages have forbidden her this hope too.

Last night I wandered for four hours, till I was exhausted, throughout Judería, the Jewish quarter, and on all the little streets around the Mosque. I left immediately after dinner. First, in the park. The cold, the rain that had fallen a few hours earlier, the fact that there was a performance of Sevillians that drew many noctambulists to the variety theater—contributed to the cleansing of the park. Toward midnight the vegetation always triumphs over the works of man. When it is completely dark and the buildings are no longer visible, you have the impression that you have left the city, that you have escaped from stone and brick.

On the bank of the Guadalquivir, to watch the moon rising—this time, sickly, yellow. I circled around the Mosque, then entered Judería—and I succeeded in coming out into the light again toward 2:00 a.m. in Plaza José Antonio. I walked slowly, seeking the darkest lanes, wandering with delight, surprised at the sound of my own footsteps, encompassed in solitude, melancholy, sometimes dreaming until fatigue wakened me. At first I heard laughter, voices, radios. Then, only whispers. From a barred window, a moan. And I seemed to keep losing my way, returning to the same places, as happens in my novella, "Nopți la Serampore."[31]

One of the things I love best is wandering at night through dark, decadent neighborhoods. I love not only the cosmic fact itself, but also the nocturnal regimen of the spirit, the abandonment to the darkness of nonbeing, to the telluric depths, the womb of all virtualities and reposes.

In the afternoon, to Arruzafa: a former monastery, I believe, a few kilometers from Córdoba, today in the process of being remodeled into a tourist hotel. Gardens, terraces. Córdoba is seen from here as I had never imagined it: ringed by mountains. Successful fiesta: a young poet recites admirably a selection of Andalusian poems. Then a Moorish "orchestra" plays long, sad Arabian and Arabic-Andalusian melodies. At nightfall, a rain chases us inside.

I say to myself that here, Arruzafa, would be an excellent place for me to withdraw and live on very little, working and economizing. Only God knows what will and what won't be possible.

✳

In the evening, at the variety theater to listen to *Carmen de Triana*. After all I saw and heard last year at Seville, it doesn't interest me.

A detail: the two young men in front of me had brought a pair of binoculars that they passed back and forth in order to look at the dancers' legs when they twirled their skirts and bared them to their thighs.

＊

In order to be able to save myself spiritually, I must dedicate myself seriously to my work. Otherwise, I'll decline imperceptibly, sinking either into madness or the most criminal sin. You understand very well what I mean. Pray to the Holy Virgin.

Córdoba, 8 October

Sunday. I enter several churches, immediately following the conclusion of the mass, to see who has remained behind, who is so unhappy that he or she cannot bear to stop praying.

＊

In Plazuela de Capuchinas there are benches of white marble. The sun has reappeared suddenly from behind the clouds, and I stop here to let it shine on me. A great peace floods over my soul. Such rare hours of peace and joy are the only things that help me survive.

＊

This afternoon at a *finca* [ranch] in Córdoba la Vieja, to see how the young bulls are run and subdued, to discover the true *toros bravos*. Gastão de Matos explains a great many extraordinary things about the run and the bullfight. Everything confirms my old hypothesis about the initiatory-ritual origin of the bullfight (see *Prolegomene*).

I try by every means to escape from Paloma, who, for some unknown reason, tires me to death. I return with Jabrier and two delicious girls. We go to the house of one of the girls, next door to the cathedral. I meet her brother—an engineer recently converted and now a priest.

In the night, long walks through Judería and San Fernando.

Córdoba, 9 October

I did not read my paper at the Congress, but I summarized it in a few minutes because the hour was late, there were only a few prehistorians present, and almost no one listened when someone was speaking.

After lunch, by bus to Medina Azahara. We had to wait more than an hour to get seats. In addition to the Congress people, an enormous number of Córdobans attend any fiesta, any excursion. A congress is a unique opportunity for amusement for many people. While a great man is speaking, young men gather around, boys stare at the bottles of wine, old women check their makeup; almost never here at Córdoba have I observed anyone listening. Everyone is content to applaud. At Colegeo de la Merced, while "El cronista de la cuidad de Córdoba" [The chronicler of the city of Cordoba] was pronouncing an "evocación colombina"[32] (on 6 October), the public watched and gathered around the refreshment tables, especially, the better to be able to serve themselves the moment the signal would be given.

Paloma found me this morning at the Congress, and we took another walk together. We arranged to meet at the bus at 3:00, but I came at 5:00. I find her again at Medina Azahara, and the first thing she says is, "Come on, drink a glass with me!" It's amusing that so many of my Córdoban friends think I'm tremendously fond of drinking. At the palace of the Marquéz de Viana they saw me holding a glass, and half an hour later I was in high spirits. And they imagined, probably, that in the meantime I had drunk a whole bottle. The truth is that I can get "tipsy" on a glass of soda water. My animation, and even my intoxication, has nothing to do with alcohol. For me, the night, the moon, the field, the woman—or anything else that's alive—suffices.

Medina Azahara. The palace descends, on terraces, to the plain below. From here Córdoba can be seen, beautiful beneath a rosy sky. And in the other direction, the Sierra Morena, on the margin of which was built this marvel of the Caliphs. The excavations have brought to light a whole city. But nothing remains save a few walls. It was destroyed and burned to the ground. The only example I know of a work of Moorish art destroyed by the Moors in their civil wars. Azahara shone for less than a century.

Meditation on these ruins. Because anarchy and civil wars razed Azahara—we were saved, in the saving of Western Europe. What would an occidental Islam, in a state of continual warfare, have been without intrigues and anarchy?

There are hazelnut and cypress trees here that already are beginning to give life to these ruins.

I meet Paloma again when it has become dark. She smells of wine.

Delicious Carmen. Student, majoring in history, who remembers where I met her: at the Fiesta Andaluza. But then she was wearing her Gypsy costume, and she danced for us—and she didn't seem to be more than fourteen. She says she's nineteen. We talk a long time.

Córdoba, 10 October

I try to read Paloma's novel *La Duquesa de Latencourt*, which she gave me, along with some photographs of herself in Andalusian costumes—but I quit after a few pages. Later.

At the museum to see again the paintings of Valdes Leal, which I didn't remember. Disappointed. When this painter is not macabre, he's completely uninteresting.

At Rafael Bernier Soldevilla's place, Encarnación, 8, to see his works in Córdoban leather. The Master had just a few pieces in progress. He is, without doubt, an artist.

We're leaving tonight. I make my favorite tour again: the Mosque, Judería, the Guadalquivir, and back to the center of the city by way of San Fernando. The sky is like crystal, without its being a hot day. On the streets a continual clamor.

I pass the last hours with difficulty. But I try not to lose a moment. I don't want to spend the rest of my life waiting; that is, I don't want to die imperceptibly, waiting for an event, something that must come, which has announced its coming, and concerning which I have no way of knowing if I will still exist when it appears.

Lisbon, 13 October

Upon returning home, I find Nina with a swollen ganglion, hardly able to close her mouth. Completely devitaminized. Her mouth is dry all the time, her teeth are loose, etc. Another specialist at her bedside, with Damaso Moura, in despair over this new misfortune, which prevents her from moving, eating, and sleeping. Horrible pains.

And, strangely, I still haven't lost hope or patience.

But I ask myself: am I not betraying my duty? Am I not betraying myself, my service, my nation, by giving myself absolutely and exclusively to Nina's illness, not sleeping nights, doing nothing all day, not even transcribing and perfecting my unfinished works? Maybe I ought to be more of an egoist. To think in the first place about the duty I owe to my service.

15 October

Yesterday I tried to return to *Prolegomene*, making corrections and adding two pages to the chapter on the aquatic theophany. I have two or three more days of work—but Nina's sufferings preclude any continuous effort.

The hours I snatch—when Nina is sleeping or when she is less tortured by pain—I waste on scattered readings. Much about ancient Andalusia, the studies of Menéndez Pidal, the life of St. Theresa (who amazes me by her extraordinary artistic abilities), and *Drogas magicas* by Milton Silverman (Spanish edition; original title, *Magic in a Bottle*). I'm surprised by the drama of pharmaceutical and medical discoveries. Vitamins were discovered as a result of the wars of conquest waged by the Dutch in Indonesia. The Dutch were being decimated by beriberi, and Christian Eijkman was sent to Batavia to find out what "microbe" was causing the terrible disease. He discovered vitamins.

Oscar Liebreich, the discoverer of chloral, died alleviating his last nights of suffering with his own drug. Mering, the creator of veronol, had the same fate, as did Emil Fischer.

Another detail: all the antithermics (antipherine, aspirin, etc.) were discovered due to an error. S. Kolbe, for example, believed that antipherine was a synthetic chemical, whereas it was an original compound.

17 October

A second blood transfusion for the amelioration of Nina's general condition. It is discovered only now—after a week!—that she has otitis and mumps! And they can't be treated, either with sulfonamide or with injections of milk, because of her extremely weak state.

19 October

The pains have continued to increase to such a degree that Damaso Moura has asked for a consultation with a professor who is an ear and throat specialist. He recommends urgent treatment with sulfonamide. In order to avert the side effects, he orders another blood transfusion. Yesterday, she began to be fed artificially through the intestine.

The professor's honorarium: 500 escudos (100 Swiss francs). A transfusion costs 1300 escudos. The daily visits of Damas Moura—3,000 escudos per month. The same for the nurses. Plus the other doctors, etc. I'm at the end of my resources—and my strength. I remember with horror the obsession that tortured me for a whole night walking the streets of Malaga in May of 1943:

I, immobilized, unable to work, lying in bed in a state of misery; Nina next to me, also sick; and Giza, bringing us milk every evening before leaving for the sordid dance hall where she worked.

20 October

Today, the third blood transfusion; in the evening the treatment with sulfonamide begins. The count of her red corpuscles made today confirms that her anemia is very serious.

Tonight I wrote several pages of the "Andalusian Journal." There are still a great many things I don't know how to say, in what form to express them. Should I still wait? Still wait for the "big book" I've wanted to prepare for years about Islamic Spain, which I'll never write, just as I've never written on Camoës, nor the book about Portugal, nor the one about Eça de Queiroz, nor about Lusitanian poetry, etc.?! Or should I say the things I know and understand in pages of simple prose, impressions, essays, memoirs, reveries? My detestable obsession with perfection will eventually make me sterile. What I'd like is for anything I write, in any direction, to be, if not the best, then at least the best-informed, the most original, etc. How absurd—and how dangerous!

22 October

"Una tristeza muy profunda" (St. Theresa, *Su vida*).

23 October

I regret nothing more intensely than the time lost in 1941–42 with the documentation and writing of the book about Salazar. That ill-fated decision I made in November 1941! When I think that for *Salazar* I renounced the projected book on Camoës, in which I'd have had so much to say about India, about ultramarine discoveries, oceanic discoveries!

24 October

Jules Sauerwein tells me, among other things, that after reading my book on Yoga he decided to change the ending of his novel, *Initiation à l'aube* [Initiation at Dawn]. As he described it to me last spring, the novel has to do with a triple initiation, performed in a twenty-four-hour period: nature, music, love. The hero is a great pianist, on the evening of a concert. He must, on the first plane, spend the night in long amorous struggles with his sweetheart. Now, both of them will be chaste. The power of abstinence (referring to the technique of *sahajīyā*, the fear of seminal emission).

26 October

For a week I've been working on the Córdoban journal,[33] following the model of my vacation journals published in [1937 and] 1939. I'm glad for the opportunity it gives me to relive certain hours in Córdoba. I use the notes I made, but I especially like to write about the many thoughts, images, etc. that because of fatigue, negligence, or chance I failed to record here, thereby saving them from oblivion.

28 October

I continue writing my impressions. In the future travel volume that I intend to publish, they will constitute a long chapter pretentiously but beautifully entitled "Córdoba, Sultana mia!" Am trying to give as much density as possible to the impressions, to go beyond the *brouillé* [draft form] of the journal, yet without sacrificing authenticity and intimacy, the only qualities that validate such prose. I have in mind constantly these lines from Gide in *Amyntas*: "*Je relis aujourd'hui mes notes de voyage. Pour qui les publier?—Elles seront comme ces secretions résineuses, qui ne consentent à livrer leur parfum qu'échauffés par la main qui les tient.*"[34] But there's nothing I can do about it.

After hesitating a long time, I've decided to "add" to the Córdoban journal the notes taken for a study about the fall of the Caliphs and the political anarchy of western Islam. I don't know if I'll ever write the study. It is better to convey, even in a precipitous form, certain thoughts to which I adhere.

29 October

Continuing "Córdoba," I've realized once again how deadly my system of writing and creating is. My refusal to note carefully the observations I make and the thoughts I organize, my laziness about working daily at putting my papers in order, the illusion that someday I'll write a book or at least a study about any problem that interests me and so it's not necessary to define it now, to write it up, etc.—contribute to the holding over from year to year of my production.

How much better is Eugenio d'Ors's system! I copy the following lines from his *Introducción a la vida angélica* (p. 44), in order to stimulate myself and to try to imitate his method: "Mi ilimitada poligrafía cotidiana me permitía recogerlo todo esencias (he is referring to "spontaneous spiritual flowers"). "Cuanto pensamiento llamaba a las puertas de la reflexión, venido de Diós sabe dónde, está abierto, hospedado y servido. Parece indudable que, en condiciones tan hospitalarias, podríamos conocer pensamientos del más vario linaje—muchos, indudablemente, de catadura más humilde—que los demás hombres de pluma."[35]

This isn't exactly what I want to impose upon myself, but it's close: to force myself to give attention to my mental life daily in some way other than through overly technical glosses buried in notebooks of future "books."

2 November

The interesting interpretation d'Ors gives to Socrates' daemon: it is a compensation for Xanthippes. The man who could not be consoled and enhanced by a woman is compensated by the presence of the guardian angel. The loneliness that marriage could not banish—is banished by dialogue.

3 November

Poor Nae Ionescu! How they laughed at him—the serious philosophers, with [C. Rădulescu-] Motru in the van and the various Bagdăzarians[36] in the rear—when, after being accused by these same "perfected ones" of basing his philosophy on fashionable ideas, he gave his famous opening lecture, "Fashion in Philosophy." Today, Nae's ideas are met at every step in the writings of thinkers ("amateurs"): take for example, the following from d'Ors's *Introducción a la vida angélica:* "¿Una moda? Bien, pero en las mismas llamadas modas, no se revela siempre—más al desnudo quizá que en ningún otro aspecto de la cultura—algún profundo cambio en la dialéctica del espíritu?"[37] (p. 153).

5 November

I have returned, stubbornly, to *Prolegomene*, although Nina has been rather bad in the past several days. I feel I can escape from sadness only by working at this book in which, if I'm successful, I will say all.

7 November

Change of government in Romania today. Vişoianu at Foreign Affairs. Will I keep the stipend with which I'll be in a position to bring Nina back to health (the month of October cost me 20,000 escudos; I receive 11,400; the rest—the doctors—I haven't paid), or will it be remembered that I'm a "fascist" and I'll simply be cut off?

I have written 250 pages of *Prolegomene*. Therefore, one-fourth is written. But to my regret, I believe I'll have to set aside 104 of those pages (about the Mystery Religions), which, amplified, I shall publish as a separate work. Otherwise, based on the proportions given to the "Mysteries," *Prolegomene* would require 2,000–3,000 pages. I'll have to summarize all those excellent chapters in 30–40 pages. Thus, I already have a book, *Le Mystère*, which I never suspected I'd be able to write so soon—a book I've planned since I was [a student] at the university.

11 November

What can it mean? Despite all the transfusions, all the sulfamidele—Nina is still very bad. She's so terribly weak. Professor Larrondé's surgical procedure to evacuate the pus from the parotid gland has not yet yielded results.

I work at *Prolegomene* to keep from losing my mind.

14 November

Last night, a great service at the Fátima Church. I pray constantly, but never have I realized as I do now that my prayers come from a soul too sinful to allow them to rise as high as they must.

19 November
　　Despair. I have horrible dreams. Can't sleep anymore.
　　Tomorrow—after another transfusion (that makes seven so far)—we begin with penicillin.

Cascaes, 20 December
　　I'm writing in our new residence—Giza's and mine—Rua da Saudade 13, Cascaes. I write at the table in my office with the ocean in front of me, only a few steps away.
　　On 20 November, at 12:30,[38] without our knowing or even suspecting it was near, without the sister's forewarning us—Nina left us. Monday, 20 November, at the hour of 12:30. Eleven years and eleven months (lacking five days) since our engagement.
　　She couldn't leave until the moment she lost consciousness. Otherwise, she fought constantly. How much she suffered in the last months and especially in the last ten to fifteen days, I cannot remember without crying, overwhelmed with despair. Did those sufferings perhaps atone for something? I can't believe that. I am sure that Nina had to endure them in order to be able to detach herself from the earth. Her love for me was so total that it wouldn't let her go. And once gone, she would have wandered in my world until my death, if those sufferings had not purified her. I don't want to think about the material causes of her death, about the long chain of disasters—the cancer of the summer of 1943, the sciatica of February 1944, the radiation treatments of June, the hemorrhages, the mumps, the sublingual gland, the left lung probably blocked by a galloping tuberculosis. The doctor says that she was defeated by a general infection. Six transfusions and three series of sulfonamide plus countless other injections could not heal this general infection, which prevented her from eating and, in the last hours, from breathing. I don't want to think about these things. Nina was taken for my sins and for her salvation. God willed to take her, in order to cast me into a new life—of which, now, I still know nothing.
　　For a long time I couldn't believe it. The first day I didn't realize she was gone forever. The one consolation—that she is no longer suffering. That she will no longer have to be tortured with each spoonful of coffee, which provoked long spells of coughing. The pus that covered her whole mouth kept her from swallowing. I couldn't stand to see her suffering so. Why, Lord, why?!
　　I read to her all that night from the Gospels. I knew that she had not yet awakened from her dream, that she was beside me, not understanding what was happening.
　　The next day, as is the custom here, she was buried. In a lead coffin, waiting in a crypt in Anjos Cemetery to be taken later to the homeland. How

much she longed to be interred in Romanian soil, how much horror she had of being dissolved into the soil of this country that she, for a year, had hated with all her being! . . .

That night I sat up late talking with Giza. We consoled each other with the thought that her suffering had ceased—and with the hope that those twelve years had been, for her, happy ones.[39]

For several days I couldn't realize that she was truly gone. I felt no intense grief. A kind of apathy, a spiritual sleep, in which I would catch myself recalling happy events from the twelve years. I went, then, to stay at Brutus Coste's place in Estoril, coming into Lisbon only occasionally to pack my library and gather up things. Often, without any kind of warning—I'd be overwhelmed by despair, by spells of weeping. Knowing that I do harm to Nina by crying, I tried to control myself by praying or by reading from the Gospels and St. Paul.

Nor did I feel the material blows any longer. Dr. Damaso Moura, through whose negligence she died (because he didn't notice her hemorrhage in September until two weeks after its onset, and by that time she had lost almost two and a half liters of blood), is demanding another 7,000 escudos in addition to the 6,000 I already paid him. The government at Bucharest informs the Legation that I am taken off the staff (why? I wasn't appointed by Antonescu, but by the democratic government of King Carol), and that I will be paid until 31 January at the rate of one-third salary—and after that, nothing. Brutus Coste, however, is continuing to give me the 2,000 Swiss francs (and not the one-third) until 31 January 1945, and after that he will pay me out of his special fund 7,000 escudos monthly, as long as he holds his post. I'm ridden with debts. I haven't yet paid the hospital (for transfusions) or a number of doctors. I'm selecting the books for the first lot to be sold. This little house in Cascaes I located for 1,200 escudos per month. But I'm perfectly indifferent to all these things.

December

Nina didn't leave me of her own accord, but God took her to make me think in a creative way, that is, to facilitate my salvation. Nina's departure will have, for the life I have left to live, a soteriological meaning. My separation from Maitreyi nineteen[40] years ago also had a meaning: I left India, I abandoned Yoga and Indian philosophy for Romanian culture and for my literature.

❄

Nina's death has impoverished me. A whole life—twelve years of youth—was validated and constantly enhanced by our conversations, our common memories. "Do you remember at Freiburg, when we got on the tram and that old man addressed us in French and offered to show us around the square?" Those questions refreshed the past, made it alive and abundant. Life consumed *together* is not lost if it is a "together" that remakes it, amplifies it, and fertilizes it continually. That "together" is lost for me now. All that was more intimate, more blessed, more dramatic—all our essential *history*—remains only in me. I can't evoke it, because it had no meaning except for the two of us—and for the two of us only. For that reason, it is probable that I'll no longer be able to find consolation for my loneliness through literary creation, but only through philosophy and theology. I have no one now for whom to recall my memories.

22 December

In order to console myself for Nina's passing, I think—in the moment when grief or melancholy overwhelms me—of the tens of thousands, killed on the fronts, in bombed cities, etc.—or about our beloved dead who died long ago. Do I lack the courage to face reality? Or is it a matter of the reintegration of "the one" into the all, "the Absolute"—the only possibility, in my view, of transcending the human condition effectively? I cannot save "the finite" except by reabsorbing it in "the totality"—and trying to attain that totality through a spiritual élan.

"Because the present form of this world is passing away . . ." (1 Corinthians 7:31).

I can't read anything but the Bible and Leon Chestov.[41] Not only because I long for and seek the consolation of faith, but also because the Bible seems to me the only reading of substance (and Chestov does nothing but comment on it). Especially, the books of Job, Isaiah, and the Epistles of St. Paul. From the reading of these texts I return with a great confidence in the creative powers of man, in the freedom of faith. Life is very beautiful if you understand how much and how easily it can be changed. For this, nothing is required of you except to rediscover the enormous creative freedom of man, which we moderns lost from the moment we considered that faith means obedience.

A series of notes and observations relative to these biblical readings that I propose to develop and transcribe. Actually, wouldn't they be more worthwhile than all those books I have in my head? Shouldn't I write them first? Why haven't I had, before now, the courage of a Nietzsche or a Kierkegaard to philosophize on my personal experience, to write in aphorisms and fragments? My passion has been the erudite study, the unreadable "contribution," or, only now, finally, the well-finished treatise. Why not a notebook, like the last books of Nietzsche? I must have this courage—and I will have it.

Even now I can't return to *Prolegomene*. The night of 19–20 November I worked until nearly 3:00 a.m.[42] on the chapter about the mythology of the moon: to be exact, the moon as the realm of the dead. Going to get a glass of fresh water to drink, I heard Nina coughing and I went into her room. She hadn't slept at all. I begged her to make an effort to fall asleep. She said she'd go to sleep if I would go to bed too. Her eyes were half open, but she seemed not to be able to see. She reached out her hand, seeking me, and she caressed my forehead. In this way she bade me farewell.

23 December

For several years my hope and my despair have had their sources in the reality of the spirit and in life after death. The awful nihilism that sometimes comes over me is unleashed in the moment when I doubt that there is anything beyond. I feel so free, then, and so indifferent that I could commit any crime or any deed outside the law. And I can bear the "passing of time" only in moments when I do not doubt the beyond. Otherwise, I sense how time is passing, how I'm aging, how I'm running toward nothingness—and then I can console myself only in orgy. My play, *Men and Stones*, confesses something about the nihilism provoked by the loss of faith in the beyond. But the same thing is said—and quite bluntly—by St. Paul (1 Corinthians 15:32): "If the dead do not rise, let us eat and drink, for tomorrow we die!" I'd forgotten that passage, although I studied the Epistles quite closely in the camp at Ciuc. (It's amazing how quickly and totally I forget any thought—mine or someone else's—that might console and strengthen me!) I sense that my childish, pagan hope—of meeting Nina again after my death—is terribly anemic. I mustn't hope this thing any longer—not this thing *only*. But with great, fiery, absurd certainty, I must believe that we both will rise, in our bodies. Only in this way can Nina's sufferings possibly be redeemed: physically, so we may experience the joys we might have had and didn't have.

*

If Jesus Christ, who was more than man, who was God—could sweat, urinate, and defecate, then everything is possible for God, everything is possible in the world. Therefore, when the moment comes that I can believe absolutely in these things—everything will be possible for me too. I shall then be free. I shall be able to make Nina not to have suffered, not to have left my side. I shall be able to abolish the past, thereby obtaining a present of bliss and life eternal.

I can think of Jesus only as seated on the wine [cup]—and defecating. And in that moment I know that he is God. I don't see him as a rabbi, I don't see him as a man—however perfect a man he might be. But God—urinating by a fence or wiping his sweat. Is this blasphemy? I can't believe it is. God can do this, and not give a damn, because he is not bound by anything. If this weren't so, Christianity would make no sense in the world—because the cosmological visions preceding it are superior to it theoretically. Christianity fulfills to the highest degree the paradox that has obsessed man since prehistory—of the coincidence of the All with a fragment. Therefore: God walks among men as a man, and he suffers the same humiliations—not the moral or the social, but the physiological ones. If this thing is true—then everything is possible.

25 December

Twelve years ago, on 25 December 1932, my friendship with Nina, which had lasted for several months, was transformed suddenly into love. It was completely fortuitous. Neither we nor our friends suspected that such a passion was possible between two friends and comrades. (I had told Nina about my love affair with Maitreyi, and I had kept her up-to-date with the stages of my relationship with Sorana, which had begun in the fall of 1932.) Nina told me that she was unwilling to share my love with anyone, and that I'd have to break off with Sorana. I promised her, and I tried, but I didn't succeed until some seven months later, in July 1933, when—after having spent ten days with Sorana at Poiana Brașovului—I broke definitively with her and announced my engagement to Nina. Those seven months were emotionally taxing for me: I loved Nina; Sorana exasperated me, but I couldn't give her up. I lied to both of them. And their sin fell on me. Because, in June, Sorana had a curettage, and in the same month Nina told me she was pregnant, and, although we weren't married, she implored me to let her have the child, even if our love would never have an official consecration. I opposed it adamantly, and Nina acquiesced. I don't know under what conditions the curettage was done, but after that she never became pregnant—and in 1943 she discovered, while at Bucharest, that she had uterine cancer. Was it provoked by the curettage? If so, am I not to blame for her suffering and death?

29 December

Forty days since Nina's passing. Requiem at the church of Nossa Sen-hora de Fátima, as also on 6 December. For better than three years we had looked at this church from the balcony of the house on Avienda Elias Garcia 147. After Nina returned from Lousá, I put her bed in the living room. From there she could see the church just as well as from our bedroom. Both of us had a boundless faith in the Lord's Mother of Fátima. In the eight months of her illness, whenever there was a service at Fátima, I told Nina to pray—and she did. On 13 October, when the ceremony with the candles began, Nina watched from the bed and we both prayed. She had even made a vow to go on a pilgrimage to Fátima as soon as she was well. She would have gone on October 13, but then the glandular swelling began, with the terrible pain. I remember that she had a horrible attack on the very night of 13–14 October, after all those prayers. But I, in despair, went out at 3:00 a.m. on the streets. I wandered around the Saõ Sebastian neighborhood and when, upon returning, I saw lights in the church, I went inside. It was 4:00 a.m., and a service for sick women was just then in progress. I believed it was a good sign . . .

This whole day I spent struggling not to cry, for despair. There passed before my eyes not scenes of happiness and love from the last eleven years, as heretofore, but fragments from her last weeks, her wonderful struggle with suffering, her strength and faith, her angelic patience, her will of steel. How she asked for raw meat juice and drank it, for a whole week, in an effort to regain her strength; how she would ask, every three hours, for some milk or soup . . . Why, Lord, did she have to suffer so much? . . .

✳

Last night I dreamed of Nina for the first time, or at least for the first time that I've remembered the dream rather precisely. I woke up and wrote it down. I transcribe it here.

An enormous lecture hall. Pangal is speaking, and at a certain moment he interrupts his lecture and lifts the telephone. "I'm speaking with Marcu at Bucharest," he says. In the hall Nae Ionescu is walking around, agitated. He was in one of his chestnut-colored outfits, with his hands in his pockets. A large number of ladies from the "outside world" whom I didn't know. Maruca Cantacuzino, Mme. Prepau, etc., approach me, offer me candy, ask me what I think about the political situation, etc.

I go outside onto the balcony where there is a huge iron wheel (which was at the same time a gate). I begin walking on it, and the wheel begins to move and to fall. Totescu stops it. An officer in the uniform of Carol II enters the hall quickly and crosses the room, saluting to right and left.

The continuation of the dream: in a park beside a marble bench, in the evening—Nina and I. She is very beautiful, young; it is she, and yet she is changed. She says to me, "After a time we will be married again." I reply, "But aren't we husband and wife now?!" Nina blushes, happy, and gives me an envelope full of foreign banknotes. I begin to thumb through them and I exclaim, "Look, pesetas! And French francs! And pounds!" Nina, on the bench, gazes at me. Behind her there appears a handsome, well-dressed man with a cane, a Don Juan type, who, as soon as he sees her, starts eying her amorously. I hide the money quickly in my pocket and approach the newcomer provocatively. I strike the stranger in the face without angering him or making him stop his flirting. Then, because many people are crowding around us, I start talking in a joking manner, in French, even affecting a Parisian accent: "Mais, monsieur, prenez garde . . . c'est ma femmé!"[43] To no avail. Nina looks at us both. I tell him that we're going to dinner. The stranger assures us that he has eaten, but when Nina gets up, he comes along too, and she takes his arm. All three of us set off down the lane, which seems very long, with steps toward the end—Nina in the middle, I holding her left arm, the stranger on her right. The dream ends with our little group leaving, ascending the lane.

Another dream that follows is less interesting. I am alone. I go down into a valley in order to defecate, but I see Lita and Calin Botez coming, and I hide. On the road, passing by, is Picky Pușcariu, who says that he has seen me. I try to climb uphill, but it is difficult. The valley seems to be a deep chasm. Using my arms, I reach the edge of the road, but I can't go any farther. I call out to a young man to give me a hand. "Are you a Legionary?" he asks, but he reaches out and pulls me up.

This is how I interpret the dream about Nina: Forty days have passed since Nina's departure from us; she meets me in order to tell me that now she is going farther away (a new postmortem stage begins after forty days, according to all traditions), but when I die we will be married again. I reply that I consider myself bound to her even now as husband to wife; that is, in my view, we won't be remarried. This moves her (she blushes). Then she gives me the packet of banknotes to hold: our wealth, that is, our common past (the pesetas equal our trips to Spain, etc.) which I joyfully reactualize (Look, here's our England! Look, here's our trip to Paris! etc.). When I declare that I consider myself her husband now, Nina entrusts me with our common past, to preserve it, to reactualize it continually, until the moment when we will meet again. But this gesture of hers, the happiness these reaffirmations of our enduring love have given her, move her, and she attaches herself anew to the earth. Then the conqueror appears, the angel of death, the true owner of the park where we are (the other realm). In vain do I strike him, in vain do I threaten him and entreat him (the ironic remarks in French); he persists. Nina dares only to gaze at us. No longer can she choose between us. However, it is plain to see that she is beginning to sense the enchantment, the magic of the other realm. Between the two of us, somewhat a captive, she ascends the steps, heading toward the far end of the lane. We two will spend the night together; the other one will only stand by. Nina's separation from the earth is difficult. That does not rule out the possibility that this is a prophecy of my approaching death.

30 December

All day yesterday and today, overwhelmed with grief. I'm remembering Nina's last weeks especially. I see her face constantly, hardened, changed by sickness, and yet so dear. And I remember as well her premonition of death, about which she told me many times. That first night at Lousã, when she was still so well (she didn't even have the edema in her legs! She had gone there to be able to sleep, because in Lisbon she couldn't, on account of the heat and the noise), she looked at me and started crying. She said, "You know, Mircea, we're going to be separated soon. I knew a long time ago that this was coming, but I didn't think it would happen so soon. I'd like to live a little while longer . . ." Then, a few weeks later, she told Giza that she was going away. Another time, she told me she had had a meaningful dream: she had seen women in Oltenian costume weeping and looking at her. Once when I came home I found her crying (she hadn't had a hemorrhage at that time) because she had heard someone singing on the street, and for her as well as for me, the song had awakened memories of our happy years in Portugal. Once, when the Herescus were with us, she heard us talking and eating in the kitchen, and she began to cry. She told the nurse that she would never be able to eat at the table again. When the Herescus left for Madrid, she bade them farewell, saying she'd never see them again. And although Herescu returned two weeks later, he didn't see her, because she wouldn't let anyone see her (someone who had visited her and kissed her—possibly Lita Botez—had given her the mumps). On the night of 19–20 November she said to Maria,[44] who slept by her bedside, that she was dying.

And how could I ever forget her long, searching looks of those last days?! Sometimes she would ring the bell to call us, saying she was afraid, alone, in the dark. A few days before she went away, she frightened Giza, who thought she was losing her mind, because she said, "Where's that little doggie? Poor thing! I feel sorry for him!" And when Giza asked what dog she meant, she replied, "That doggie that was following *me* in North Station." The symbolism is clear enough: the station = leaving. The dog = psychopomp. And I myself dreamt of a dog on the night of 18–19 November. I have the habit of writing down my dreams, but that night I woke up and wrote without turning on the lamp. Later I could decipher only "the dog that . . ." The night before, I had dreamed of three nude women who embraced me one after another. One of them was my Aunt Lina, who died in 1929; another, Corina;[45] the third, I didn't remember.

And the series of bad omens in connection with Lousã! When I went in Calin Boetez's car to see what the sanatorium was like, we met a funeral procession. Two days later, when I was taking Nina there, the same thing happened. Almost every time I went to visit her, I would meet a funeral coach or procession (once a coffin carried by two men). And the day Nina came home, there was a hearse at the Fátima Church.

31 December
Last night's dream: on 15 December I write Nina a long letter, which I address to our old house, Avienda Elias Garcia 147. I don't realize she has

gone, although I know we are separated from each other. I go outside the city to a church. In front of it I see an enormous funeral procession, with music, an honor guard, etc. I go to the church to take part in a choir rehearsal, but I realize that I've passed our church and am standing in front of a strange one from which a funeral party is about to leave. I go back a few tens of meters and find our church. I enter the choir loft. Haig is there too. Then I find myself at a session of an organization where I have to give a talk. I even have a typed manuscript in my pocket, but I see that the lecture has been postponed. A great many of my lycée classmates are there, as well as buddies from the army. I put the letter to Nina in the envelope and give it to Paşcu to post. Everyone is embarrassed. "But this is 15 December!" someone says.

Another dream: Our house, in a large city, is located near the ocean (as we are located now, but seemingly, in the dream, even closer). I look at the sea as if I were looking through the window of an aquarium. Suddenly, three submarines appear, one after another.

Then—the dream of the dog in Paris.

✳

"Il faut se délivrer de passé, il faut transformer ce qui fut en ce qui n'a jamais été"[46] (L. Chestov, *Athènes et Jérusalem*, p. 190). Undoubtedly, the most courageous thing that Chestov says—that any modern can say, perhaps.

The possibility of man's abolishing the past, of making a thing that has been not to have been, or to be in a different way than it was—was envisioned by me as early as the time I began to study Indian mysticism and magic. Cf. my novella, "Nopţi la Serampore," where a scene from the eighteenth century is repeated concretely and yet is modified by characters from the twentieth century.

✳

Relative to what Aristotle said, that happiness presupposes a minimum of wealth, I read in Samuel Butler: "To love God is to have good health, good looks, good sense, experience, a kindly nature, and a fair balance of cash in hand."

✳

Chestov (*Athènes*, p. 397) corrects Descartes in this way: "Mais il aurait dû raisonner autrement: je ne dispose pas des preuves de mon existence, mais je n'en ai pas besoin; par conséquent, certaines vérités, des vérités très importantes, se passent complètement de preuves."[47]

＊

From S. Kierkegaard: "On ne croit que lorsque l'homme ne découvre plus aucune possibilité. Dieu signifie que tout est possible."[48]

". . . un maître merveilleux qui sait tout mieux que vous, mais qui n'a ignoré qu'un seul problème: le vôtre" (La Répétition).[49]

". . . la lâcheté humaine ne peut supporter d'entendre ce qu'ont à dire la folie et la mort" (La Répétition).[50]

＊

I can think of almost nothing from my recent past—because the memory of "that time" that I lived with Nina pains me; and the Lusitanian landscapes, the trips to Spain, etc., not only have lost their savor, but they have become inimical to me, they overwhelm me with their fatality. Sometimes I find myself trembling, melancholic: I had been thinking about England, Germany (our unforgettable summer vacation, taken with a few thousand lei), Paris. Impossible! Those territories are forbidden to me. I could travel in countries unspoiled by our common memories: Sweden, for example, or America. But could I really travel?

I gaze out the window at the endless beauty of the Atlantic. But what good is it, if I experience it alone?

At night, when the terrace is bathed in moonlight and the moon brings the ocean closer to me, I say to myself: why wasn't I granted to see this too with Nina?

No; history for me must come to an end.

5

The Journal, 1945

2 January

Reading Dilthey, Heidegger. All good: philosophy begins with an existential analysis, with the difference between *res* and *sum*, etc. But all these analyses start from the man of today, the European of today, with his science and culture as background! This is not man in general. If a yogin succeeds in walking on hot coals, in swallowing razor blades, in levitating, in making himself invisible, in realizing a state of apparent death, etc.—can't these things also be taken into account? Why do we always take as our object fallen man, the European man of today? Why don't we take account of other men's capacity for freedom, of their creative will, of their possibilities for transcending "fallen man"? Modern existential philosophy, as well as speculative philosophy, are valid for their authors—and for no one else.

Job, in the end, gets back his wealth, and God gives him other children. But this thing does not console me. Who recompenses Job's sufferings? In order for him to enjoy life and God again, it would be necessary for all that he suffered, all his past, to be abolished: things would have to be exactly as they were in the beginning, when he had not suffered, had not been tried. But this "history" remains: God does not abolish it. God does not make that cease to be which has been. If Job loved very deeply his first wife, how could he be consoled with the second wife God gave him?[1] And the memory of his sufferings—did this not plague his newly obtained happiness? And, especially, the memory of his children, dead because of him, because he, Job, had been tempted by God?

3 January

My thoughts run from one book to another: now I want to take up *Cosmos și Istorie*, now I return to *Prolegomene*, now I'd like to write a book challenging the modern world, an invitation to the absolute freedom I decipher in certain myths and discover still in certain persons even in our age (yogins, mystics:

the phenomenon of levitation, the incombustibility of the body, clairvoyance, prophecy, etc. that demonstrate the autonomy of man vis-à-vis the laws of matter, the freedom that man could obtain if . . .).

What tempts me most of all is a rebuke of Hegel and historicism. I feel that I possess an intuition that could result in a great vision of the whole. But I can't concentrate. I can't decide to get down to work. I'm afraid I'll never be able to finish any book . . .

✳

I struggle against despair in two ways: through an effort at faith (in the sense of absolute freedom) that brings me very close to Nina, and through stupefaction in the historically concrete: the thousands killed in the war, the condition of my country, the disasters of my friends (I don't know which ones are free, which still alive, etc.). Besides, the historical present is so incredible that my personal sorrows no longer seem real, no longer have substance. And yet, how distant I seem from my country, from Europe, from 1945—how alien to me are all these things, whose tragedy seems mechanical, exterior to me.

4 January (*transcribed from pages written in the night*)
I sense there is something I will never attempt, come what may: to become resigned. This would not be the way to find Nina again. I don't want to renounce the finite, splendid, palpitating fragment. Nothing can satisfy me but the conquest of the finite. Only God can give me the power to recover the finite. But, please, don't confuse me with Kierkegaard![2] There is in both of us the same passion for and obsession with the real, properly speaking, in our surroundings, for the concrete and the evanescence of the fragments, of finite things. But for me the fragment can coincide with the Whole; while remaining in finitude, man can nevertheless grasp the infinite. Through his rites and myths, archaic man knew how to remain in and enjoy the concrete world, yet without "falling" into the world. This conviction that I've acquired in the past eight or nine years of ethnographic research—Kierkegaard did not have. Hence his terrible despair—and my mere melancholy. He repeated and discussed to the point of exasperation the examples of Abraham and Job, casting himself (but only with his mind) into an Absurd, which would allow him to recover Regina Olsen. But I observe that Abraham and Job have a vast prehistory back of them, that man obtained "repetition" through a whole series of rituals (cf. *Cosmos și Istorie*, where I mean to take it up), that, therefore, the "repetition," the abolition of "history," the suspension and regeneration of "time," was possible not only for a few chosen and tried by God, but for the whole of archaic humanity.

My mission in the culture of the twentieth century is to rediscover and make alive the pre-Socratic world.

4 January (toward 3:00 a.m.)

"To believe in spite of reason—is a martyrdom," writes Kierkegaard. Is that really true? Always, purely and simply a martyrdom? But are you not sometimes attracted irresistibly to the irrational, which invites you to neglect reason, to contradict it or to ignore it completely? Doesn't this attraction give you pleasure, even a thrill? And another thing: the act of believing, which is a creative act (because through it you affirm your freedom, you obtain a new mode of being)—doesn't it bring you a state of bliss? Does the simple fact that reason is always beside you mean that every act of faith is always an act of martyrdom? The liberation through faith; the enthusiasm with which the believer affirms the absurd (Tertullian's *De carne Christi*, for example: "Crucifixus est Dei filius . . . , et sepultus resurrexit; certum est quia non possibilis");[3] the plenary, almost orgiastic feeling of the "creatural," that your faith is creative, that *how* you believe *makes* the world, that your free act of faith is not only a sotereological act but also a cosmological one—don't all these things give you any joy? That is, you believe, you create, and you bear witness—and all these things do not console you, all these things only make you suffer a true martyrdom, just because you "believe in spite of reason"?

It seems probable that Kierkegaard, who had long since lost his faith, also had lost the memory of it.

5 January

No one has guaranteed me a long life. On the contrary, both the "history" happening around me and my inner drama make me believe, rather, in a near end. I must begin to say quickly, even in a summary and imperfect form, those things I have to say to my contemporaries. The ideal would be to compose hurriedly several small treatises, emphasizing their philosophical implications and consequences, passing in haste over cultural morphology. Even *Prolegomene* ought to be simplified. The writing of the integral version will require at least two more years.

And for the time being, no concern for artistic production. Later on, we'll see.

✳

Now I realize, having reviewed all my theoretical and erudite works, that I have never written history, that I've never composed a work of history. Always I have been concerned with the decipherment and promotion of the meaning of a ritual, a custom, a literary work. Never have I been interested in its history, its evolution, its stages of development, etc.

My passion for the history of religions, folklore, ethnography betrays primarily an interest in a world of freedom that modern man lost long ago.

The same interest explains my inclination (since lycée) for the occult sciences and magic: the freedom that man obtains through such techniques. I'm not sure now if the occult sciences are "real." But, at least, their world is invigorating: a world where man is free, powerful, and the spirit is creative.

6 January
I like Chestov. He's a man who fights against *necessity*, who believes that freedom can be something more than the obligation to submit to laws discovered by reason. He has the courage to understand Genesis in its true spirit and its letter: that is, God is the God of Abraham, Isaac, and Jacob—while Adam is man, free and creative.

If I were able to meet Chestov today, I'd draw his attention to the fact that the creative freedom of faith, which Adam lost in choosing reason, critical thought, general and necessary knowledge—that this freedom is permitted also to the man of today. God means that all things are possible, Kierkegaard repeats. There are people who believe this so strongly that for them almost anything is possible.

I began several days ago to transcribe neatly my fragmentary notes, scattered in numerous "jackets," correcting and amplifying them in places. I've undertaken this business because, in the first place, it's not very hard, it doesn't require me to concentrate very long on the same thought. But also, out of the need to leave something more worthwhile behind, in case I have to quit this life sooner than I think. (This morning I woke up sobbing. I'm more and more disconsolate.) A large number of reflections and observations will find their way into a book or study many years from now—if indeed they find any place at all. All the books I'm writing—not to mention those already published—testify to stages long since superseded. No book of thought is "up-to-date," none is contemporary with me. Not even *Prolegomene*, which cannot go beyond the history of religions, although the understanding of it will be completed only through an anthropology.

Transcribing the notes, I observe another amusing thing: almost none of my recent "discoveries" (for instance, those about history and the abolition of history in archaic conceptions, etc.) are recorded. Ordinarily, the notes are thoughts somehow lateral to the great problems. But at least they don't betray me.

The simple fact that I'm writing in this journal consoles me. Not particularly because I'm speaking about Nina—but especially because it obliges me to concentrate on things that interest me at that moment, thus helping me to break out of my passivity. When I simply sit doing nothing, just thinking and suffering, I'm disconsolate. As often as I can, I pray—and I believe. I believe with all the strength of my being that I will meet Nina again, that our love will begin anew, that our bodies will rise some day in glory. And when I believe all these things, I feel I'm a man. Why can't I keep always the certainty and freedom I have then?!

7 January
Long intervals of loss of the sentiment of time. Staring out the window, I forget I exist.

But the attacks of despair continue with the same intensity. I can't free myself from the obsession with things that might have been done, and weren't. Why wasn't I a better man, why didn't I do more, why didn't I demand more of myself, etc., etc.?!

And when I come out of these hells of despair, I sense with a terrible fatality my eternal passion of the body, my craving to lose myself in the most concrete sexuality. Never have I been more clearly convinced of the functional ambivalence of man, the polarity of his instincts, as in these last weeks. What will become of me? Already an abstinence of almost two months threatens to destroy even the modicum of vitality and responsibility that my attacks of despair and melancholy have left me. If this ascetic regimen continues, without the assurance of a steadfast spiritual life and some religious consolation, I'll end up losing my mind or committing suicide. In spite of my despair, in spite of my upsurges of absurd and paradoxical faith (as any act of faith must necessarily be), in spite of my attacks of melancholy—I'm seized, as soon as I emerge from those moments (which, however torturous they may be, are spiritual moments), by a frenzy of the flesh, by a wild passion for the body, for concrete love, however venal, with any woman, with all women, anyhow, anywhere, etc. These orgiastic seizures I can control for the time being, by invoking Nina's sufferings. But I feel that what I'm doing is a sacrilege. I feel that the memory and love of Nina must not be involved in my corporal hygiene, my physiological equilibrium. I'm more ashamed of this than I am of the erotic invasion itself.

What a splendid expression Søren Kierkegaard's father used: "calm despair"! Kierkegaard's comment: "Where did my father ever find these words!"

I'm inclined to write everything in this journal, which I seek out eagerly and which I keep always at hand. But will I have the courage to confess also my terrible secret? I don't believe I could survive the confession. I couldn't do it unless I knew that, *nevertheless*, I'd be forgiven and saved.

✳

Why am I incapable of using my despair, or my melancholy, or even my moral lapses—for creating, for writing, as Kierkegaard did? Why do I let myself be consumed in my hours of acedia and despair, when at the bottom of my heart I still believe that a human experience, communicated and explicated through an act of creation or simply by a correct formulation, can help another man, can enlighten him and make him fertile? I realize I'm not writing anymore in hours of victory, of absolute faith, when I understand the vanity of culture—but I don't have the right to take refuge in a void, to lose myself in idleness, when I'm suffering or struggling.

8 January
Kierkegaard calls existential philosophy "an absurd struggle of faith for a possible."

✳

These days, I've been reading constantly from Kierkegaard (*Enten-Eller* [Either/Or], *Post-Scriptum*, *L'école du Christianisme*, *Journal*, etc.). I brought back from Paris last year some twelve volumes. J. Wahl I had long ago, and I return to him several times a year. Kierkegaard excites me, but he also exasperates me at the same time. He is laconic and prolix, he is poignant, ironic, and boring. Sometimes he's simply unreadable. The comments he makes on certain contemporary works or books lack interest for me completely. Kierkegaard saves himself by his genius and his prodigious existence (I'm not thinking of Regina Olsen only, but of the intensity with which he lived, his superhuman efforts to create, his struggle against despair, etc.). I believe, however, that he suffered from a certain graphomania that forced him to write continually—and write, and write . . . It mustn't be forgotten that S. K. stimulated himself not only with coffee, but also with an enormous number of readings. This existentialist had a library of over 20,000 volumes. He read and browsed constantly in order to stimulate himself, to make rejoinders, to alternate the "conversation."

The first time I read Kierkegaard was in my first year at the university: it was *Diary of a Seducer* in an Italian translation. He excited me, and since, at that time, he hadn't been translated into French and I read German with difficulty (especially Kierkegaard!), I sought and found other Italian editions: *Erotica muzicală*, *In vino veritas* (this last in the series, La Cultura dell'anima, edited by Papini, admirably prefaced by Knut Ferlov, who later translated K.

into French). In 1926 I published in *Cuvântul* a somewhat pretentious feuilleton, "Sören Kierkegaard: Logodnic, pamfletar și eremit" [S. K.: Fiancé, Pamphleteer, and Recluse], which was rather successful, and which, I suspect, was the first article about Kierkegaard published in Romanian.[4]

My commerce with Kierkegaard has lasted almost twenty years, but even to the present day I haven't read him in his entirety. Something resists me constantly, keeping me from devouring him; it is, perhaps, the Kierkegaardian irony (I have no fondness for irony), or perhaps it's his prolixity, his running in place, his stimulated euphoria.

This time, here at Cascaes, I'm reading him with as much enjoyment and understanding as ever.

Leon Chestov, recalling the lightning bolts hurled by Kierkegaard against Falstaff (referring to the latter's meditations about bravery: "Can honor give a man back his arm?" etc.), says, "Actually, this person ought not to have let himself approach philosophical problems." An admirable formula that I propose to adopt myself. Certain "speculations" and reflexes take place on such an inferior level that we ought to be ashamed to discuss them, even to refute them. How, for God's sake, can you discuss anything with a positivist, a psychologist, a Marxist, a racist, etc., etc.?

Since 1 January, thanks to Giza's luck in discovering a Radio Romania broadcast for the provinces, we listen every evening to the bulletin of internal news transmitted to the newspapers. For the first time since the armistice, we're finding out what's going on in the country. That nothing good is happening, we expected. What sense would it make for me to lament the trainloads of materials that leave the country daily to be unloaded in Russia? Etc., etc. All these things are spelled out in the armistice convention. In order to be able to survive, we have to pay—to the brim and running over. We were blamed for fighting at Stalingrad; now we're fighting on the front line at Budapest and in Czechoslovakia. There's nothing to be done about it. When you're small and stupid, etc.

Among other scraps of news, I learn that, in conformity with an article in the armistice convention, all books and other publications that have been withdrawn from circulation will have to be withdrawn also from the public libraries, put in boxes in special rooms, and sealed under the direct responsibility of the director of the library. This news makes me wonder if today I have ceased to be an author accessible in Romania. Being a "fascist," I've been removed from the staff, and, if it becomes necessary, my citizenship also will be taken away. Undoubtedly, *Salazar* and *Întoarcerea din Rai* were withdrawn from circulation immediately. But even my most recent publishers—Cugetarea, Publicom—probably are abolished today. The books republished in the last few years at Cugetarea will be sold in cellophane wrapping, in the best case (because they could be used as packing for cornmeal!). *Meşterul Manole*, since it was published at Publicom, is probably banned. It could very well be that my whole oeuvre will be put under the ban.

✴

"Genius is like a thunderstorm: it goes against the wind" (Kierkegaard).

✴

Kierkegaard, who did not believe (he himself confesses that he lost his faith while very young), has penned the most penetrating analysis of the religious sentiment, and he contributed, as did no one else in the nineteenth century (perhaps only Schleiermacher brought a more fertile contribution: evidence, at any rate, Otto's *Das Heilige*), to the establishment of the autonomy of religious experience, to its definitive dissociation from ethics and metaphysics. Nae Ionescu had a similar destiny for Romanian culture. No one more than he contributed, between 1920 and 1940, to the promotion of religious concerns, to the authentication of extrarational experiences, to the popularization of theological doctrines and terminology among the laity. And yet Nae Ionescu struggled ceaselessly, as a young Christian, to succeed in believing. He was constantly tortured by doubt. A good part of his systematic thought takes no account of God; it is built without the aid or presence of God. Actually, I know that as a young man Nae had lost his faith—and, according to his own statements, he had regained it while studying in Germany. But I wonder, did he really recover it? And did he lose it again? I don't know what to say. The fact is that a facile, "total" faith would not have been creative of culture as was Nae Ionescu's lost and "refound" faith. His adventures in search of God were fertile for the youth and rejuvenating for Romanian culture.

9 January
    I awake this morning in a state of deep sorrow, bathed in tears.

✴

I've never realized the enormous harm done to me—both to me personally and to my work—by eros and the flesh, with all their invitations to skepti-

cism, to Epicureanism, to an "I don't give a damn" attitude. The attraction of
a life of pleasure—that is, to be more precise: a life of erotic adventures—has
macerated me constantly, and a great many of my most noble tensions have
been nullified by the return of that ridiculous leitmotiv: what's the difference?
You're still young, take advantage of things now or you'll regret it later, etc.
This mixture of the poignant and the banal, of ecstasy and cheap carnality, of
the eternal and "drink, drink, and forget!" has been a true curse for me, but
even more so for my work. To the tendency toward cheap, convenient, erotic
adventures there corresponds, on the creative plane, the tendency toward scientism, erudition, and philosophical lukewarmness.

My horror, up till 1938, was that I might be considered an amateur in my
training—and for that reason. I published unreadably erudite studies. This fear
of dilettantism only betrayed a secret struggle with skepticism and scientism. I
didn't dare separate myself—as I wanted to, in reality—from positivism, although
I didn't consent to enlist in the ranks of the "savants" either, because I despised
them. This attraction for scientism, erudition, "culture," etc. was homologous
with the physical attraction for one cheap, easygoing adventure quickly followed
by another. My poignant love for Nina as well as my Legionary adventures correspond to my passion for the Absolute in metaphysics and religion.

How I admire those who can "unravel the thread of memories" (as they
say), who can relive, year by year, their childhood, adolescence, and youth. I, as
soon as I make contact with the past, as soon as I get caught up in memories,
am so overwhelmed, so devastated, that I risk being dissolved by despair and
sorrow. From early youth I have had a horror of the onslaught of memories,
which have always made me suffer terrible melancholy. The feuilleton *Împotriva
Moldovei* [Against Moldavia]—which caused such an uproar at the time—I wrote
to cure myself of one such attack.[5] I believed then that my melancholy was an
unconsumed holdover from adolescence, or else the influence of my Moldavian
heredity. Only in recent years have I understood that melancholy is the only
religious experience God has allowed me. And it can arise out of anything,
but especially from the remembrance of things that used to be. Since Nina's
passing, I don't dare recollect anything personal. I recall only things concerning other people—and then only when Giza is present or when it's absolutely
necessary. General things, pertaining to objective history. I can't look anywhere
except into the future. The past freezes me. When I feel I have to go back to
a certain year (1934 or 1938, for example), I do everything I can to evoke it
historically and not biographically.

Why does Christianity—true Christianity especially—equate *suffering* with
the love of God? Why does the person who is loved by God have to suffer, and

why does the suffering prove God's love for the sufferer? Religiously speaking, wasn't the Judaic view a truer one—namely, that God's love for a man is shown by his contentment, his happiness, his prosperity? Isn't the religious experience that saves the concrete, the material assets, the truer one? No, says Christ, since through faith we can ask for mountains to be thrown into the sea. Therefore, faith can do anything; it can make the material world obey us: we can command well-being, good luck, health, etc. And the more a person believes in God, the happier he will be here, on earth, since "All things you ask in prayer, believe that you have them, and they will be yours" (Mark 11:24).

In this regard, I believe Isaiah (3:10): "Blessed is the righteous man, because it will go well with him, and he shall enjoy the fruit of his deeds." God rewards here on earth, and he blesses with material goods, with good fortune, and lusty physical pleasures. The inclination of the Jews toward luxury and the material, toward wealth and the good life, with large families, etc.—is perfectly justified. Why this craving for suffering and martyrdom? The greatest happiness God has made possible for man—is it not the "saving" of the concrete, giving it a religious meaning, making it possible for man to enjoy himself in the flesh while remaining in the spirit? Should religion reintegrate the concrete whole—as I believe—or should it control it, ignore it, despise it?

10 January

Kierkegaard wrote *Either/Or* in eleven months. In the French translation I have, *Ou bien . . . ou bien* (N.R.F., 1942), the book has 600 large pages with many lines to the page. Everybody talks about the creation of this amazing work in such a short time, as if it were a miracle. Actually, *Either/Or* has approximately 1300 pages of the size I'm writing on and in the handwriting I use. In 330 days, Kierkegaard composed about four pages per day—which, for a production considered a miracle, is rather few. When I work on a novel, or even *Prolegomene*, I write ten to twelve pages without too much effort. And yet, in spite of this, I haven't written, for several years, a book of even 300 pages. It's because I lack what Kierkegaard had in prodigious measure: continuity of labor. Each day he completed the number of hours or pages he had set for himself. Every day—not only in those eleven months of *Either/Or*, but for four and a half years, until he completed *Concluding Unscientific Postscript*. Thus is explained his massive output—compared, for example, to the meagerness of my own writings in the past five years. I'm capable of writing a treatise in a week, or a novel in a month—but I can't do it, because as soon as I've made a vigorous start on a work I'm stricken with an attack of disgust for the current project, and I feel demonically tempted to undertake something else. Ashamed, furious, I don't start to write the "something else" that might please me, and then the days flow by, dead and unproductive.

✳

The internal news report that I heard last evening on Radio Romania announces new purges: professors and men of culture who openly supported Fascism, Hitlerism, rightist ideas, etc. I hope I'm on the list; since I don't have any position (having been purged on 23 November when I was removed from the staff), it is probable that my books have been banned and my citizenship suspended. If I'd been in the country, I'd have been arrested. And how I regret that I wasn't! On the one hand, because I could have hoped for death in the near future, perhaps with torture, which would have brought me closer to Nina; on the other hand, because such an arrest and eventual assassination would have ended my biography as a Romanian writer in a glorious way.

So, being at a distance, my isolation from the Romanian public forces me to begin writing for the few friends who will survive, and for the readers of tomorrow. I have taken almost five years' leave of my readers: I've written nothing for reviews since April 1940, while the books I've published since then have been unable, certainly, to compensate for my absence from "the middle of things." But now the rupture is definitive. Because none of my old books will be allowed to be republished. New generations of adolescents will grow up without *Maitreyi*, and new generations of youths without *Întoarcerea din Rai* and *Huliganii*. How surprised they'll be when they discover them later! . . .

Meanwhile, what if God separated me, in the same month (November), from both Nina and my public, in order to dedicate me completely to the new work he requires of me? But what is it?!

I must compare, someday, in an article, Kierkegaard's "stages" with the four stages necessary for the perfection of a man in the Indian tradition: disciple-pupil, married and parent (until the marriage of the first son), withdrawal from civic life together with his wife, then complete seclusion after one member of the couple is left alone. Lacking is the Kierkegaardian "stage of aestheticism." Instead, there is the perfected religious modality, because the man dies alone, as a recluse, face-to-face with God. And yet he is not antisocial, because he has performed all his civic duties.

It must be repeated to all lovers of great religious experiences that both Abraham and Job, after they had passed through their terrible tests that define for us Christians the most precise relationships that man can have with God until the coming of the Savior—both Abraham and Job *returned to their concrete worlds*, they resumed their ordinary lives of physical abundance and spiritual blessing. They gave up nothing. They abandoned nothing of what they had *here on earth*—even though they had touched the extreme limits of despair and faith.

But are we moderns able to imitate them? Can we return to the historical concrete after tasting the Absolute? Obviously not, and to me this seems a decline from the primordial dignity. "Mysticism" is a late invention of men who were no longer able to endure the flesh in proximity to God, who had to choose.

11 January
There are hours when I can't bear being separated from Nina. At such times, I don't know what to do. Nothing can console me. I can't pray. Then all of a sudden, I come to my senses again. I am, if not reconciled, at least resigned. My finite existence has a purpose once more.

I'm sure that these deliverances from attacks are due to help from above.

✳

Should I be ashamed of the autobiographical substance of my entire oeuvre? Listen to Kierkegaard: "An author must always give something *of his person* (French: *de sa person*—but I don't like that), just as Christ feeds us from his body and blood" (*Journal*, 838). And he knows whereof he speaks!

✳

Did Gide read Kierkegaard? Torsten Bohlin, whose excellent monograph I'm finishing now, claims that *La porte étroite* is steeped in Kierkegaard, that it is the same problem as *Fear and Trembling* (the jealousy of God: Alice sacrifices Jerome to God, etc.), that "the novel is a legitimate child of that Kierkegaardian spirit," etc. But in Gide's *Journal* there is only one sentence cited from Kierkegaard (p. 335), and a rather ordinary one at that. In 1911, I wonder what Gide could have read of Kierkegaard, or about him, in French—because German was always hard for Gide to read.

12 January
"Elle est retrouvée."
"Qui?"
"L'éternité."[6] (A. Rimbaud)
To be used in the chapter on the regeneration of time in the book *Cosmos and History.*

✳

How can I work on *Prolegomene*, how can I write anything that involves rereading and "amplifying" the books from last spring, summer, and fall? It all reminds me of reality, of the fact that I have lost Nina. I tried to reread certain pages from Jane Harrison's *Themis*, and I was projected back into mid-August—and I relived Lousã, the edema, and the injections sent by Dr. Wagner. It's not only that I've lost interest in *Prolegomene* except to the extent it could be the basis for an anthropology—but even if I wanted to return to it, for the time being it would be too difficult.

13 January
    I woke up this morning to find a blizzard blowing in the window. Snow-flakes larger than I've ever seen in Portugal. (It's true that since Christmas a "polar air mass," as the newspapers call it, has been upon us, and last week five persons froze to death.) The ocean is gray, thrashing about. I stand watching the terns, which don't know what's happening, flying disoriented above the snowy waves, trying to lift themselves higher and being tossed by the wind. There only a few of them attempting to fly. The rest, the usual flock, I discover crouching on the rocks in front of the house, almost stuck to the stone, losing their color in the curtain of snowflakes.
    When I go downstairs, the blizzard intensifies. I kindled the fire earlier than usual and stuffed paper around the doors and windows. I shut the door to my office, where there is always a difference in temperature of several degrees. The waves are breaking against the walls of the terrace now. Among the rocks in front, strange geysers erupt now and then, as if they were springing out of the stone. The cast-iron stove is almost red hot, but still the room is cold. We think about what we would have done at Elias Garcias 147. And I think of a great many things that were, and that will never be again.

    I transcribe from L. Chestov's *Kierkegaard* (what a loose, problematic book—but how admirable!), page 276: "L'acceptation et l'endurance sont-elles réellement les seules réponses que l'homme puisse donner aux horreurs de la vie?"[7]

    My life is—and, above all, it will have to be—a fragmentary and disordered reliving of the history of philosophy. In a great many moments—qualitatively different from one another, of course—I realize the theoretical positions of all the philosophers in turn. The Cynic Antisthenes says: "I'd rather go mad than to feel pleasure." Why? It is completely absurd for a Cynic. Nevertheless, I too have felt this philosophy.

I will be asked, "Why are you always talking about 'primitives,' about people so low on the scale of evolution, so unfortunate, etc., and never take us, the civilized, for your examples?" I'd like to reply in the following way:

Imagine that on a beach somewhere there are five civilized men, all of whom have long since become sexually impotent. In addition, one is deaf, one blind, one crippled, another has a stomach ailment, another a nervous condition. All, however, are well-dressed, very clean, cultured, etc. They are watching a group of "savages," almost naked of course, who are playing, dancing, singing, and, especially, making love—right there, under the eyes of the observers. The blind man won't see them, but he will hear their voices; the deaf man will see them without hearing their music, etc. All will know they are making love and that, in this respect, at least, they are infinitely superior. And they will say, "It is true that they can do what I can't anymore, but they're dirty, ugly, naked, cold, they eat badly, they're barbarians and ignorant—and they don't even believe in the true God."

✳

If Marxism triumphs in the world and Christianity is abolished, it will demonstrate that man cannot endure the paradox of being man: that is, of being finite and ephemeral, yet having a nostalgia for the infinite and eternity, attempting all experiences and knowing all shortcomings, in an effort to obtain coincidence with the Absolute, reintegration and regeneration. Then, because this paradox is so cruel, because men suffer and make others suffer (the exploitation of man by man, etc.), because the world in which the paradox of Christianity (and, in general, of any religion, any metaphysics) has been possible is a bad world, unjust, mediocre, etc.—then it is better to put an end to the human condition, to abolish the mode of being in the Universe that is proper to man and return to the natural, biological state, renouncing the spiritual freedom that we have profaned and that, to tell the truth, we almost never have taken advantage of in an effective way.

14 January

I find in an old issue of *Ecoul* an article by Miron R. Paraschivescu[8] in which, mentioning me, he writes, "Little Master Mircea Eliade, the one from India and Portugal . . ."

I'm always amused by the prose of this intelligent lad, so full of resentment for me. The existence of a Mircea Eliade, contemporary with him, simply exasperates him. But I understand him. To have been to India, to have loved and lost Maitreyi, to have been to Himalaya and returned; to have written some twenty-five volumes, to have become the favorite author of the public and to have driven away this public of young women and lycée students with hard, unreadable books; to have been able to lose everything (your university post, the right to publish, freedom, health—and only by chance not to have lost your life also); to have received blows (the trial at the University, the death of Nae Ionescu, the death of friends, the passing of Nina), and to have known the bombing of London—to be a novelist, essayist, scholar, philosopher, and dramatist, without sterilizing your life, without becoming old before your time, without getting rich; to be at age thirty-seven poor, turned out on all sides, without having had a single moment of victory (because when the Guards came "to power,"[9] Dimăncescu remained Head of Press Services at London and I, as luck would have it, received nothing, not even a greeting); to have had such an existence, full of intense, dramatic, creative events; to have been chosen by destiny to reactualize misfortune and yet not be defeated by despair—how could all these things fail to exasperate Miron R. Paraschivescu? He, even when the country was waging war in Russia, was free, was at Bucharest, writing for *Timpul* and *Ecoul*, and writing what he thought, that is, pro-Communist articles, etc. He didn't risk losing his health—not to mention his life!—because he wrote an article that was not to the Censor's liking. He wrote about Serghei Esenin[10] in 1942, whereas I couldn't write about Eminescu in 1938 (cf. the articles censored from *Vremea*).

I understand him, and I forgive him. I always forgive resentments directed against my genius, my work, my existence. But not his taking the air of a martyr, because it doesn't befit him. The "little master" has worked sixteen hours a day for over twenty years in order to learn, to know, and to create—and today he lives on a subsidy given him by a friend, Brutus Coste. And his trials, undoubtedly, are not yet ended.

I discover in Kierkegaard's journal the contempt he had for Goethe: ". . . the perfidy of human egotism which seeks to defend itself from impressions produced by the misery of life, in order not to disturb the voracious joy of living." To be "à la Goethe" was, for Kierkegaard, one of the most terrible insults that he could bring to anyone. So, for example, he denounced Bishop Mynster.

I understand Kierkegaard's viewpoint, but I can't share it, not even in moments when I find myself close to him, as now. Why this unhealthy horror of any concrete happiness? Why this withdrawal from life? Christ never told us that we must suspend finite life; he told us only to believe, and anything we ask, praying and believing that it will be given us—we will have. In other words, a Christian can enjoy anything in life. And Goethe can be disdained for the fact that he, not being a believer, reduced considerably the possibilities of living in the concrete—but not in any event for "the voracious joy of living."

15 January

Unpleasant discussion with Vasconcellos, owner of the apartment on Avenida Elias Garcia, who is asking me for another 2800 escudos, that is, a month's rent, for damages found. The well-known Portuguese system: foreigners have money, diplomats have plenty of money. Squeeze out as much as possible.

Al. Burilianu has been transferred to the Legation at Paris. Good news! This means there's a possibility of our leaving for France at the beginning of summer, a plan I made a long time ago, in fact. We shall see.

16 January

The days of deep melancholia continue. I can't talk. I sit for hours in the same room with Giza without uttering a word.

This afternoon I began the novella *Un om mare* [A Big (or Great) Man], based on a dream I had at Lousã, the first night I slept there. (I believe I mentioned it in the journal.)[11] I dreamed then how I grew (was it I or a friend? I don't remember which) to monstrous proportions. Now I understand the meaning of the dream (that which I give it in the novella): the isolation of the man chosen by God or by fate—of the genius, of the saint, of the "individual" (in the Kierkegaardian sense)—his absolutely incorruptible isolation, his cursed inability to communicate by means of signs, etc. I wonder if that dream of last July at Lousã, where the end was prefaced for Nina (because everything began from that place: from Dr. Damaso Moura, from her edema, from Wagner's injections, etc.), did not portend my present isolation? The fact is that for the last several weeks, especially, I've been "growing," just as in my dream—and in my novella. Will I stop in time?

18 January

The beginning of the great Russian offensive could bring the armistice sooner than I had hoped. A terrible convulsion will come over Europe. A new thing will be attempted. We shall experience apocalyptic times—or uplifting ones. Do the "well-cured" truths of old Europe still have any meaning?

20 January

Two months since Nina's passing. In the past several days, a terrible sadness. Nothing to be done.

I go to say a prayer at the Church of the Mariners. Very close to the house where we stayed in the summer of 1941. As I am leaving, two funeral coaches cross the road in front of me. I hope it is a fatal sign. Actually, almost all I've loved and all I've felt a bond with—are beyond. Here, I have nothing but memories. It's depressing to begin life again at thirty-seven, with an empty heart and twenty years of memories continually interposing themselves between yourself and the world.

Continuing to write *Un om mare*. As soon as I finish it, I'm thinking about writing another, larger, novella, in which I can say even more.

Interesting observation of Kierkegaard (*L'École de christianisme*, p. 128—an excellent book from all standpoints) that Peter would not have denied Christ if he had considered him simply a man, however perfect—but only a man. What troubles Peter is that the Son of God, whom he has never doubted before, is powerless now, paralyzed, like any other man. Peter is not upset that Jesus has let himself be captured—but he denies him in the moment he sees that the Son of God, who could sweep them all away with one finger, is behaving like an ordinary prisoner. It is not fear that makes him deny, but a "mental flaw," that is, his great doubt, his unbelief. If Jesus had been a Zealot instead, and Peter had been his disciple, he would have stood beside him at his torture and at his death. Don't all the political leaders in the world today have their followers who, at their orders, endure even the most terrible tortures? Didn't Peter have at least as much strength as an SS or Communist youth? Obviously, it's a matter of something else entirely: of a lapse of faith in Jesus as Son of God.

21 January
Sudden transitions from great depression to bliss, from the most terrible sadness to serene reconciliation.

When I reflect on all that has happened to me in the recent past, I realize that each blow has pursued a precise purpose, and each pain has played a definite role. I regain freedom with respect to "society," I find myself again, I become alone before God once more. I will not write hereafter to fulfill contracts with publishers. No longer will I devote the greater part of my time to earning a living. I have no worries and very few needs. My terrible passion for erudite scholarship and learning is spent. I'm capable today of selling all my books—and I may be forced to do that someday. If I were to hear that my library in Bucharest had disappeared, that all my note slips had been burned—I'd shrug my shoulders. I know that dozens of studies and unwritten books are there in the drawers—books of Indology, the history of religions, ethnography, philosophy of culture. But I can't help it. They don't interest me anymore. For the time being, nothing interests me except essential problems. Nina has bound me to herself more tightly, freeing me from many illusions and helping me find myself again.

✴

Long walk with Giza after sunset, in the direction of Boco do Inferno. It was our favorite walk—the three of us—in the summer of 1941. On the way back, I think about a fantastic novella in which I can evoke a number of adventures. We keep hearing a little owl.

✴

Today we invited the Burilianus to dine with us. Luiz Reis Santos came too, in order to embrace me, etc. He told me a strange story having to do with a lottery number. "There are many things beyond our understanding," he says. He adds that he is working hard to prepare for the position of director of the art museum at Coimbra.

✴

Why does Gala Galaction always translate *skandelon* as "sminteală" [folly, hindrance]?[12] The whole biblical sense of "an occasion for scandal" is lost. I didn't understand it until reading a French translation of the Bible.

23 January
This afternoon I finished the novella *Un om mare*, 51 pages of this size. I begin this evening a new novella, which I've been thinking about for several days.

24 January
This morning, a walk to Marinha. Sunny.
This afternoon and evening I work on the novella. I write a good part of the journal of the young Briton; it's the most interesting episode and the easiest to write. I evoke our walks of February–March 1941, just after our arrival from London.

25 January
Awakened by a storm. The waves are breaking against the rocks in front of the house, and from upstairs, from my bed, I can see bits of spume being tossed toward the sky. The ocean is dark, furrowed with billows as far as I can see. I'm reminded of that absurd trip, in which I nearly lost my life, with our boat, *Hai-Hui*, from Tulcea to Constanța. Those two days and two nights—driven by the storm into the open sea for I don't know how many miles. The second day the mast broke. No food, no drinking water. A seaplane from Constanța was sent to look for us. My curious mental state (I kept thinking of the flower

garden on Strada Melodiei). *Apologia del buddismo* in the water at the bottom of the boat.

Even today I carry traces of that adventure of 1923. I still become either hysterical or depressed by thunder and lightning.

✳

"On est devenu savant sur la personne de Christ d'une manière illicite, car ce qui est permis à son égard, c'est de devenir croyant."[13] (Kierkegaard, *L'École du christianisme*, p. 44.)

✳

I shall remain forever grateful to Kierkegaard for his courage to have said, in 1848, that he knew only one danger: that of religiousness—and to have said that his leaving of Regina Olsen was a world-class event infinitely more important than the appearance of Alexander the Great.

According to Kierkegaard, I can say that Nina's death is greater even than the catastrophes of the homeland that have followed in succession since 1940. And if everything I write from now on will be related in one way or another to Nina and her passing, I am perfectly indifferent to all the criticisms that, undoubtedly, will be made of me—that I don't understand the historical moment, that I don't take historical realities into account, etc. For me, the historical moment reduces to 20 November 1944. The rest seems unauthentic; and if someday I should create something on the basis of this unauthentic material, I will do so just to earn a living—as I did so often in 1934–40.

✳

Other than the Bible, I can read only authors like Chestov and Kierkegaard, or, occasionally, private diaries. For example, I always return with great pleasure to the journals of Gide and Julien Green; I enjoy rereading little notations having no universal value.

✳

I've known for a long time, and have liked, Kierkegaard's obsession with finding "the idea for which I would live and die." But I was surprised today, while studying more closely the excerpts from his journal of 1835, that he spoke about this idea at the age of twenty-two.

✳

It's after midnight and I don't believe the storm is abating. The billows keep breaking constantly on the rocks, shaking the house. And the wind has intensified again. Sometimes I hear strange cries; I wonder if they're birds (but what kind of birds?) or the cold wind whistling over the waves. This house of ours has suddenly acquired a sonority previously unknown.

I'm sitting alone in the little room with the terrace. The fire in the stove has gone out. I can't keep on with the novella (have reached a point in the Briton's journal where I don't know what to say next), and I persist in returning to Kierkegaard's journal (yet how hard it is!). But the waves obsess me. I listen to them sometimes for many minutes: a great slithering sound, as though the waters were gathering together, then an outpouring, thunder, the first muffled explosions on the rocks, and the great repercussion, the gigantic fall—after which the silence seems awesome.

✳

I believe I've already copied in this journal Kierkegaard's remark about Christianity, but I repeat it once more because few men could verify its validity better than I: "Il en va du christianisme ou de se faire chrétien, comme d'une cure radicale qu'on ajourne aussi longtemps qu'on peut"[14] (9 October 1835).

26 January

It's unbelievable how quickly the weather can change on this Atlantic coast. After the storm of yesterday, which continued with fury for a good part of the night, I wake up to a warm, sunny morning. A real summer day. We leave for Guincho. At the entrance to the municipal park, we stop briefly at the zoo and watch the monkeys. I remember with an unbearable acuity the afternoon in August when we took refuge in the zoological garden at Bunfica. Again, sadness makes me silent.

Wherever I go, whatever I do, I meet something tangible from the twelve years I lived with Nina.

✳

I can't continue the novella. The urge for literature has passed. (In all, it lasted six or seven days.) In order not to waste the afternoon, I work on a commentary for *Glossarium*.[15]

But with such a short breath, what will I be able to do of lasting value?

I understand Nietzsche's need to write aphorisms—to liquidate a mood or a new vision of the world, in a few lines, or, at most, a few pages.

✳

The majority of the notes for *Glossarium* were written with a view to possible studies or articles. Their point was to be amplified, or else they were to be copied precisely, in their abbreviated, summary form. What I am doing—what I'm content to do—harms rather than helps. It destroys the spontaneity of the notes, and yet it does not yield in exchange the gravity of an article. But I need to continue *Glossarium* whether I want to or not. I haven't the time to write those innumerable studies and essays; they don't interest me now. And it would be a shame if all those observations—some of them fertile—were to be lost forever.

For several months now I've had a copy of Nietzsche's *The Will to Power* (unabridged edition), but I haven't succeeded in reading it through. Along with astonishing fragments, dozens of hodgepodge sentences, dreadfully mediocre. All that he writes about (or rather against) religion, Christianity, Buddhism, is external, badly informed, feeble; it's as though I'm reading a commonplace atheist. The theoretical level is that of a Socialist of 1880. I am amazed at Nietzsche's capacity to resist symbol, myth, mystery. The genius sees nothing in religion other than what his contemporaries could see—men whom he, with good reason, despised.

In Kierkegaard's journal, 1836: "Dieu me damne, je peux faire abstraction de tout sauf de moi-même; je ne peux même m'oublier quand je dors."[16]

I'm making *Glossarium*, as well as my other copybooks with comments (for example, about the history of religions, travels in Spain and Portugal, etc.), in order to detach definitively from this journal several hundred pages that I had promised myself would have to be taken out sometime, just as I must separate out, for example, the "Journal of the Novel *Viață Nouă*" and the datebook of 1940–41.[17]

27 January
Great agitation in the heart of the Romanian community: a Swedish vessel, commissioned to make an exchange of Turks and Germans, may be able also to take Romanians from the Iberian Peninsula. The ship will pass here on 1 March. And whereas until just the other day everyone was talking about how eager he was to return home, now they're worried, they're raising questions, wondering if they would be making a big mistake going back during the typhus epidemic, etc.

As far as I'm concerned, my mind is made up. I'll return only if I have the assurance that my old books can be reissued and I can publish my new ones. Having been removed from the staff of the Legation, with no university position, without savings, without the possibility of earning a decent living—and, in addition, running the risk of being arrested at Ana Pauker's[18] first attack of indigestion—I have no reason to return to the country. I prefer to vegetate in Cascaes where, at least, I have the most precious thing in the world: freedom. Of course, I'll stay here only until I can leave for Paris or America.

28 January

From Kierkegaard's journal, 1837: "Qu'est l'amitié sans échange intellectual? Un refuge pour âmes faibles qui ne savant respirer dans l'éther de l'intelligence mais seulement dans les exhalaisons de l'animalité."[19]

The explanation of my sterility of 1940–44.

Where is it coming from—this anxiety accompanied by a delightful disconcertment at the thought that I might be able to go to Paris sooner than I had hoped? This strange sentiment has persisted for an hour, ever since Brutus telephoned from Sintra that the former counselor of the French Legation in Bucharest, Spitzmüller,[20] who is on a mission to Lisbon for a week, wants to see me in order to discuss the possibility of my going to Paris. The appointment is for 5:30–6:00. I'm waiting with genuine impatience.

✳

Spitzmüller knows *Yoga* and *Zalmoxis*. He is interested in the history of religions. We talk for nearly two hours. Exciting particulars about the coup d'état of 23 August. He assures me that as soon as I want, I can address him and obtain a visa for Paris at any time. (He told Brutus that Picky advises me not to return to Romania.)

29 January

"Dichten: Das unschuldigste aller Geschäfte" (Hölderlin).[21]

30 January

Brutus gives me the telegram to read—M.A.F. [Ministry of Foreign Affairs] no. 8191, 1944 (received 23 November)[22]—by which I am removed from the staff: "Be so good as to inform Mircea Eliade that, on the basis of new legal dispositions and through the High Royal Decree No. 2134, he is dismissed

from the staff of Ministry of Foreign Affairs as of the date 1 November 1944."
Signed F. Filotti, Secretary.

31 January

The bulletin of internal news transmitted last night by Radio Bucharest announced that among those to blame for the disaster of the country are its leading writers, such as Ioan Al. Brătescu-Voineşti, who has been arrested.[23] It's getting more and more beautiful!

1 February

Against ritualism: "For the pure, all things are pure" (Titus 1:15). How much I understand from this generous but imprudent statement! I think in the first place of love: in the area of sensual pleasure, everything is allowed to a lover. Basically, any lover is a "pure" man, and his rights are unlimited.

"Rejoice always in the Lord. Again I say to you, rejoice!" (Philippians 4:4). How does Kierkegaard comment on this text? I would be interested to know what value he gives to joy, so categorically affirmed by the Apostle. It's true that he adds, "in the Lord." But it is no less true that the command is, "Rejoice!" The imitation of Christ, therefore, does not imply—as Kierkegaard believes—suffering and martyrdom. Or, more precisely, however much suffering the militant Christian may endure, his heart must rejoice unceasingly in the Lord. It is not a matter of sadness or solitude or drama. "Again I say to you, rejoice!"

2 February

The waves I heard last night, from up in my room, reading St. Paul . . .

The sentiment that I have been sent into the world to solve mysteries. I must be bolder. I must say, more and more clearly, what I think. Time is passing.

Thus I've decided to write for *Glossarium*, but in an extremely abbreviated form, the defense of Judaism on which I've been ruminating for several weeks.

✳

What freedom to create is afforded by music! Does any other contemporary art form dare to say so much and in such a frankly grandiloquent way as music? All excessive impulses, all the great naivetés that transform the biological condition of man into a destiny, make it truly a modality proper to his existence in the Cosmos. All the "big words" (love, God, solitude, tragedy, etc.), all simplified conflicts, all fundamental problems—are presented in music, whereas in drama and the contemporary novel they are bent, shrunken, flat-tened, owing to the resistance of the materials, to an excess of prudence and intelligence, to the refinements of good taste, etc., etc. In what novel can you "speak" of God, or happiness, or loneliness—as "any composer with a modicum of genius speaks"?

The science that says no with respect to phenomena, that does not believe that they are as they seem to be, that says, "You are not like that, but you are atoms, or you are electrons, neon, etc.; you are not matter but a center of electrical energy, etc."—these modern sciences have discovered the attitude of the Upanishadic sages with their famous "*Neti! Neti!* You are not this, not that!" who refused to identify the spirit, Brahman, with cosmic phenomena, identifying it rather with ātman.

To be developed (in *Glossarium*): concerning St. Paul's spiritual sons. "To Titus, my true son in the faith we share . . ." (Titus 1:4). "I appeal to you for my child whom I bore while in chains, I appeal to you for Onesimus" (Philemon 10). The regeneration by faith is assimilated by the Apostle Paul to the act of birth. To Titus he gave birth through faith—his own and that of Titus. Conver-sion—the marriage of two spirits: that of the Apostle and that of the convert. St. Paul creates spiritually—and nevertheless in the order of life. The differences between a father (procreator in the natural order of life), an artist (creator in the spiritual order), and a saint (spiritual creator in the order of life).

In order to make this journal useful, to turn it into an instrument of defense against the nothingness that threatens me on all sides, I would have to meditate with it beside me, to return repeatedly to the pages already written, to annotate them, to recall here certain events I have passed over too summarily or failed to record at all. Only in this way will I collect myself—or recollect myself completely. I could abandon myself here to that past that obsesses me. I could save the "lost time" by remembering it. I must not be afraid of filling too many pages, of wasting too much of the time I still have left to live. It may be that many of the books I want to write I won't be allowed to finish. Why don't I just concentrate on myself, on my life, my salvation, and my health, making this journal my true oeuvre?

So much the worse if nobody ever reads it. I, in any event, can only benefit.

✳

"Why do you keep thinking about Nina all the time?" a friend might ask me. "What does the loss of your wife mean, compared to the world catastrophe in which tens of thousands of persons are losing their lives daily, when cities are being annihilated and nations devastated? Why are you so egocentric? Why can't you view things objectively, looking at reality as a whole, not just the sector in which you live?"

I would answer: "Imagine a young man, in love for a long time, who one fine day succeeds at last in embracing his sweetheart. He is happy, and in reaction to his outburst of happiness, you say to him, 'What difference does it make that today you've possessed a woman?! In the same hour as you, all over the world, at least a million couples made love. What happened to you is nothing extraordinary!' And yet he, the young man in love, knows that what happened to him *is* extraordinary!"

3 February

I didn't fall asleep until 4:00 a.m. A troubled insomnia: despair overwhelmed me. I realize very well how great the sin of despair is, how close it is to nonbeing!

I'm in despair whenever I see ahead of me no alternative: more precisely, when I feel that whatever I do, the result will be despair. I can endure more easily the past, despite all its horrors. When Nina's departure overwhelms me, I still see a way out of the suffering: my own death and our meeting again. But the despair provoked by consideration of the future is terrible. I say to myself, I don't know how much longer I have to live, so I must take advantage of my life. And I have the alternative: if I were to throw myself again into "experiences" (that is, erotics), I'd consume myself in vain, since no amount of sexual pleasure is able to console you the moment after its cessation. (Am I consoled by the fact that I have held Rica, Maitreyi, Sorana, and several other women in my arms? An erotic memory never consoles you; everything is completely consumed in the act; you remember the love, the friendship, the history connected with the woman, but that which was the erotic essence, the act as such, becomes nothing the moment it's over.) Thus I tell myself to be content with a physiological equilibrium obtained without mental involvement (an ordinary, convenient adventure), and to concentrate on my work, letting life pass by without making an effort to taste it, change it, or get very close to it. But I'm afraid that later on I'll regret these years when I've failed to take advantage of the immediacy of life. I'm afraid I'll suffer regret—when it's too late. As I've regretted for the past five years certain liberties of which I did not wish to take advantage—with the result that every spring I suffered from neurasthenia. (I must make it clear that my neurasthenia was provoked originally by the sentiment that life is passing—along with youth—and that I am no longer free, being married. There were times when I wished I weren't married, but my love for Nina was so strong that I couldn't conceive of separating from her; on the other hand, I suffered from being bound, from having made a choice. And then, from 1939 to 1944, my despair derived from the fact that history was irreversible, that things had happened that had banished me from my youthful state of *disponibilité*, when I was free to enjoy any adventure, erotic or otherwise, when I was not tied down by anything, etc.).

If I decide to live, simply to live, I could regret later having wasted time on illusions. If I were to withdraw from life in some way or other—a monastery, isolation, continuous creation—I could regret that I had wasted my youth (what youth I still have left—that is, twelve or thirteen years) instead of taking advantage of it now, and devoting myself to my work later on. And there's a third alternative, which drives me even more forcefully to despair: not to live, not to "create"—but to seek to perfect myself spiritually, to enter into zones that only I know, to become "One" . . . This is a great mystery . . .

Thus, in a sense, I can say that despair and melancholy, nourished day after day by Nina's departure, is preferable. I can't be consoled always, but her presence in a future more or less near, the certainty that we will meet again, sustains me. In any event, I don't have a sense of nothingness, as I do when I consider the alternatives for the future—when, no matter what I might choose, I'm afraid of choosing wrongly.

✳

No despair is bearable. For several hours, Nina's departure seemed so terrible that, other than my own death, I could see nothing, then, anywhere, no way out.

4 February

"Depuis bien longtemps et de nos jours, on a complètement perdu de vue qu'être écrivain, c'est agir, avoir l'obligation d'agir et, par suite, avoir un mode personnel d'existence"[24] (Kierkegaard, *Point de vue explicatif de mon œuvre*, p. 39).

The accent falls on the personal mode of existence. That is, in the first place, on the capacity to hold out against the surroundings and the daily press, "the symbol of abstract and impersonal information."

I too understand the mission of the writer this way, and not as a simple incorporation in a mass, as Communism proposes.

From Kierkegaard's confessions, I understand that for almost five years he wrote daily for a certain number of hours, that he imposed this schedule in order to restrain the superabundance in himself; because, if he had abandoned himself to his inspiration, he would have written so much of the time, day and night, that he would have gone mad. This schedule explains, to a large extent, Kierkegaard's prolixity. If he had written without schedule, he might have written more concisely, more sharply. But the daily hours of work allowed him any loitering, any fantasy, any digression. There are utterly unreadable pages in *Either/Or*, and even in his extremely dense books like *Training in Christianity*, the inspiration sometimes languishes, the style is dull, and repetitions abound.

Today, Burilianu came with Maddy in order to make a farewell visit to Estoril and Cascaes before leaving for Paris. They have lived in Portugal for three years. In a few days it will be four years since our arrival here. And now, at their departure, it seems they are leaving with a part of my life. What value does a past have, when you are the only witness to it?

He asked me to return to him Galaction's translation of the Bible, which he lent me last summer. From 20 November until last night, I couldn't go to sleep without reading several pages from the Bible. I know I can get a copy tomorrow from Brutus, but when I gave this one back, it broke my heart. It was the one with which I watched by Nina's bedside. It was the copy with which I spent so many nights this winter. With this volume I had ties of confidence. I know the text is the same in any other copy of this edition, but I feel that something of a witness has been taken from me that nothing else can replace.

5 February

Melancholy or despair, torpor or temptation, whatever may be—my duty is to work, to write the several books I've begun or planned. I can't see anything else; I don't know what else I could choose. Perhaps all the sufferings I've endured and still endure, perhaps the melancholy itself that becomes increasingly worse, are given me in order to perfect an oeuvre which otherwise would be in danger of getting lost in erudite ephemeras and juvenile fiction. This oeuvre could comprise a series of personal books: journals, reflections, autobiography, etc. The fact that I can't publish anything I might write in Romanian ought to encourage me to write exclusively posthumous works.

Glossarium has reached 65 pages.

✳

The thought that I might be able to publish excerpts from this journal earlier than I had decided (that is, before 1967)—will it intimidate me so much that I won't dare confess everything? I must banish this thought. Because, even if I were to publish it before the date of my sixtieth birthday (whether or not I'm still living), I will choose only excerpts.[25] That's what Gide did, and Julien Green does likewise

Therefore—be brave!

6 February

"Die Philosophen sollen Grammatiker, und die Grammatiker sollen Philosophen sein"[26] (F. Schlegel). Use as the motto for *Glossarium.*

7 February

On this day four years ago, we had finished our preparations for leaving England. Mrs. Sassoon, our landlady at Oxford, was disconsolate. She believed, however, as we also hoped, that we would be able to return to England in the course of the year 1941, bringing Giza too. My idea, when requesting an exit visa, was this: to go to Romania and have a long talk with General Antonescu, then to return immediately to England. V. V. Tilea[27] also entrusted me with certain things to say to the General. My personal message was the following: (a) the Romanian government believes that England is losing the war, and is behaving accordingly, but this thing is by no means certain; (b) nevertheless, supposing England does lose the war, this does not mean in any event that Romania can dispense with England, that it can mock it in a ridiculous way through the radio and the press, etc., because, as we know, the second day after the defeat of Germany in 1918, the most important diplomatic post after Paris and London was Berlin. Therefore, even in the case of a German victory, London will continue to be an extremely important place, and it makes no sense to anger the English, to offend them, to irritate them with nonsense, etc.

I had one other thing I wanted to say to General Antonescu: London was saved during the blitz by the Home Guards, the civilians. The only possibility of surviving in the face of massive bombings is to organize the civilian population.

On arriving at Lisbon,[28] I found the confirmation of my appointment to the post of press secretary here. I wrote, then, a report to General Antonescu that I intended to send through Vardala, who was returning to Bucharest from London. At the last moment, I abandoned the idea and burned everything I had written.

I remember now, hour by hour, those last days in England. Nina's happiness, and mine, that we would see Giza again, that we would be seeing friends (about whom we had heard nothing since the rebellion).[29] Dinner with Buxell. Evening at Farnam Common with Vardala, Munteanu, Ion Bianu, V. Cornea, and Radu Florescu.[30] Our last night in Farnam Common where I had known so many joys and so many fears (when Romania was "Slavicized";[31] when a bomb fell unexpectedly in the vicinity; the rebellion). Long conversation with Victor Stăncea, who asked me to take a ring to his father, and, shedding tears, told me he knew he would never see him again, that he wouldn't be able to return to the homeland; he believed that England would win the war, and he was in love.

At the end of January 1941 we received a telegram from O. W. Cisek (the first not signed by E. Bulbuc):[32] "Please stay there and wait for instructions."[33] Nina started crying (she supposed that the rebellion had been real, that Bulbuc had been arrested). Mrs. Sassoon's happiness.

The tragedy of Kierkegaard is not that he lost Regina Olsen by renouncing her, but that he had met her, loved her, and was loved in return. All that followed—his sufferings and his drama—were due to the irreversible fact that he had met her and was loved by her. This thing could not be abolished.

My tragedy was not consummated on 20 November 1944, but on 25 December 1932, when the friendship I had had with Nina up till then was transformed into love—which led later to our marriage, with all its joys and all my melancholies. 25 December 1932, was irreversible. Sometimes I wanted to get free, but even if I had succeeded in doing so, the simple fact that I had loved Nina had modified everything. Destiny had intervened, and then history. Unfortunately, I could not make things that once had been no longer be. Only God can do that.—And, I hope, death. I hope that in death all will be fulfilled for me, without my suffering for being divided, for having chosen, for having lived the fragment and the finite.

The whole world is in flames. The fusion taking place today has only one advantage: that the metal liquified at such great sacrifice can be poured into any kind of mold. If the three—Roosevelt, Stalin, and Churchill—will have political genius and good faith, they will be able to pour the world in fusion into perfect molds. If not, we will have to remake everything with the old, worn-out forms. But later it won't be possible to do anything. ("Strike the iron while it is hot!") Since after a third world war, the world will not melt again.

8 February

The importance of peace, of absolute calm, not only for you, man, but also for the Cosmos, in order for it to understand itself, to find itself again. Any violent movement in Nature confers on it the advantages of life—but also separates it disjunctively, fragmentarily. Dynamics—a false modality of being (esse). The refinding, the gathering together, the total possession of the self—a conquest of peace. Calm = reflection = consciousness.

✳

Four years ago: the last night at Oxford.

9 February

Four years ago. We left Oxford in the morning in Radu Florescu's car. We stopped by Mitrany's[34] place; he gave us letters for his mother (they never reached her, because the diplomatic bag was confiscated). Then, to London. We all ate at the Savoy. At 3:00, the train to Bristol. The parting at the station. How carefully I guarded the sealed valise, although I hadn't been told that it contained anything important.

We spoke to each other hardly at all the whole way to Bristol. We were in a highly emotional state and hid our feelings from each other. We didn't know if we'd escape being bombed, because Bristol had suffered some terrible attacks during the preceding weeks. Neither did we know if we'd escape in the airplane. The evening before, there had been a search of V. Cornea's place.[35]

It was night when we arrived at Bristol, and an alarm was in effect. The station had been almost entirely destroyed. No porters, no taxis. A fine rain was falling. With the greatest of difficulty we got out of the station and onto the platform. I set the luggage on a trolley, put the bouquets of flowers we had been given at the other station on top, and began waiting. After a quarter of an hour, seeing that the "all clear" had not sounded and that no taxi was in sight, I left Nina with the luggage and set off in the darkness. Now and then I could hear the antiaircraft batteries firing, but I was used to that. Finally, I found a taxi. The driver hesitated to take me, but I promised him ten shillings extra. We reached the hotel at 10:00. The restaurant was closed. We could get only sandwiches and tea. I didn't realize that the hotel where we had our reservations was the only one that hadn't been destroyed by the air raids, and that only one wing of it had escaped. Not until the next day, when we were leaving, could we see the disaster of Bristol.

In our room, I hastened to write a letter of thanks to V. V. Tilea. Nina wrote to Mme Tilea. Then I went down the hall to take a bath, but bombs falling in the vicinity interrupted me. Nevertheless, they didn't hit the airport. We slept half-dressed. We had to be up at 6:00, because the car was coming to take us at 7:00.

✳

I reread in *Insula lui Euthanasius* the articles I had written about Gabriele D'Annunzio. In *Solus ad Solam*[36] the poet asks himself, "Who will give me back my wild, wonderful strength to which I owe all my victories? . . . Why don't I cast the cadaver, the dead weight, far away, and seek strength and pleasure in other places? Why do I persist so stubbornly? What else am I waiting for?" Formerly, such urges to heroic amorality—which I myself experienced between 1927 and 1933—troubled me. The eternal immoralisms in Gide, in D'Annunzio. When I read them, I suffered in my condition of husband and writer: weighed down by projects, exhausted by needs. Such passages encouraged me in all sorts of liberties, because they helped me to return to what I had once been, to what I had ceased to be on the day I decided to pass the hardest examination of my life: to get married, to accept all the risks of becoming mediocre and failing through poverty and dependency, in order to verify my true strength, to find out if my genius could withstand any environment and any destiny.

Now it makes me smile to read the naughty Gabriele. The whole problem is not to cast off the dead weight (any adolescent can do that), but to live with it, to create with it, to fly with it—if you can. The lead on the wings, the cadaver in the soul, etc.—are excuses for mediocre spirits, for failed minds. Not to run away from reality, to look it constantly in the face—and continue to be yourself. This, yes.

10 February

Four years ago. We left the hotel in the dark, at 7:00 a.m. In front of me sat an officer with tired eyes, chain-smoking (he was the one who would search me later). As soon as the car started out, we began to be aware of the disaster of the bombing raids. We passed between what were, purely and simply, ruins. Now and then, a building still standing, but through its windows we could see the sky. It was a sinister sight that haunted me for a long time afterward.

We arrive at the airport at 8:00. There are just we two, plus a young Englishwoman (secretary of the Legation in Madrid), a young foreign man, and the crew. We are left for last. We wait in a large room with a reservist beside us, dressed so strangely, in a uniform too large for him, that we wonder if he is an agent of the Secret Service who knows Romanian, sent to eavesdrop on our conversation. I am called, alone. I take the diplomatic case with me. When I present my diplomatic passport to the functionary sitting beside the captain at a table, he looks over the list of the accredited diplomatic corps. I am not there, because Tilea had not succeeded in getting those of us in the "cultural service" put on the list. So, in spite of my diplomatic passport, I am invited to hand over my billfold, etc. They find nothing. The captain gets up from the table and turns me over to some special agents who proceed efficiently with the body search.

When I found myself naked, I had a moment of silent revulsion. I seemed, in my own eyes, completely abased. The agents searched with such dexterity that I'm sure that if there had been a sign made with a pin on one of my shoelaces, or if I had marked my tie with imperceptible dots, I'd have been arrested. Nothing could have escaped them. They pried the heels off my shoes, they examined the buttons, seams, linings—in a word, everything. On the airplane, I found out that Nina had undergone a similar radical search. At the same time, in another room, a search was being made of our toiletries—the toothpaste, powder, lipstick, etc. were pierced with pins, taken apart, etc. Our luggage, as we learned only at the airport in Lisbon, had been opened and gone through, piece by piece, and then had been closed up with a foot—somewhat irritably, evidently, because the search had taken nearly three hours and absolutely nothing compromising had been found. In their haste to shut the suitcases—the airplane had been kept waiting two and a half hours beyond schedule—the handle was torn off one bag, the clasps on the valises were damaged, etc.

When the captain reappeared, he told me that, not being in the Diplomatic Corps in London, I could not take the diplomatic bag, despite the fact that I had courier papers. I refused then to leave. But he pointed out that without me the plane would not leave, and in that case I would have to sign a legal document obliging me or the Legation to pay the sum of 1,000 pounds. I asked to be allowed to telephone London. Impossible. He did let me send a telegram. For the briefcase, he gave me a receipt that I still have: it's amusing. On a piece of paper with the heading "British Air Mail," it is stated that they have received from me a sealed valise.

I meet Nina, who is in tears. We run to the airplane. The captain comes after us, now very affable. He wishes us bon voyage, and to me he holds out his hand. There, in the sight of all, I have the satisfaction of not shaking it. It was my only revenge.

The flight lasted almost nine hours, because the plane veered sharply toward the Atlantic, then drew near the coast, east of Viana do Castélo. I don't know why, but I had the feeling of impending disaster. If they were sure that I might be dangerous, since I was the first Romanian to be leaving that besieged fortress, I said to myself, they wouldn't hesitate to cause a disaster to the plane. The crew was Dutch. The life of the secretary of the Madrid Legation would have been sacrificed . . .

We arrive at Sintra in the evening. Nina has an attack of nerves when she sees what a sorry sight our luggage is. We don't want to accept it, but we are obliged to, by Customs. We telephone the Legation. [Minister] Cămărăşescu tells us he's been expecting us. We leave Sintra by taxi. We can't believe our eyes when we see the lights. Waiting for us at the Legation are Cămărăşescu, the consul Bastos, and Jean Antohi. The evening newspapers carried the news that England had broken diplomatic relations with Romania. This explains everything, Cămărăşescu says. Indeed . . . I telegraph the Foreign Ministry in Bucharest that my diplomatic case has been confiscated and that I have suffered a body search. (Later I heard that the telegram made Antonescu indignant, and he complained to Hoare.[37] The fact is that all who left England after we did—the group of lower-rank officials, Bill [Gh.] Munteanu, Vardala, Captain Câmpeanu,[38] and Costăchescu[39]—suffered nothing.) We were told that the only room that could be found for us was at the Hotel Suisse-Atlantico. (We would stay there nearly three months.) The dinner frightened us: sixteen different kinds of food! And the lights of Lisbon . . .

Playing with Maybe's two pups today, I was suddenly reminded of the following scene: one morning in November Nina begins ringing her bell. We hadn't gotten up yet (I knew that at that hour the nurse bathed her and gave her an injection). Giza woke up and ran to the kitchen, which, for several days, we had made to be Nina's room (the living room was too gray, but the kitchen was bathed in sunlight all day). Speaking with difficulty in her hard, dry voice (which to me was so dear), with the bandage around her throat, Nina says, "Maybe has given birth! Go, see the puppies!"

This detail suddenly revives the infinite grief I believed was dead. I thought I wouldn't have to contend with anything but melancholy and despair. And, lo, grief returns—the sentiment of the irretrievable, from which I can relieve myself only by crying.

The flames of hell—do they not fulfill the function of "drying" the soul, of separating it from the "humidity," that is, the passions? The symbolism of water is too vast to summarize here; I've devoted a chapter to it in *Prolegomene*. But I recall that water dissolves, disintegrates, comingles. "Water is death for the soul," says Heraclitus somewhere. Water is the principle of decomposition and of regression into the amorphic, the undifferentiated. Now, punishment in hell aims precisely at the desiccation of the soul, at the elimination, through terrible sufferings, of the waters (the passions that have, on earth, mingled man with matter, "silt").

✳

Long walk, in the dark, alone, along the shore of the ocean. I return reinvigorated; something from the predictions of the hero of my novella (the English aviator with the V. C.; I still don't know his name, and I haven't settled on a title for the novella—the characters haven't transmitted it to me). I go back over the manuscript from the beginning. His journal is almost finished (I wrote it in two days), but the several pages at the beginning of the novella don't satisfy me. (That was the reason I stopped working on it.) I'll have to rewrite them. But I have this unfortunate mania of being unable to redo a text, to rewrite a page. How much I admire Gide and Julien Green for their ability to rework their books.

11 February
Four years ago. The first stroll in a sunny, springlike Lisbon. A walk to the Legation. Lunch with Cămărăşescu. I telegraph to Romania, requesting travel money be sent me. Cămărăşescu tries to convince me that my post is here, that it was announced already in November, that I have been placed on the list of the Diplomatic Corps. (Ten days later I would receive a telegram from Nichifor Crainic[40] confirming me in the position of press secretary at Lisbon.)

I try to remember hour by hour my first full day in Lisbon, but I don't always succeed. The feeling of beatitude I had then makes the days run together.

✳

"La plus grande réalité correspond d'abord à que l'on mange,"[41] writes Gaston Bachelard (*L'eau et les rêves*, p. 161), after he has cited several surprising passages from *La mer* by Michelet.[42] I transcribe them too:
"Ces eaux nourrissantes sont denses de toutes sortes d'atomes gras, appropriés à la molle nature de poisson, qui paresseusement œuvre la bouche et aspire, nourri comme un embryon au sein de la mère commune . . . La nourriture microscopique est comme un lait qui vient à lui . . . Ses infants pour la

plupart semblant des foetus à l'état gélatineux qui absorbent et qui produisent la matière muqueuse, en comblent les eaux, leur donnent la féconde douceur d'une matrice infinite où sans cesse de nouveaux enfants viennent nager comme en un lait tiède."[43]

Indeed, if "the greatest reality corresponds first of all to what one eats," then poverty is nothing but a larval state, a regression to the embryonic modality. In that case, Marxism is right to accord a primordial importance to hunger and the struggle for bread. The class with which Marxism is concerned, the proletariat, is an exploited humanity, a hungry humanity. For it, the real is that which it can eat. Thrown back into the fetal phase, impoverished humanity cannot separate itself from living matter, it cannot obtain the freedom to contemplate that is possessed by the adult, the liberated man, that is, the man who controls the means of production. The error of Marxism begins when it generalizes its fetal dialectics to all regions of the spirit. Marxism is justified as long as it expresses the viewpoint of the oppressed, the poor, the hungry—for whom "la plus grande réalité correspond d'abord à ce que l'on mange."

Error: to solve a problem by the way you formulate it.

Daliez's excellent rejoinder (in *Le méthode psychanalitique*, II, p. 495) concerning Freud's definition of religion as a "collective delirium": if there is anything that is characteristic of alienated persons, says Daliez, then it is above all their lack of sociability. The mind of the alienated one is autistic: he cannot make contact with other intellects.

Only now do I understand the deep meaning of a certain Indian custom: the spiritual master, as a sign of great love, feeds the disciple from his own hand. So the Swami did to me at Rishikesh: he put nuts into my mouth, one by one. I thought it was just a token of love. Today I understand: the disciple is a newborn, like any neophyte at an initiation ceremony. He is still an infant; he cannot feed himself. In many "primitive" initiatory societies, the candidate forgets how to talk, forgets how to use his hands, and is fed by his parents like a baby, having food put into his mouth.

Sad people are unloved unless they let themselves be consoled, unless they can give others the rare satisfaction of knowing that they are good, generous, and strong. A sad person who refuses consolation becomes boring, uninteresting, tiresome. The would-be comforter cannot reveal his great goodness, he cannot satisfy his legitimate pride in consoling and encouraging—that is, his feeling of being strong and generous, of growing in his own moral estimate. How much more agreeable, on the contrary, are those unfortunates who let themselves be consoled and encouraged, whom you find in tears and leave with a smile on their lips, saying, "Thank you for coming! Your being here has done me so much good," etc., or "What would I have done if it hadn't been for you in such difficult moments?"

13 February
    For the first time since Nina's passing I feel an interest in erudition and culture. Yesterday evening I reread some notes taken a long time ago having to do with *Cosmos și Istorie*. It's true that I've been thinking again recently about this book, but only about its philosophical theses. Yesterday, in contrast, the erudite and cultural parts interested me too.
    I notice the awakening of this interest when reading, as I do every night, from Kierkegaard. This time, *Coupable?—Non-coupable?* [Guilty/Not Guilty?][44] seems unbearable. I can scarcely read a few pages. I return, gladly, to the Bible. Sometimes Kierkegaard's prolixity exceeds even the extreme limits of decency. I'd like to make someday a "complete edition" of Kierkegaard's readable texts. They'd make two excellent volumes.

✳

    I've begun working on *Cosmos și Istorie*. I chose today because it's a Tuesday and it's the 13th!

14 February
    Last night, a terrible case of insomnia until 4:00.
    Today, soup for twenty poor people, for Nina's soul.
    Several times, overcome by a grave, unprecedented sadness. I persist, nevertheless, in working on *Cosmos și Istorie*. With the greatest difficulty I write three pages. Oppressed by the tremendous number of things I know and want to say—but without losing the readers in a labyrinth in which I myself walk today with perfect certainty. I need to summarize, and yet I cannot leave out a great many little-known facts that, in my opinion, have been interpreted incompetently.

15 February
    Last night, insomnia until nearly 4:00 a.m. I get up rather late, and since I know I must go to Lisbon I don't start work on my writing. I read *O*

caminho da culpa [The Road of Guilt], which Ioaquim Paço d'Arcas sent me. In the book, Doctor de Morais discovers that the woman he loves has cancer. Now I understand why Paço d'Arcas was embarrassed to give me this, his latest novel.

At Lisbon from 3:00 to 8:00. Brutus Coste gives me compensation for the months of February and March from a fund at his disposal. What would I have done without him? Because, since 1 February, I've had no position, no right to anything. I see Herescu, who is ill and bored. He tells me in jest that he doesn't want to die in Lisbon, that he'd rather die in Paris.

16 February
I write all day on *Cosmos și Istorie*. I can't say I've created anything, my work today being mostly a summary of results published six or seven years ago (*Cosmologie și alchimie babiloniană* and *Comentarii la legenda Meșterul Manole*). But I have to start from things known to the readers in order to arrive at other, new things. Besides, I have the impression that my so-called scientific publications haven't been read very widely, or at any rate they haven't been read by people who could understand them. *Cosmos și Istorie* is addressed in the first place to philosophers.

This evening, a long walk alone, all the way to Boca do Inferno. All day I've felt depressed. I found no justification for my survival other than the writing of the books that I've proposed to myself to give. My most revolutionary thoughts in metaphysics and mysticism will remain, however, unpublished. I have the sentiment that they are, still, incommunicable. "Terriblement en avant des siens"[45] (Montherlant).

18 February
Sunday. I don't work at anything all day. I allow myself, for the first time in a month, a vacation, to see how I'll react tomorrow.
. . . What do I have left to do? Nothing but to maintain my courage to be unpopular.

✳

"Comment n'être pas enragé de ne pas vivre, aux heures où l'on travaille, et inquiet de ne pas travailler aux heures où l'on vit?"[46] This text, from *Service inutile*, which I've known for a long time and which has fallen under my eyes again, sums up a good part of the drama of my youth. Should I believe in the prophecy Montherlant makes? "Dilemme quotidien, et cet que la fatigue, la vieillesse, ou la maladie, en nous interdissant de vivre, peut seul résoudre"[47] I attempted another solution, especially in 1928 and 1933, that of "living" with so much intensity that I would empty myself completely, attain the supreme limit of disgust, dreaming of a beatitude of studious solitude, creative effort—anything other than the flesh, experience, tragedy.

19 February
I continue with *Cosmos și Istorie*. Have written so far thirteen sheets in the format of *Prolegomene*.

✳

Three months ago I was working till long past midnight on *Prolegomene*, in order to defend myself from despair. Nina was getting worse, but I didn't foresee the end; I couldn't believe it. Now, when I look back, or when I look ahead, I can see no meaning to my life other than the completion of my oeuvre. And with what difficulty I embark upon the books that have been asking so long to breathe. I'd be happy if I could say everything in a few pages, and then rest.

20 February
Three months.
Herescu comes to dinner, and we take a long walk together. But my thoughts are elsewhere, and after he leaves I sit alone on the terrace for two hours, trying to understand and console myself.

21 February
Among the many brief treatises I'd like to write—brief, even laconic, because I won't have time to write them all—will be one devoted to the postmortem problem. The surprising thing is the fact that each one meets the after-death universe that he has accepted through religious tradition or has conceived through personal thought. The Buddhist will find the regions and forms known in his mythology and rituals; a mystic or Buddhist metaphysician will find the Void, the bliss of nonbeing, etc. A Muslim, a Jew, a Christian will pass through the thanatopic, postmortem geographies known, learned, or rectified during his lifetime. While a nonbeliever, one to whom it seems that everything ends here (it only seems so to him, because such a statement cannot be based on fact), will meet the void, nothingness, nonbeing. For him, death means the end. He was right, but only insofar as he was speaking of himself. The others know a new modality of being—debased, provisional, but neverthe-less a new mode of being.
This is why Jesus says that he has come to rescue people, to save them. Those who believe in him will know a postmortem fate superior to those who practice only an Old Testament devotion and ritualism. Jesus truly saves persons by revealing to them an eschatology of a higher type. Dying with the thought, with the knowledge, of this celestial glory, the good Christian will find glory,

etc. That is why Jesus says that those who do not believe in him will not survive after death, but will perish. Indeed, the atheist or the materialist has every chance of finding, beyond, nothing but the interaction of natural forces. He will not be anything; he will be reintegrated into cosmic energy. From the standpoint of the human person, he will be lost, he will perish.

The indispensable chapters in the treatise: the certainty of survival, the uncertainty of immortality; survival—the stage of depersonalization: what dies first in man, after he has died physically? How long (in historical, concrete time) can the deceased person "descend" to earth in some form or other (in the dreams of those who loved him, as a presence in certain meetings, etc.)?

The overwhelming importance, for the one who has passed beyond, of what is happening on Earth: for example, he is still linked to Earth so long as he is remembered, missed, mentioned, etc. The moment the last person who knew him in life passes into the land of the dead—the one beyond becomes completely detached from the Earth.

A chapter that I consider sensational and that I don't know yet if I'll dare to write will be that devoted to this problem: what happens after the supreme detachment from Earth? To what extent can one speak about survival after that?

22 February

It is one year today since Nina became ill with—as we supposed—sciatica. We were coming home at night from Estoril in Călin Botez's car, and Nina felt sciatic pains for the first time. I remember the date so precisely because we had been to Estoril to celebrate Brutus's birthday. It was the last social event in which Nina took part in good health. Until July we went to several diplomatic dinners and dined with friends, and we were obliged to give a few luncheons—but Nina was sick, and she endured her sciatic pains by taking aspirin.

This evening we were invited to Brutus's home—Giza and I, the Burilianus (who haven't left for Paris yet because their French visas haven't arrived), and the Constantinescus. I was very depressed all evening. At the table, a terrible attack; I had to excuse myself and go to the bathroom, where I washed my face with cold water. I couldn't control myself any longer. I've observed that people tire me, cheerful conversations depress me, laughter exasperates me. I know I have no right to bore others with my sorrow, and for that reason I avoid as much as possible going out, meeting friends or acquaintances. There are days when I can't stand any presence, even Giza's. I sit, then, staring at the sky or the sea.

26 February

I've lost the last several days fighting melancholy and neurasthenia. Incapable of doing any serious work.

I reread Ecclesiastes, that terrible book. Astounded by its sadness and despair. I took a few notes. I read it last night, in bed, and annotated it. It would be interesting to write a commentary. A point of support for pleasure, for the good life, and for Jewish sensualism; the philosophical justification for "eat, drink, for tomorrow you may be dust." Exactly the attitude St. Paul would have had, had he not met Jesus. "If there is no resurrection, then let us drink and eat, for tomorrow we shall die."

I reread *Oedipus Rex*. I work a little, and badly, at reading a book of Sir [James] Jeans, *Physics and Philosophy*, which I found in a Portuguese translation.

It gets harder and harder to bear Nina's departure.

And yet, time passes. And I'm not doing anything. News from Romania contributes to my depression. Ana Pauker is trying to overthrow Rădescu.[48]

27 February

I read with greatest interest *Le temps et la vie* by H. Lecomte du Noüy. I have a series of notes. In connection with Ch. E. Guyl's axiom: "C'est l'échelle qui crée le phénomène" [The scale creates the phenomenon], I transcribe an observation of H. Poincaré that I didn't know: "Un naturaliste qui n'aurait jamais étudié l'éléphant qu'un microscope croirait-il connaître suffisament cet animal?"[49] I ought to inscribe these words as a motto for *Prolegomene*. They agree, in any event, with all my theoretical works. In all I've written in this field, I have done my best to show that by looking from underneath at an object of knowledge, the object loses its true meaning and does not reveal that which makes it exist as such.

Extraordinary experiment of Fisher (cited by Noüy, p. 167): two fragments from the heart of a chicken, placed side by side in a so-called culture of tissue, palpitate in different rhythms: for example, one beats eighty times a minute, another fifty times. But these fragments grow, and at a certain moment they come into contact with each other; then, it is stated, the rhythm becomes identical. Synchronicity is reestablished; the two fragments palpitate together. "Ainsi, bien que l'oiseau soit mort depuis longtemps, bien que ces petits cubes de muscle séparés de son cœur ne soient pouvres ni de circulation sanguine, ni de système nerveux relié à un réseau central ils se reconnaissent, pourrait-on presque dire, dès qu'ils sont en contact, et persistent à effectuer le travail pour lequel leurs cellules avaient été crées, non pas au hasard, de façon indépendante, mais ensemble et de façon coordonnée. Ai-je besoin de dire qu'il n'existe pas le début d'une explication de ce phénomène si curieux?"[50]

I don't know what explanation, if any, biology will find for this phenomenon. But I was moved to tears reading it; it was as though I had heard a call from a great distance, from the depths of living matter—a call exceedingly troubling and mysterious.

28 February

Radio Moscow announces today the resignation of Rădescu. It is just what I expected the moment the unfortunate general dared to declare war on "those without country and without God," Ana Pauker and Vasile Luca.[51] I was amazed that he could be so naive, that he could believe in justice, gratitude, and other big words. Actually, the only thing that counted was to be on Ana Pauker's side. He was not received. His fate was, inevitably, sealed.

In the six months since the armistice, the first two stages have been accomplished. The first was the National Democratic Front [FND], which ended with the resignation of Sănătescu.[52] The break between the Liberals and the Peasantists on the one hand, and with the FND on the other, marked the second stage, with Rădescu. Now we will have, probably, an FND government. Maniu[53] is liquidated. A plebiscite will follow, etc.

4 March

I'm writing these lines in bed, at night. In the daytime I feel too great a reluctance to go down to my office and write. Today I had the worst attack yet since Nina's passing. I fell asleep late, at 3:00 a.m., and woke up at 6:00, convulsed by an infinite despair, to which was added my usual neurasthenia; between 6:00 and 7:00 I tried to calm myself, taking massive doses of Pasiflorina. Desperate, I wept, showing myself to Nina: "See what a sorry plight I've come to! See what's happened to my poor nerves!" I remembered how Nina wept at Lousă, showing me the edema: "See, Mutzi,[54] what's happened to my legs!" And I said to myself that just as Nina suffered in the flesh, and little by little her body wasted away so that looking at it you were filled with pity, so I am cursed to suffer the same pains in the spirit, until the final "wasting away," insanity. My great attack began on 21 February, when we celebrated Brutus's birthday. Am I destined to repeat Nina's cycle of suffering of last year? If so, 20 November 1945 will equate to my mental collapse.

I know very well there's nothing to be done. In order for me to recover my equilibrium, I would have to live a normal life. My sensuality will bring me down. Should I unchain it? That won't solve anything. There are so many other things back of it . . .

5 March

Am reading again from V. Rozanov.[55] I'd have written the way he does if I'd had more courage. If I had dared, always, to be myself.

✳

Frightened by the recent attacks, and in order not to regret later that I hadn't tried everything within my power to save myself, I returned today to physiology. In one hour, I embraced three times the same woman—who was a little surprised, it's true, at my indefatigability. Tomorrow or the day after, I'll consult a neurologist. I mean to try everything. I'd be devastated to find out, for example, that my neurasthenia and melancholy are due to the wonderful seminal functions. Not that I'd have any contempt for those precious gifts. But I'd wonder, then, what would I have done if I had been confined to a camp or prison for several years? Why can't I have at least the satisfaction of being the master of my own body?

"Ce que je veux et réclame de tout homme que j'entends vraiment reconnaître, c'est qu'il ne pense le jour qu'à la catégorie maîtresse de sa vie, et qu'il en rêve la nuit"[56] (Kierkegaard, *Coupable?—Non-coupable?* p. 125).

8 March
Yesterday I proposed to Leontin that the two of us go on foot to Fátima. This thought brought me peace immediately. I know how much Nina wanted to journey to Fátima last October. The pilgrimage I'm making will be, in the first place, for her. In the second place, for the salvation of my mental integrity.

In the course of my readings I'm continually coming across reports and observations of explorers, missionaries, travelers, etc., relative to the unnatural ability of certain natives to talk with animals, to predict the future, etc. The last, in *Mythologie primitive* by Lévy-Bruhl, p. 56. It would be very interesting to collect all these statements and publish them—without commentary. Actually, they are "impossible" for us because they don't conform to the current state of scientific knowledge. But can this be an absolute criterion? Can we invalidate several thousand exact observations, just because they don't agree with what we've become accustomed to accept as real, as "true"?

9 March
Thirty-eight years old. And for the first time since 1934, I don't wake up to find a present from Nina. Today, Giza gives me a device for sharpening razor blades—something she knows I've wanted for a long time.
This evening the Burilianus leave for Paris. Later, the Constantinescus, the Costes, and the Grigores come to our place. Formerly, 9 March was a day for having a party.

13 March
This morning I listened to the radio broadcast of the ceremony at Cluj.[57] Greatly moved, hearing the shouts and applause that greeted the King. Surprised to hear Vishinsky[58] speaking Romanian. What will be the outcome of this event? Will we succeed, after all, in preserving a scrap of independence and autonomy? Or, as happened with Rădescu (called, last fall, by the Russians), will Groza[59] be dismissed as soon as he refuses to become the instrument of total sovietization? However it turns out, I'm excited. I'd like to be in Romania, whatever the risk. And it seems to me that a return is becoming less and less probable. I shall have to get accustomed to a new life: that of an emigrant.

I tell myself that I must do more for my fellow human beings. To love them, help them, write books for them, and teach them to value life—is not enough. I ought to declare my entire message to them, even though the times are not favorable. (But, actually, what does the historical moment matter when one is talking about a new quality, a new dimension, of life?) Because, I can teach them at least this much: to transform their lives, to take a greater interest in them, to live a thousand times more intelligently, more authentically, *more fully* than they do today. I ought to write a novel or a play revealing this message, addressing my contemporaries straightforwardly.

14 March
Where has it come from—this sudden, unexpected cheerfulness? For the past few days, the attacks of nerves have abated, the melancholy has left me. I'd be distorting the truth to reduce my inner equilibrium to the liquidation of a moral crisis by my decision to make a pilgrimage to Fátima. It's not just that—although, as always in my case, the moral crisis plays the preponderant role. I sense my whole being urging me to throw myself into that which, with a genteel euphemism, I learned long ago to call "life"—that is, unlimited erotic experience, constant adventure, licentiousness. Portugal is not the ideal country for such a vocation—but I shall try it here too. I will repeat my well-known technique of liberation through excess, of purification through orgy. I'm very lucid; I know I'm writing these things on the eve of making a pilgrimage to Fátima for the repose of Nina's soul and for my own benefit. But, as usual, I want to know exactly what's wrong with me. I want to know whether or not my melancholy has physiological roots. I want to free myself from any seminal influence, even if this liberation will entail the seduction of a hundred women. I want to stand alone, all by myself, and then to look at myself, judge myself. I'd be humiliated to judge myself while carrying in my flesh and spirit the phantoms of the women I haven't had. What I'm writing is very incoherent—but it's true.

15 March
Three months since we moved to this house in Cascaes.

*

Imperceptible transitions from despair to vulgarity, the dark desire for "experience." And then, melancholy. I'd like to formulate in some way—in a play, a novella, an essay—the sad reconciliation I feel sometimes in the late-night hours: the cosmic alternation—the day that follows, without fail, the night, no matter what happens; spring that follows winter. The eternal return. This myth must be revived, if life is to have any meaning, if it is to be worth the living. *Cosmos și Istorie* treats only the anthropological problem of the despair of modern man, who lacks any living myth that could justify, explain, or recompense the sufferings, deceptions, and injustices endured on account of history. Yet it is not only this problem of the "terror of history" that demands resolution, but also the other, equally urgent one of the reconciliation of man in time, of his salvation by virtue of the simple fact that he participates in a temporal, rhythmic Cosmos, rich in alternations.

16 March
Have been to the nerve doctor, Professor Bernardes, a pupil of E. Schneider. A rather intelligent young man. The consultation lasts 45 minutes. He tells me it's nothing too serious. My attacks of melancholia have nonphysical causes, and he can do nothing about them. But, unfortunately, there are the other attacks, which he explains by my unsatisfied hypersexuality. My equilibrium can be regained only after realization of sexual equilibrium.

18 March
Tomorrow morning Leontin and I are leaving, on foot, for Fátima. It will be a journey of 160 kilometers. I have high hopes for this pilgrimage, which I make for the repose of Nina's soul and for the salvation of my spiritual integrity.

(19–26 March transcribed from the black notebook.)

19 March
Cascaes to Sintra, 14 kilometers. We make it, without stopping, between 8:30 and 11:00. Splendid weather. Sudden melancholy at the entrance of Sintra. I was here last summer in June with Nina and Giza. Nina was feeling almost well then; she climbed up Santo Pedro, and on our return to Lisbon she also climbed—on account of my stupidity—the two kilometers from the Campolide

Station to the first taxi. I saw her beside me today all the while, from the time I entered Sintra.

We eat at Hotel Nunes (where we ate the last time too; we were amused and annoyed alternately, because it was a Sunday and, on account of the crowds, our table wasn't served for *three* hours!). The first time I was here was with A. Cotruș and the Antohi family, in February 1941. We had just arrived from England, and I was waiting for money to enable us to fly home. How could I have imagined then that I would stay in Portugal four years, and that things would turn out as they have? . . .

The inexpressible charm of Sintra: the antique color of the ancient walls. And now, in springtime, the wisteria that we meet everywhere. I repeat mentally the only verses I know by heart from "Oseminte pierdute" [Lost Bones]:

> *Atât amar de ani e de atunci!*
> *Glicină tu, tu florile-ti arunci.*[60]

We set off at 2:00 for Mafra. Before arriving at Granja, we meet to the right of the highway a lake, exceptionally clear and deep, in an abandoned stone quarry. We take off our shoes and cool our feet. On the damp stone where I'm sitting, a striped snake is sunning itself. It slithers away into the water. I watch it swim toward the bottom. Overhead, two trainer airplanes keep circling around. As we sit with our feet in the lake, we watch the airport opposite us. All is very peaceful. Back on the road again, our feet start to hurt. Twenty kilometers, and we're wearing dress shoes with crepe soles (the only kind we have).

At Pero Pinheiro, the landscape begins to resemble that of Lousã. Revived memories: my hike up the hill, leaving Nina at the window watching . . .

At 6:00 we arrive at Cheleiros. In a valley; a white village with dark-red roofs. We cross a long and famous bridge; the riverbed is almost dry. On the left, a church; Romanesque entrance. We climb, fatigued. We've covered 34 kilometers, and there are still seven and a half to Marfa. The blisters on my heels smart, but I remind myself that Nina suffered as many as eight injections per day, and she was weak and in pain all the time, and couldn't eat—yet I never heard her complain. Remembering this strengthens me.

Up on the high ridge the wind strikes us for the first time, on the chest. Leontin is walking with increasing difficulty. Two proposals: to dress more warmly and to eat chocolate and oranges.

We enter Mafra at 8:30, exhausted. We locate the sad, mediocre Pensão Duarte. Miserable room. But all the windows open toward the Palace. Superb night, cool. Moved, I listen to the cathedral clock striking.

The city is full of soldiers. Maneuvers. When we came into town, we saw a house on our left with girls, waiting for the troops.

I'm writing in this somber, shabby room. How many forgotten things from my travels in adolescence and youth does this stuffy cubicle call to mind! The first hotel room I slept in at Tulcea in 1921, as a Boy Scout. The miserable hotel chambers in Athens and Constantinople in 1928.

20 March
Mafra. Morning. I look out into the courtyard: camellias, lilacs. From the kitchen a pretty girl emerges and begins picking beans. A pigeon takes flight. The monastery bells again.

We leave at 11:30, barely able to walk on account of the pain. At the edge of town, furious that the road sign indicates more kilometers than the guidebook says. The road winds uphill and down, passing between forests of eucalyptus and cork oaks. We save two kilometers by cutting across a valley. I ask Leonid the time: it is 12:30. Four months ago, at this hour, Nina left, without saying a single word to us. I stop in the shadow of an earthen wall and say a prayer. Sad, but reconciled.

Hard journey to Gradil. There we eat lunch on the grass, in front of a church. From a tavern I bring a liter of black wine and two glasses. From a pharmacy, a bottle of mineral water and vaseline with boric acid to rub on our heels. The pharmacy was a little general store: toys, buttons, kerosene, newspapers, shawls, etc. The boy who waited on us, selling us what we needed, tells us that one kilometer ahead there is a van that runs to Torres Vedras; it costs only 5 escudos per person to ride.

We leave Gradil and cover almost six kilometers of difficult road, which brings us to Molveira. Impossible for us to reach Torres Vedras by evening, 16 kilometers farther on, as tired as we are from our effort. We return to Rosario to wait for the van. On the way we stop twice at taverns to get something cool to drink. There's nothing but wine. We create panic: "Estrangeiros!" [foreigners]. At Rosario, an amusing conversation with a beggar who thinks we are English. About the King of England: "O George também é uma boa criatura!" [George is a good man too!]."

We pass through Turcifal, in the van, regretting that we didn't get this far on foot. An hour later, we arrive at Torres Vedras. No room at the hotel: a conference of agronomists. We will be able to eat here and even take a bath, but we shall have to sleep at a pension. Actually, it is an inn on the edge of town. We enter a bar, walk across it, pass the kitchen, climb a wooden staircase; a few little rooms on the courtyard, with two rustic privies next to them. Weak light. We're given a little room with two beds.

In the evening, after dinner, at the café. As usual, I try to spend this hour like a resident of the town, to think and feel like one. The young man playing billiards.

21 March

Torres Vedras. I slept badly on a bad bed. When I awake, I find my feet swollen. We put our packs on our backs and go to the hotel to eat and take a bath. The bed for the night cost seven escudos.

We leave at 11:30. We cross the city: the church, the market. The street is colorful, picturesque. Above, on the hill, a ruins. The fragrance of barrels of wine.

After Ramalhal, completing ten kilometers, we stop in the woods for lunch. It is simply divine. The sky is soft, limpid; only the tips of the pine branches are trembling. The grass is abundant, variegated, despite the drought. And all around us we hear birds. But Leontin has swollen tendons and can hardly walk. He stops beside a bridge to wait for the van to Bombarral. I push on alone in the heavy, oppressive heat.

At 4:00 I arrive at Onteiro. The road runs between cornfields and forests. I reconstruct again, mentally, a part of my life spent with Nina. What awaits me at Fátima?

I begin the ascent to Bombarral. Toward evening I arrive. I find Leontin at Pensão Central with his ankles wrapped in bandages. Pensão Central is the only building in the small town that isn't depressing. The palace of the Duke of Bombarral, with a gorgeous coat of arms. A part of the courtyard is rented to a trucking company, which has built a fine garage. We stroll around the town in the evening. Complete darkness, misery. "Cafe la Bar." At night, I wait two hours for a telephone connection with Cascaes. I speak with Giza. The lobby of the pension where I wait for the telephone is full of British propaganda leaflets. The table—laden with magazines containing the same propaganda. I wonder why the English have spent so much money to convince people who are already convinced . . . The fellow who keeps writing all the time, illumined by his own ardor, self-hypnotized. He is a traveling salesman. Also in the lobby are two other travelers, waiting for the night train, with their modest toiletry cases on a chair. The proprietor knows them all very well. The familiarity of a boardinghouse.

22 March

Bombarral. Leontin leaves on the train for Caldas de Rainha. I set off walking, alone. Superb day, with a little breeze. The landscape becomes archetypal: all of Portugal is here, under a clear sky, on the crests of hills—furrowed, coppery, with grapevines, pines, eucalyptus and cork oak trees. I'd like to preserve forever this image—so pure, linear, and comforting.

At San Mamede I make my first halt, with my eyes captivated by the undulating hills.

My only sorrow: my spiritual poverty. All day yesterday and today—obsessed with sex.

1:30: Lunch on the grass, opposite the citadel of Obidos. I was here in the fall of 1943. I repeat over and over, "In our narrow circle . . ." I live this hideous destiny. All my concerns, confessed and unconfessed, of recent times are reducible to stupid ephemeras from a very narrow circle.

An old man meets me on the road and, passing, says in English, "Good afternoon!" I reply and, considering me an Englishman, he approaches. He speaks very good English. He is a sailor, 61 years old; he's been everywhere, and for four years has been unemployed. He is walking to Lisbon. I admire him. He asks me for an empty bottle. I don't have one. I give him a little chocolate, hardtack, and cheese.

I arrive at Caldas de Rainha at 5:00. Leontin comes out to meet me on a bicycle, to show me the way to the hotel. He admires me: "You walk like a god!" I've made only twenty kilometers, but I feel fine.

At the hotel, a stroll in the park. The town of baths. I've passed through here many times in a car. I remember Bostanian's laments. He, like all "undesirable" Romanians—had his forced domicile here. He told me he spent every day at the cinema (there are three of them).

The walk downtown in the evening. At the café I entered, a group of young fellows are trying to amuse themselves with a bottle of mineral water. Two women from Lisbon pass by, and the group leaves immediately to follow them. A happy age! . . .

The old man laughing to himself, reading a section of a newspaper.

23 March

On foot from Caldas to Alfeizirão. We eat lunch in a strong wind, sheltered by a broad ditch with thick grass, in the shade of a eucalyptus. Twelve kilometers. We climb two more, to a *pousada* [inn] where we drink a cup of coffee while waiting for the van. Leontin still finds it very hard to walk. We are told that we're mistaken, that the van to Alcobaça doesn't pass through here, but down below, where we ate. We return, Leontin barely able to make his feet carry him. At 4:20 the van arrives.

We enter San Martinho do Porto, an adorable little city with prim houses; I remember the naval station and the city of hills. At Nazaré. The vehicle stops in the port. Those famous boats on the beach, with the fishermen in their plaid shirts—how long have I known this image, from how many pictures?! I think I'll come back here in May.

Clouds have gathered. The van climbs the ridge toward Alcobaça. Before we reach the city, the landscape changes abruptly: a river is running alongside the road: poplars, oaks, a mill, lumber. Images from Germany return. My fatigue encourages them. I slip out of time; I relive those happy years of 1934–37.

In the evening we arrive at Alcobaça. Did I think I'd ever see it again? I enter the cathedral. It seems, somehow, even more beautiful. It has a plain, ascetic sobriety. And never have I felt more completely the thrill of transcendence that verticality can give. The simple fact that man is crushed by this architectonic space defines his precarious position.

At night, a long discussion with Leontin about Yoga. A steady rain is falling.

24 March

Alcobaça. After a night of rain, a splendid morning. A little too warm. I wake up feeling sad. My sense of loneliness is painfully acute.

We decide to ride the van to Batalha, twenty kilometers, in order to be able to make the rest of the trip, another twenty kilometers, on foot. But at 12:30 we are informed that the van, already an hour late, is full. We set out. Lunch two hours later. A rain overtakes us seven kilometers from Batalha, and we climb aboard a truck loaded with barrels. The driver, after inquiring about our nationality, tells us that the Germans pay better than the English. Until a year ago, he carried wolframite to Algarve, where it was picked up by a German submarine. We make a detour through Porto de Mos, where we wait for an hour. A castle with beautiful windows, restored, on the hill in front of us.

We arrive at Batalha at 6:30 in a torrential rain. The walls of the monastery seem red now, soaked by the downpour. We find out that the bus service to Fátima has been suspended on account of a lack of tires. We are forced to take a taxi for these last twenty kilometers, which we make in the rain. It is uphill all the way. The time is 8:00 when we arrive at Fátima. An overwhelming sadness engulfs me, as I remember all that Fátima meant for Nina and me, from 13 November 1941, when we witnessed for the first time the procession from the church across the street from our house, until those terrible days of October–November 1944, when Nina's last hopes were fixed on a miracle of the Lord's Mother, revealed to the shepherdess at Fátima. With that same sadness I entered the little church—the cathedral isn't finished yet—and prayed. The same sadness, walking on this desolate plateau, still wet from the heavy rain of today.

We are almost alone in the inn. It is an improvised hotel, seemingly made of faience, with a lobby of tables crowded with plants: the atmosphere of a mausoleum. The pendulum clock, when striking the hour, also plays approximately the hymn of Fátima, a melody very familiar to me, having been neighbor for three years to the church on Elias Garcia. Again, I am dissolved in grief. Nina's presence.

I have written all this in my room, between 10:00 and 11:00, by candlelight. Can't sleep. A strange sadness, of a different order from that of my well-known attacks of melancholia and neurasthenia. It's as though the life has been drained out of me.

25 March

Fátima. Up at 6:30 in order to attend the first mass at 7:00 in the Carmelite chapel. It is the Catholic Palm Sunday. We walk in the rain and darkness about a kilometer, guided by a servant woman. The church is full to overflowing with country folk. During the time of the service, the sky clears. I emerge into the sunlight. Consoled, but without a sense of exultation.

We leave Fátima at 9:30 in a van that takes us to Vila Nova de Ourem. From there another van carries us to Tomar, where we arrive at 11:00. Adventure with the tipsy porter, who escorts us around to the taverns he knows. Then, to a pension to leave our bags. Visit to the Castle of the Templars, with the famous Manueline window in the shape of a ship. Too listless to write any more. Admirable view of the hills with olive trees and cork oaks.

After dinner, in the park. The river, the abandoned mill, the pillars with wisteria. Martial music. The sunshine. Sitting on a bench, I ask myself to whom will I relate now what I have seen, to whom will I deposit these fragments of my life and memory? All those melancholies you endure in your youth in the hope that someday you will confess them to your life companion, thereby making up for them. My youth has lost its witness. Hence the void that threatens me on all sides. (A void I feel only in my hours of erotic obsession.)

The black backdrop—storm clouds of summer—that frames the Castle at 3:30, just as we are about to leave. Tomar has pleased me so much that I promise myself I'll return here with Giza.

From Tomar to Entroncamento, on a train of a secondary line. We learn from the newspapers of the massive crossing of the Rhine and the lightninglike offensive of Eisenhower. It's the best news we could have—the rapid termination of the war.

✳

Cascaes, 29 March

Since returning, my sadness has persisted with such great intensity that I can't read anything but newspapers and detective novels. I observe that only the latter make me forget my desolate state. Brutus shows me, in a letter from Tilea, a few lines addressed to me. They have been grieved by the news of Nina's passing, they send me condolences, together with the hope that it can be arranged for me to come to England.

Râmniceanu[61] tells me that Spitzmüller has written him concerning my coming to Paris. He says for me not to make any requests through the Consulate, but to send the papers directly to him. This news lifts me out of my lethargy for a few hours.

I've let my beard grow. This reminds me of my crisis in September 1930. Actually, it was necessary for me, at any price, to invent a "new man"! . . .

2 April

For several months I've had the sentiment that I was lost in a labyrinth. I advance with difficulty, not knowing what direction to take, if I'm getting closer to the exit or sinking even deeper. Sometimes there's a ray of light; I feel regenerated, optimistic; I view "the future" with confidence. But immediately afterward, I fall back into miasma and despair.

"Physical labor," the doctor said. I ride a bicycle. I swim every day.

Am rereading *The Possessed* in a complete English edition. As usual, I admire Dostoyevsky's "devices." Never does a character come completely out of his room; he steps to the threshold and says or does something unusual. If he doesn't come of his own accord, he is called by the host. Characters break off speaking, change the subject abruptly, or become silent. Everything possible is done to "hold" the reader. A day occupies several hundred pages, and even if nothing sensational happens, the reader has the impression at the end of each chapter that a catastrophe has occurred. It's simply brilliant!

6 April

I receive a second letter today from the minister Grigorcea, sent from Vatican City. The first, six or seven weeks ago, asked me to authorize the publication of an Italian translation of *Maitreyi*. This second one informs me that *Maitreyi* is in press, and that the Caravela publishing house is offering another 10,000 lire (the same as for *Maitreyi*) for *Huliganii*. I accept, although I doubt, from past experience, that this translation will ever appear. *Maitreyi* was translated into Portuguese in September, and on account of a lack of available printing facilities, it hasn't gone to press to the present day. My translator, Egidio Amorim Guimarães, writes me that Coimbra Editora is asking for my entire oeuvre.[62] But will it ever appear?

10 April

Brutus Coste shows me a telegram he received from the Ministry of Foreign Affairs and signed by Stoica, through which it is pointed out that we three, those dismissed from the staff—Cădere, Leontin Constantinescu, and I—can return to the country if we want.[63] How should this telegram be interpreted? That I can return to the homeland without fear? That I'll be judged innocent of the nation's "disaster"? Or, as a warning: I've been given notice that I can come back; if I don't return it means I'm taking a political stance, and as such I risk being penalized, losing my citizenship, etc.? For the time being, since there is no possibility of my returning, the statement remains without any practical consequence. But it forces me to examine once again the attitude of the Ministry of Foreign Affairs toward me, and toward press counselors in general. I believe I've written very little about these matters in this journal. This is a suitable occasion to write about them now: because they're not without interest, and because I need to be drawn back to this journal again, so much neglected of late.

The hatred of the "Foreign Affairs people" for the "Press Service" is a well-known fact. And for several reasons: (1) we too have diplomatic passports, we are registered on the lists of the diplomatic corps, etc., although we are "outsiders"; (2) we were, at one time, better paid than they; (3) sometimes we were appointed directly as "counselors"; (4) we were "more active" than they (receptions, teas, "connections," etc.). This hatred takes no account of personal worth. It is enough to be "from the Press" for "Foreign Affairs" to detest you. An example: when our services were placed under Foreign Affairs in April 1944, I was downgraded from "Counselor" to "Secretary." I regret very much that I didn't understand the matter correctly then (I thought it was just a bookkeeping oversight), so that I could have resigned. When I did find out, the coup d'état had occurred, we were all recalled, and Nina was gravely ill.

The first thing the Ministry of Foreign Affairs did after 23 August 1944, was to abolish the press services abroad. I was recalled on 9 September when the Russians had not yet entered Bucharest. I was taken off the staff in November, without the Russians' having requested it. Quite exceptionally, I was given 2,000 Swiss francs per month for Nina's illness (an illness that was costing almost double that amount monthly!). Since 31 January I've been given nothing. All I've received since then, I've gotten thanks to the friendship, courage, and intelligence of Brutus Coste.

I thought for a while that we were the first sacrifices, that our heads had been demanded, that others would be recalled, etc. I was wrong. Not only has no one been recalled from Foreign Affairs, but they have been named to other positions, even those who were recalled during the summer: Ciontescu to Lisbon, Râmnicianu to Madrid. The Rador agents also were reappointed: Munteanu to Lisbon, Mme Popescu (Barbul's sweetheart, the one in the Capşa, etc.) to Madrid. Our secretary at Press, the excellent Mica Paraschivescu, was recently reappointed. The Secret Service, anathematized with frenzy by Foreign Affairs, continues to receive one-third pay, being only recalled. Therefore, it was not any kind of "budgetary economizing"; only we "counselors" were removed definitively from the staff, pointed to here as "Nazis," etc. If it weren't so tragic, it would even be funny: Mircea Eliade sacrificed—and queers, nonentities, second-raters with no backbones, etc., etc. holding jobs. When I think how a Totescu or a Dinu Cantemir bowed down before the German minister! When I think that not one of the foreign ministers, other than Brutus, dared even once to hold an opinion different from the official one—that is, the Marshal's,

Ică's, the pro-Germans'—and today these brave fellows, who have never given a dinner, who have deposited massive savings in the bank, who don't give a damn what happens in the homeland so long as they receive their salaries, who today are looked up to as martyrs to a political cause—when I think about all these things, I say to myself that I have no right to forgive them, that I must write a novel someday with "Foreign Affairs" in it and bring to light the strange "freemasonry" of these "individuals." And write it I will!

11 April

I return with determination to this journal, hoping to regain an appetite for work through the effort I must make to write. Because, indeed, it is an effort. I believe that never in my life have I experienced a drier season than this, beginning from 21 February (when I broke off work on *Cosmos şi Istorie*). Since then I've been able to write almost nothing: just a few journal pages and some note slips from a study on the Davidic kingship. For several weeks, nevertheless, I managed to read works of ethnography and history of religions. Then, not even that much—just essays and novels. Dostoyevsky's *The Possessed* was the last novel read. I abandoned myself for a few days to biblical readings, without which, since 20 November, I've been unable to go to sleep.

All these things I lay to the account of my nerves, but I know very well it all comes down to a ridiculous obsession, to a psychological detail of no importance, which poisons every free hour that melancholy and despair leave me. I have written obscurely and vaguely, but I wonder if I could be more explicit without betraying the complexity of my attacks. Actually, it's a matter of two distinct experiences. The first is that of melancholy and despair, related, ordinarily, to the remembrance of Nina. The second is a neurasthenic attack, nourished, of course, by my lack of sexual satisfaction (although since 5 March I've resumed a somewhat normal routine; but this is not enough: I need a lover for both day and night). This neurasthenic attack is provoked by the psychological detail mentioned above.

These spiritual and mental miseries with which I struggle keep me from working, writing, taking notes. But it's strange how lucid I am sometimes, even when I slip into the most monstrous abyss! If only I had the power (more precisely, the appetite, the disposition, *l'envie* [the desire]) to write down, to note, fragments of my meditations. I return to the world more pessimistic—and nevertheless with a new, reckless hope. Pessimistic with respect to the present condition of man. I'm depressed sometimes by the immense role that vanity still plays in the life of almost every man—greater than that of sex, hunger, or fear of death. I'm convinced, too, that the male "in general" is more stupid than I thought up until a few years ago. The lucidity of males is a myth. I know a great many men today who have been chosen, led by the nose, and "caught" by completely uninteresting women—without their even suspecting their passive role. Excellent women often pass over such men who have a very high opinion of themselves; but because, out of pride or timidity, these women do not attempt to "grab" them, they fail at life—and the men become the husbands of homely or stupid females, hags or tarts, who have contrived to "trap" them. In a great many households I've known in the past seven or eight years, the wives are on a lower plane than their husbands, but infinitely more clever and able than they, as proved by the fact that they have them! On the other hand, almost all the really admirable women I've known in that time period have remained unmarried—because no man has known how to choose them.

I believe that the man almost never does the choosing anyway. He is always chosen. How else can I explain the large number of absurd couples I know? The stupidity of men is never more evident than when, after many flirtations and adventures, they decide to marry. Almost always the wife "chosen" is the most inferior of the women with whom the man flirted, etc. The recent case of the Secretary of the Budapest Legation who was accosted one evening by the famous prostitute Zeta (she was charging 3,000 to 4,000 lei in 1936), and ended up marrying her. (In parentheses, what amazes me in this case is not the marriage; actually love and marriage purify even a prostitute—provided, of course, that she takes the vows seriously; what is amazing is the consent that his superiors in Foreign Affairs hastened to give the Secretary of the Legation; and after the wedding they sent him to Budapest where, probably, there were a dozen Hungarians who had slept with Zeta for several thousand lei.)

I've been drawn into these petty obscurities only because I wanted at all costs to write, to get back into the habit of writing. But I didn't mean to dwell on them. It's not just about the vanity of man and the stupidity of males that I've learned new things. I foresee a new ideal for man: free, strong, perfected; liberated from superstitions, tabus, fears; conscious that a life can mean a great deal, that each hour can be transfigured into eternity, that the millions of years of life that lie back of him are waiting to be transformed into self-consciousness.

12 April

Five years ago I was in Paris, en route to London. Those few unforgettable days spent with Emil Cioran! I had set foot in Paris for the first time—on the eve of the catastrophe. And for the first time in my life, I had a good salary; I had forgotten about the cares of tomorrow. But in Paris I had no money [with me] at all. I borrowed 500 francs from I. Dragu, then head of Press Services in Paris.

13 April

The death of Roosevelt. No use to fight it: destiny has decided; the Soviets will win the war and the peace. Romania is thrown backward 120 years, to the era of the Russian protectorate. On Radio Bucharest we hear nothing but news about what the Soviets are doing, thinking, saying. Our poor governmental leaders are just tools. At the first gesture of autonomy they will be removed. And so, probably, they won't make any such gesture.

14 April

All day yesterday, laid low by a great sadness. At night I reread "Sărmanul Dionis" [Wretched Dionisis]; less enthused than previously. In places, Eminescu's language is viscous, artificial; cacophonies abound.

Today, I struggle in vain against melancholy. Definitively detached from my oeuvre, from culture, philosophy, life, salvation. All I want—is to lose myself in nothingness, to rest, to forget myself.

Nina's presence continues.

15 April

I've taken up *Isabel* again, in order to correct and modify the text for a possible new edition. (I'm incapable of any creative work, so I've decided to review my old books.) Have reached page 120. Quite as enthusiastic as I was when I reread the whole novel last summer. Although, disconcerted sometimes by my lack of literary talent; some chapters are written in a language that could be anything but Romanian. I never would have believed that I could write so badly; there are sentences that are simply foreign, strident expressions, improper terms, etc. I remember that there were days in 1929 when I wrote in a terrible heat and with a mad effort: each sentence was extracted with forceps—something that never happened to me again except with certain chapters of *Lumina ce se stinge*. The novel is, nevertheless, exceptional, and I understand the enthusiasm and the hatred it evoked upon its publication. For a certain group of readers, *Isabel* could become my most interesting work.

Because I have a free hour, and because I've wanted for a long time to write what I think about *Isabel*, I will note a few observations and perplexities. First of all, I must state that although *Isabel* includes a great many autobiographical elements, the principal character, the "Doctor," is very different from me. These things are true: the life of the boardinghouse of Mrs. Axon (Mrs. Perris), my subversive flirtations with Verna and Isabel, the piano lessons and gymnastic exercises, the nervous breakdown in "The Dream of a Summer's Night," the "Doctor's" passion—which is also mine—for adventure, travel, the tempting of girls, etc. I resemble the "Doctor" with respect to my adolescence: when I was thirsting for "the Absolute," when I beat myself on the back with a wet rope every night in order to purify my dreams, when I believed that the fulcrum of life is the will. But I don't resemble him in the following traits: I have never believed in the devil; I have never had an obsession with evil; I have been, and I remain, amoral with respect to sex; all my attempts at asceticism of 1923–25 and later had as their aim the verification of my will; I have been, and remain, a sensualist, whereas the "Doctor" boasts of not being one, adding that only moral experience interests him; I have never had the sentiment of spiritual or carnal sterility—on the contrary, ever since my "launching" at *Cuvântul* in 1925–26 I have had the consciousness of being able to create in any literary genre; and the myth of "bewilderment after victory" is invented.

The book seems all the more interesting to me in that the material, in places autobiographical, was used in creating an exceptional character who resembles me only incidentally. The "Doctor," like Manuel in *Lumina*, was created in the period when there was a conflict in my soul between magic and the thirst for authentic religious experience. Manuel is primarily magical; the "Doctor" has a religious problematics too. Lacking any living religious experience, obsessed nevertheless with sacrality, familiar with the terminology, structures, and preoccupations of mysticism, my inner tragedy was—and remains—a strange spiritual hybridism: on the one hand, convinced of the reality of religious experience; on the other hand, incapable of knowing it, lacking any sentiment of sin, a Dionysiac from all points of view. Melancholia has been my only concrete approximation to religious experience. Probably it was my need to "realize" sin that made me write that scene of homosexuality in *Isabel.*—A scene that, in any event, I can never understand. (I hope no one will doubt my courage; if I had the least inclination toward homosexuality, I'd confess it in this journal.) I needed a "sin" that shouted to high heaven, so I invented it with Tom. My authentic sins with the minor, Verna—I did not recognize as such.

A detail that troubles me—the accent I placed on sterility and impotence. They are, undoubtedly, reflections of the lessons of Nae Ionescu and discussions with Sandu Tudor[64] and Mircea Vulcănescu.[65] But I've wondered if my refusal (in the novel) to possess Isabel might not have been interpreted psychoanalytically as an obsession with impotence. I have never had this obsession. But I wonder, nevertheless, from whence comes this refusal to possess a girl who offers herself to you, complicated with the sadistic pleasure of seeing her possessed by another man. Quite probably this question has been asked by others too. I remember that Sorana, after a "heroic day" in the lodge at Poiana Brașovului in which I embraced her ten times, admitted that my vigor had surprised her; having read *Isabel*, she supposed I was almost impotent. Alarmed, nevertheless, by my resources, she confessed them to Lili Popovici, whom, she assumed, had had a number of experiences with men. Lily told her that if she hadn't known me, she would have believed I had been on drugs, that I had taken pills, etc. What's even more amusing is that I'd never realized I was so "good." It had always seemed to me that any man, if a woman pleased him and he was not tired, could embrace her ten times. Later I understood that this is a rather rare privilege.

The problem of potency or impotency has never concerned me. Where, then, have these suspicious details come from? With regard to the "abortion motif," I observe that it is present in *Întoarcerea din rai* and *Nuntă în cer*; it corresponds to my refusal—at that age of 26–30—to have children, and to real experiences of the summer of 1933. Is my refusal in *Isabel* structured on the same complex? Does my hero prefer the child of another man because he refuses on principle to continue his existence on earth?

In any event, my real refusal (in 1933) cost Nina her life. And, yet, in 1941, I wanted with all my heart to have children. I suffer all the more knowing that I am capable of having them.

16 April

In contrast to many, I do not believe that "civilization" necessarily annihilates man. If modern man is less healthy, is degenerate, neuropathic, uprooted, etc., this is not due to the fact that he lives in an industrial society, that he resides in a metropolis, that he has a radio, motion pictures, etc.—but simply to that fact that man has not yet succeeded in adapting to the new cosmic environment created by his own discoveries and means of production. There is, still, a discrepancy between the modern milieu and man. Until he becomes adapted, he will suffer, will degenerate, will make himself sterile—precisely as happened in periods of transition from the stage of gathering fruits and seeds to the stage of raising cattle, or from nomadism to agriculture. It is certain that the first nomads who settled down and cultivated the soil seemed "degenerate" as compared to their ancestors; the latter were free, strong, not shackled to the earth, not tempted by wealth, etc. From the "hygienic" point of view, it is certain that the agriculturalist, at first, seemed a degenerate compared to the shepherd; he was exhausted by hard labor, he was physically stunted, etc. But a few generations later, when agriculture had been perfected, the cultivators of the soil—being better fed—acquired a physical condition superior to that of the herdsmen. (What was lost forever was the moral strength: the telluric mystique brought with it the orgy; proprietorship exacerbated the sentiment of possession, it promoted the passive and fatalistic attitude toward the Cosmos—rains, droughts, invasions were beyond man's powers—it encouraged opportunism and even cowardice—because the poor man had to learn to get along with the invader, etc.)

To return to the point: I don't believe that the simple fact of living in a civilized and highly industrialized society entails physical degeneration and disequilibrium, or spiritual sterility. I believe we have not adapted ourselves to the environment; and in a city with skyscrapers, etc., man can maintain contact with the cosmic rhythms, can "realize" the miracle of the day-night alternation, of the lunar cycles. The universal drama—life and consciousness, fragment-All, becoming-being—is every bit as immediate in a factory as in Himalayan hermitages. The modern city is not necessarily cut off from nature; only urbanistic heresies have excluded gardens; but the cement and iron can be incorporated perfectly into the vegetation, etc., as elements of the natural landscape; evidence the camouflage of fortifications and factories in this war. Etc.

17 April

I continue with the correcting of *Isabel*.

Have read the mediocre but pleasant biography by H. W. Nevingon, *Goethe: Man and Poet*. I gave this book to Tantzi Coste in 1943, and I asked her for it a few weeks ago, to try to get back "into my work." Biographies of Goethe have always stimulated me. I observe again this time the striking similarities of our destinies: the enormous amount of time lost by both of us in scientific works of no use (nay, to the contrary!) to artistic creation; the inability to devote ourselves to one thing until its completion; spasmodic creation quickly interrupted by a new cultural passion; contempt for the critical spirit, for doubt, etc. (the Goethean "Tell me what you believe in, since I have enough doubts already"—I cite approximately, from memory); our interest in myths of reintegration, etc. Until the loss of Nina, I used, with the same success as he, the Goethean method of fleeing from passional complications that could rob me of creativity, of looking ahead always, of believing in life, in man, in the future, etc. I observe, however, that Goethe was far from living like an Olympian all the time. His hours of attacks, his periods of despair, and sterility (for example, after the death of Schiller).

18 April

I dream of Nina, sick, not as I knew her in illness, but suffering from a curious affliction that causes purple spots on her cheeks. I wake up feeling sad, tired. I abandon the idea of going to Lisbon as I had planned. Instead, I propose to finish correcting *Isabel* and begin revising the typescript of "Córdoba" (but with great anxiety! Those pages from October 1944! . . .).[66] Yesterday I dictated to Giza some six pages of *Prolegomene*, thereby finishing the typing of the chapter called "The Earth." While dictating, I became aware of certain rough places in the text that had escaped my notice when reading it. I am not made for perfect writing; but I realize that I don't succeed in "combing" my prose, in purifying it, in perfecting it, except by repeated readings of the typed copies—readings of the whole, and not of sentences or paragraphs. After a first summary reading of the manuscript, a second slower one, then a third, and so on. The same method for proofreading of galleys and pages, since I discover the typographical errors only by reading over the corrected text a second or third time. Y. Byck told me that no typographical error escapes him because he reads the page six or seven times.

"Le secret de presque toutes faiblesses, c'est cette affreuse modestie dont je ne parviens pas à me guérir"[67] (Gide, *Journal*, 14 July 1914). The very same malady from which I also suffer.

I finish correcting *Isabel*. I try to reread certain pages from *Şantier*. Alarmed by how much I revealed in that semijournal (Kramrisch, Tucci, M[aitreyi], D[asgupta], etc.). Also, the unnecessary brutalities.

19 April
Sadness. Trip to Lisbon.

20 April
Five months since Nina's departure. Hard morning.
This evening I deposit at the Romniceanus the forms for requesting the French visas, which they will send via diplomatic bag directly to Spitzmüller. Today, the waiting begins.
At night, sitting on the terrace, I think again about Nina. Unintentionally, I find my thoughts turning to *Prolegomene*, to the new chapter I intend to write. Suddenly I'm at peace, confident. Nina liked that book tremendously. I'm sure that my neurasthenia is due, in large part, to her sufferings, and that she is suffering, primarily, from my sterility and failure. When I begin working again on *Prolegomene*, she will be at peace. A calm happiness descends upon my soul tonight: it is a sign—a sign, certainly, for me who has experienced it, though not for a skeptic who would know how to explain this happening as a very complex and delicate psychological process. But I must learn to have courage, even at the risk of seeming superstitious.

23 April
I'm thinking about all my friends named Gheorghe, whom I don't even know if they're alive or dead.
I have carefully avoided following military events in this journal. For several weeks we've been waiting from day to day for Germany to collapse. There is savage fighting in Berlin. Hitler has succeeded at least in this: reactualizing the destiny of the Nibelungen, and, in the mythological order, of realizing the Ragnarök, the final catastrophe. Back in 1934 I wondered how a revolutionary

political movement could assimilate itself to a pessimistic mythology that of necessity ends in the Ragnarök apocalypse. Germanic mythology, which Hitler tried to revive, presumes the final combat between the "heroes" and the "giants," a combat that ends in a definitive defeat of the heroes. How can you ask a nation to follow you by assuring it that, to the extent you understand the mission, you arrive inevitably at destruction? This paradox has obsessed me for eleven years, and every time I've discussed the problem of Hitlerism, I have spoken of it (the last time, at Paris, in November 1943, to Cocteau).

All day long I've been tormented with getting started on *Prolegomene* again. The psycho-mental barrage holds me back until midnight, when, with obstinacy, I sit down at my table and write for one hour.

24 April
I write two pages for *Prolegomene.*

26 April
Giza left the day before yesterday for Fátima, with three girlfriends, by bicycle.

27 April
I write two pages for *Prolegomene.*
Full moon. With Leonid till 2:00 a.m.

28 April
I leave with Mica P. and Călin Botez for Tomas, in a van. I find Giza with an injury to her face from a serious fall off the bicycle on the first day of her trip.

We stroll around all afternoon and late into the night: to the castle, the park.

29 April
Mica, going to the castle again this morning, learns from the guide that Himmler reportedly has surrendered [Germany] to the Anglo-Americans. We await the fall of Germany. We didn't think Himmler would be sanctioned to do it. I observe that the Portuguese aren't especially happy: it's news they've been expecting for a long time. The war is fizzling out; the enemy is destroyed, and yet the victory is only approximate.

30 April
We returned last night to Cascaes. News of the execution of Mussolini. Exposed in the city square.

1 May

Tonight we learn from the radio the news of Hitler's death. The rumor of his death has been circulating for several days.

5 May

We leave this morning in the Botezes' car for Nazare, to celebrate Easter. It is Great Saturday. For several days I've been able to maintain myself in a state acceptable to people around me only by taking two or three Pervitin tablets. I took them this morning too. The memories are too acute.

We eat lunch on the green grass, beyond Turcipol. As a matter of fact, we are retracing a part of our journey to Fátima. In the afternoon, we go bathing in a lagoon at San Martinho do Porto. We arrive at Nazare at 6:00. Our rooms are at Pensão Madeira, on the square, facing the beach. The only live, active, functioning beach. I record several observations for my projected Portuguese commentary.

6 May

Last night, party with champagne till 3:00. Călin and Lita Botez are celebrating their tenth wedding anniversary, and I didn't want to spoil their good time with my melancholy. I took Pervitin, I drank champagne—and I became once again the man of the good old days, merry and "witty."

We go bathing on the beach at Nazare, then take a ride in the cable car.

7 May

We leave at noon. Stop at Torres Vedras to eat. Then, to Ericeiro, so Călin can meet with the Romanians in forced domicile. There we found out that Germany has surrendered. A foreigner runs through the square shouting, "La guerre est finie! A guerra acabon!" The first—and only—enthusiast.

At 10:00 p.m. we go to the Costes' to "celebrate the victory." The same ambiguous sentiment, of something that has fizzled out. For two months no surprise has been possible. We all knew that things were going to end this way—the massive surrender of the German armies in the West and Italy seemingly had anticipated the armistice.

10 May

The attacks of nerves continue. Only with Pervitin do I keep going.

The day before yesterday I went to Lisbon to see the "Victory Day" observance. You wonder what is authentic, what is just a release of pent-up energy, and what is "internal politics" in these demonstrations. António de Souza, whom I saw, tells me that everyone is sad. Especially those of the extreme

Left, who were expecting to be brought to power immediately upon the fall of Fascism and the end of the war. But Salazar, who committed a blunder in ordering a state of mourning for the death of Hitler and was denounced by the Anglo-American press—repaired the error by breaking relations with Germany, closing the Legation and banning all the German organizations. So, today, he too celebrates the "victory."

15 May

Today we attended the ceremony at the Museum of Ancient Art (Janelas Verdes) for the donation of a Vasco Fernandes painting by the heirs of Sir Herbert Cook. The only persons attending—with the exception of the Minister of England, the Portuguese Minister of Education, and other officials—were artists and historians. We were listening to that elderly, refined, and likeable Englishman Sir Eric MacLagen telling how Cook's collection was born, when suddenly, flushing, I was reminded of my painful degradation. I saw myself, in a flash, back home, among people who believe in art, ideas, books. That is my destiny, that is my vocation. And now, what have I come down to? Preoccupied with whether or not I have success with women, whether or not I'm a "remarkable male"; preoccupied with my youth and vigor. Discussions with my Romanian friends are on a lamentable level—and I have to force myself to be agreeable, like any other clever fellow. My only noble acts: my melancholies, my attacks of nerves. At least through sadnesses, through my love for Nina, and even through my neurasthenia, I maintain weak points of contact with the world for which I was destined, and which, almost without realizing it, I have betrayed.

✳

For fear that it will not be secure, I've taken the journal out of the safe and brought it home. Today, I reread several pages from last summer. I wrote almost nothing about the progress of Nina's illness, but still the reading was overwhelming.

16 May

I have seen the photographs from Piazza Loretto in Milan; the profile of Mussolini beside his mistress who was shot with him; then the picture of him hung up by his feet.

My last fragment of esteem for the Italian people has disappeared. A race of stooges, traitors, and pimps. Some five thousand workers in Milan filed past Mussolini's corpse, and each one declared his anti-Fascist sentiments, kicking Il Duce as he hung upside down. They had the courage to do this, of course, because they were kicking a corpse. What were these anti-Fascist workers of Milan doing for the past twenty years? How many plots, how many insurrections?

The whole affair is disgraceful. Mussolini tries to save himself instead of committing suicide. Mussolini is caught along with the entire Fascist-Republican government, although there still existed in Italy a German army of almost a million men, in the process of surrendering. It was possible to capture him because he was betrayed. He was betrayed because he was surrounded by Italians.

17 May

I can't remember anything from my dream of last night except Nina's words: "I am your bride and you are my dearly beloved bridegroom. The world tries to separate us, but even oblivion binds us."

18 May

I reread *L'école des femmes* without any interest. False classicism, false simplicity, false generality. Robert is, without a doubt, unbearable; but what flaw does Eveline have? A petite bourgeoise without any vocation, who feels all of a sudden that she has been deceived by life, that her husband is mediocre, etc., but who wants at all costs to be free, to regain her autonomy. The truth is that both husband and wife are mediocre persons, and so long as love bound them together, she had a very high opinion of Robert. The only fault is borne by love, which was and now has ceased to be.

When I think that Gide wrote this book at sixty, after having debuted with *Walter* and *Les nourritures*...!

20 May

Six months since Nina's departure.

We are invited to Tantzi Coste's. We don't stay very long. I keep remembering Constantin and Elena from last year. Nina was rather well then.

22 May

Giza rereads *Huliganii* and is quite enthusiastic. Intoxicated by her enthusiasm, I try to read it again myself, but I give up after an hour. The exasperating sexuality and brutality of these characters simply makes me ill. Philip Leon[68] wrote to me in 1936 that if *Huliganii* truly reflects my soul and my being, I'm an unfortunate case: my sexuality makes me incapable of a spiritual transfiguration. I believed, then, that he was exaggerating. Today, however, this destiny depresses me—this turbulence, this insatiable carnality—which undoubtedly prevents me from "realizing" my true potential.

23 May
      I've worked on a few pages per day of *Prolegomene*. Am making a great effort to reduce the proportions, so I can finish within the limits of a thousand pages, as planned.

24 May
      Reading the lamentable *Le déliverance de Tolstoi* by Ivan Bunin: loose, prolix, 80 percent of it consisting of quotations that are not always relevant. But, again, I think of Tolstoy's destiny: not of his life, so inhumanly tumultuous in its final years, but of his spiritual destiny. This man was obsessed even in youth by what are called "great problems." He was no dunce (at least not according to Bunin's sources). He had a library of 14,000 volumes, and he meditated daily, took notes, analyzed himself in journals, etc. And yet, what extraordinary "philosophical" platitudes, what theoretical mediocrity in all those Tolstoian "thoughts" about personality, loss of self in the impersonal, etc.! *Ivan Ilyich* anticipates the whole existentialist philosophy. But his pseudo-Buddhistic reflections, his elegiac meditations on life and death, are in the worst taste. That peerless Tolstoy who raised literature to the level of an instrument for gaining knowledge—when he undertakes to philosophize "in his own words," sounds like a seminary student. His *Journal* is interesting only where he records events, moods, memories. And yet, how much effort he expended to make this *Journal* not only a candid book, but also one of wisdom! He carried it with him everywhere, he wrote in it constantly, and on his last journey—on the great flight—he dictated to his daughter while lying in bed with a high fever! How greatly he desired that none of his sublime thoughts should be lost!

29 May
      I've just heard tonight on Radio Romania that Mihail Sebastian[69] died yesterday, at 12:30 p.m., as a result of a traffic accident. This news moves me deeply by its absurdity: Mihai lived, undoubtedly, a dog's life for the past five years. He escaped the massacres of the rebellion of January 1941, the Antonescian prison camps, the American air raids, and all that followed after the coup d'état of 23 August. He saw the fall of Hitler's Germany. And he has died in a traffic accident at the age of thirty-eight! . . .
      I recollect our friendship. In my dreams of the future, he was one of the two or three persons who would have made Bucharest bearable. Even during my Legionary climax, I felt close to him. I gained tremendously from his friendship. I was counting on that friendship to enable me to return to Romanian life and culture. And now he's gone, run down by a truck! With him goes yet another large and very beautiful piece of my youth. I feel even more alone. The majority of those persons I loved are now beyond.
      La revedere, Mihai![70]

2 June

    Huliganii has been engaged by Coimbra Editora, and now I'm obliged to reread a copy of it very attentively, in order to correct the typographical errors, before my friend Egidio Amorim Guimarães begins the translation.[71] The second and third chapters of Part I—weak. In general, all of Part I is inferior to Part II. Otherwise, the novel stands up well, it is admirably structured, and I repeat my opinion, that if it had had two hundred more pages it would have been a masterpiece. But how much brutality! There are chapters that sicken me simply by their savagery. The characters are sometimes inhuman, although they're alive, you feel them living. I wonder how I wrote such a book at twenty-seven! How did I see then that life could be so cruel? The only explanation I find: my exasperation on returning from India, the failure of those experiences of the Absolute.

8 June

    Burilianu telegraphs me from Paris that, according to what Spitzmüller told him, my visa is assured. The delay is due to my own hesitations: instead of asking for the visa in March as we had agreed, I didn't ask until the end of April.

    I've succeeded in extending our lease on this adorable house at 13 Rue de Saudade until 15 July. Till then, I will endeavor to write as much as I can of the difficult and complex chapter on sky gods. After that, I'll sell part of my library; another part of it I'll store at the Legation, in anticipation of better days. I hope I'll be able to take the absolutely indispensable works with me to Paris. The transportation of my manuscripts and note slips also will be complicated.

13 June

    For three days, terrible heat (40 degrees C. [104 degrees F.]) in the shade). I go bathing frequently on the beach in front of the house. The shutters at the windows remain closed from dawn till sunset. Stifling.

    Memories of afternoons of last year pass through my mind, and all the phases of Nina's illness. Am struggling harder and harder with melancholy.

    I'm reminded also of my summers in India. I try to connect that personage of 1929–31 with the one of the present day, in order to rediscover the elements of unity, to see in what respects I've changed, in what direction I have evolved. The constants: the problem of death; alternation; symbolism.

20 June

    Six months. The same terrible sadness that does not pass.

23 June

    All this month I've worked, rather productively, on *Prolegomene*. Have almost finished the chapter on celestial hierophanies and divinities of the sky, and I can congratulate myself for having written a little monograph that is clear, is tightly connected, and contains many original interpretations concerning this vast and complex subject. The writing of *Prolegomene* keeps me above melancholy and sadness. Unfortunately, while writing, there "come" to me many new, admirable, and suggestive personal viewpoints about religion, culture, and history that I have no way of introducing into the chapter I'm working on. I content myself with summarizing them haphazardly and burying them inside the "jackets" of notes. God only knows if the time will ever come when I'll develop them. And yet, they're the most interesting things.

25 June
   I've begun to make bundles of the books I want to sell. A large number of them are in French, and I'll be able to buy them again at Paris. But will I buy them? . . .

9 July
   Working. Finished the chapter, "The Sky and 'Manic' Gods." Have decided to stop work on *Prolegomene* and concentrate on *Mort et initiation*. The 100 pages about the Mysteries, written last year, will be pulled from *Prolegomene*, amplified, and completed with a few chapters about primitive initiations and the problem of death, thus making a volume of some 250-300 pages, which I dream of being published by Payot. Otherwise, two or three years would have to pass before *Prolegomene* could be published, and who knows what might happen in the meantime?

✳

   I receive a long letter from Emil Cioran. He is surprised by the fact that I was dismissed by Buzeşti, Minister of Foreign Affairs. "It was hard for me to imagine that your 'heap' of volumes doesn't entitle you to be an exception. The ethics of the Mioritic space!"[72]
   Amused that Şeinescu from Stockholm—with the Secret Service in the time of Moruzov, then the most zealous supporter of Ică and the Marshal, the only person who hastened to set up a Romanian exhibit at the German anti-Bolshevist exposition, the only one who "compromised" himself with his pro-Germanism—was reappointed press counselor at Stockholm. About this fellow, who didn't even know how to write reports, Dimăncescu told me some precious things.
   And so, Şeinescu is reappointed, Gh. Munteanu is receiving a salary of 16,000 escudos (his back pay, 50,000 escudos, he received last month and lost at the casino), all the flunkies and opportunists are confirmed or appointed

to positions. And these things are not done on orders from Russia, but at the request of the Ministry of Foreign Affairs.

10 July
On 7 July Herescu left for Paris. Now I'm in suspense, waiting for a telegram from him.

✴

Mme. Brigette Popescu, here in Lisbon, has received telegraphically from a "special fund" the sum of 20,000 Swiss francs, that is, ca. 125,000 escudos, or some thirty million lei at the inflated rate. And she was just a sinecurist, a protége of the Ică regime. Has anything changed in the country? Nothing! Mircea Solacolu, who did business and ran errands at Lisbon, is now Under-secretary of State in the Groza government.

14 July
Seven years ago, at 4:00 o'clock on a sweltering afternoon, the group from Siguranţă ["Security"] came and arrested me. From then on, misfortunes have followed in an endless series.

Today, I tell myself that something new and good has to happen. I want to begin again to live. I'm waiting for the French visa as for an emancipation decree.

✴

Last night, for the first time in ten or twelve years, I dreamt of Maitreyi.

19 July
We have moved, for twelve days, into a house the Botezes rented for us, at the end of our street, opposite a fish market. Yesterday afternoon I began unpacking, and today I'm writing at my desk, with my library already arranged on shelves. Arranged for twelve days! Because then we'll have to move again: into a *pensão*, or to the Constantinescus', or to a different house—I don't know yet. It depends on the response I receive from Herescu.

I've seated myself at my desk and have begun working. I can hear again the noises of the city, after seven months of hearing nothing but the echoing of the waves. I lived seven months with my back to the city and my face turned toward the ocean. Now I return to the world.

I think back over all my departures. I say to myself that my life is made up of them.

22 July

Puiu Grigoriu, here from Madrid, tells me how he received the order, telegraphed from Romania, to pay Brigette Popescu the sum of 90,000 pesetas.

Răzmerița, who is calling himself "Minister of Romania at Lisbon" now, spends every night at the casino. Everybody knows him. He's "the life of the party." He stops the orchestra and sings *fados* [popular songs], makes a spectacle of himself. And everyone knows he was a general secretary in Romania, that he came here at the head of an economic commission, etc.

Bill Munteanu lost so much at the casino once that he borrowed from Cassă, giving his word that he would pay his debt the next day. He didn't pay it, and he was threatened with being denounced at the Legation. He went at night to Minister Dianu, borrowed from him, and gave his word of honor that he wouldn't gamble anymore (just as he had given it to Brutus)—but he continues to play.

I've written all these things in order to heap scorn on my own sentimentalism. Last evening at the cinema I saw *The Adventures of Tartu*, with Robert Donat, who played the part of a "captain of the Romanian Iron Guard." It was not the fact that it attacked the Iron Guard that made me angry (I attack it more virulently), but the fact that Donat, in order to appear "Romanian," dressed smartly and slicked down his hair, behaved like a flunkey and a cad, etc. I was so angry I left the theater. I couldn't watch my people being insulted—and I expressed my indignation. But now I recognize I was being ridiculous. Romanians are known and evaluated by the way they're seen abroad. And, abroad, that's the way they are! The English director was not wrong. Romanians are like that in Lisbon and Paris and London. A few thousand more or less likeable flunkeys and cads serve to define our nation. In vain does the Romanian peasant exist, in vain an Iorga, an Eminescu. And these Romanians are validated by every Romanian form of government.

25 July

Telegram from Herescu: "Eliade arrivera dans un mois environ." I decide to stay in this house where, at least, I still have a part of my library at hand.

A young man, Hirsch, who was in the International Brigades, spent time in concentration camps in France, studied chemistry (I believe), and lacking a Romanian passport (he had sent, through the Legation, six requests to Romania that a passport be issued him, without receiving any response), has requested and obtained a Yugoslavian one, and any time now he is leaving for Belgrade. From there, to Romania. I note all this because young Hirsch wants to return to Lisbon as a press counselor or something of the sort. Maybe he'll become even more than that. Perhaps his return to Romania with a Yugoslavian passport will have interesting results for certain members of the Legation here.

Meanwhile, a great many people are playing up to him. Soon, if he stays much longer, he might even be invited to dinner by a Dinu Cantemir.

The spectacle is extraordinarily interesting.

26 July

Overwhelming victory of the Labourites; the day of the workers! I'm reminded once again of what Th. Besterman[73] told me in 1940: Churchill is the last bourgeois head of state. "He will, perhaps, conclude the armistice, but he will not, in any event, make the peace. After Churchill, there will follow only a Socialist government."

✳

I read the journal of Count Ciano,[74] in *Primeiro de Janeiro*. Can it be authentic? I wonder if pro-German and other paragraphs have been suppressed.

Depressingly mediocre. The *Memoirs* of [Paul] Reynaud, published in *Diário popular*.

✳

How happy [Iuliu] Maniu will be to hear about the victory of his friend Attlee![75] How much encouragement it will give to Romanian democrats! Actually, the reelection of Churchill would have been fatal for us Romanians. The Russians have no faith in "reactionaries," and they would have taken steps to secure their position. With a Labour government, they can (I hope!) no longer allow themselves suspicions, reservations, hostilities.

The world is moving toward the Left. Perfect. Toward what is called, vaguely, socialism. But, as a Romanian, I'm not afraid of socialism, or even of communism. I'm afraid, purely and simply, of Russia and its imperialistic policies. We have nothing to lose through socialism; everything, through Russification.

28 July

What I regret most about these years spent in Portugal is the bidimensionality of my life here. I have lived exclusively horizontally, as has been true, probably, of people in all neutral countries. I yearn for the third dimension, the vertical, for the life that advances by leaps. Only such a life can reveal more to you than your biological condition.

31 July

Today, riding on the train from Cascaes to Lisbon, I suddenly had the plenary sentiment of total freedom, the freedom I get from the simple fact of being alive, of still living on the human plane, of being *disponible*. It was a sudden illumination, like a revelation. I understood (with all my being!) that I am free because I'm alive, healthy, young—free to do evil or good, to choose ideals, to think, to feel, to write whatever I want. I'm setting all this down very badly, but I want to be reminded always of such a virile, invigorating flash.

1 August

In B. Mussolini's book, *História de une año*[76] (less sensational than I'd expected), I liked especially his "intuition of destiny" on the morning that followed the fatal meeting of the Great Fascist Council. Il Duce sensed then, in the air of Rome, in the atmosphere of the streets, that destiny had become hostile to him. I wish he had said more about these troubling premonitions.

2 August

The farther I advance in the writing of *Prolegomene* and the more I coordinate the materials collected over many years, the more clearly I understand what constitutes the great merit of my works: it is the demonstration—copiously illustrated—of the logical, coherent structures of any religious experience and any mystical or cultural "form." Heretofore, religion has been viewed as an irrational thing, as a predialectical experience (R. Otto, etc.), or as an ensemble of social actions (the French sociological school, etc.), or as a rational activity, provoked by the desire to find an answer to the problem of causality (Who made the Cosmos? etc.: the Catholic school, W. Schmidt, etc.). I demonstrate that the very morphology of religious experiences—experiences to a large extent irrational—is coherently elaborated and presupposes logical structures. Not even the most demonic experience, not even the most "chaotic" ceremony, is entirely irrational; it is framed in an ensemble of beliefs and rituals that is perfectly consistent with an integral and rational vision of the world. Only, instead of clear ideas and syllogisms, we find symbols and ideograms. What is important is that this coherency is manifested even in the deepest strata of human consciousness; that even there, where we encounter pathogens or archaic psychic structures, we discover the archetypes frequently in their most "rationalized" religious forms, and we discover them fulfilling the same functions in the spiritual economy.

In a neurasthenic, a primitive, and an ultracivilized person, for example, the archetype of the "labyrinth" plays the same role: it "centers," it "concentrates," and it defends his spiritual being from external, noxious influences that threaten it with disintegration and annihilation. In turn, the labyrinth is framed in a large ensemble of beliefs, myths, and rituals. It is not the product of historical circumstances, nor is it the creation of a certain people and a certain historical moment—but it is an "immediate given" of man's coming to consciousness in the

Cosmos, a revelation. The history of religions is comprised of such revelations, of hierophanies. And every hierophany can be formulated in logical terms; each one reveals and organizes (gives "form," validates) reality. As I understand it, the history of religions constitutes the point of intersection between metaphysics and biology (all economic, erotic, and social aspects can be incorporated in the sphere of biology); more precisely, it introduces—or reveals—on biological planes the models or "problems" of metaphysics. The irrational is infused with the structures of the rational. (To be continued and explained.)

7 August

The newspapers today publish the first information about the atomic bomb the Allies have dropped on Hiroshima. The world has entered a new phase, Churchill has rightly said. I wonder how war will be possible in the near future if this bomb is perfected? It is probable that the ultimatum issued by Truman and Attlee entails not only the Japanese but also the Russians. For the time being, the Allies have this great military superiority; in ten years the Russians could achieve it. For that reason, the Anglo-Saxons are in a hurry to announce it.

There is another aspect of this invention to which I shall return sometime.

9 August

Coup de théâtre: Russia has declared war on the Japanese. With the atomic bomb, it is certain that Japan will capitulate in a few days, or a few weeks at the most. Now, however, with the USSR involved in the war too, the victory will be an "Allied" one. And at the peace treaty, the USSR also will have its say in the Far East.

Actually, it had to be this way. Stupidity has to be paid for—always and by everyone.

✳

Last winter I wrote a gloss on the biblical passage: "If you eat of the tree of knowledge of good and evil, you will surely die!" The newspapers are quoting the declarations of authorities who do not hesitate to assert that the atomic bomb could bring about the annihilation of civilization and even the extermination of the human race. This bomb is nothing but the last step (so far!) of the itinerary begun at the Tree of Knowledge; it is, in other words, an ultrarecent product of reason, of scientific knowledge, etc. Between the first syllogism and the atomic bomb there exists no discontinuity.

Logic, mathematics, physics, etc. have all made their millennial contribution to its construction. And such a bomb could confirm the Bible: the death of man as a biological species.

10 August

I don't know how I happened to acquire Alphonse Daudet's *Sapho*, which I have taken, together with other novels, from my library at Cascaes for Giza to read. I remembered *Sapho* from lycée, when I read it, as a sad book, and as an indirect criticism of "cohabitation." I remembered with precision only the ending of Chapter 1: the four flights of stairs that the hero climbs, with increasing difficulty, carrying the woman in his arms. That's why I was surprised at the extraordinary impression I had on rereading it. I could hardly put the book down. Where did this morbid, irresistible attraction for a sad and mediocre drama come from? Really, why have I been left so moved by the tragedy of the "cohabitation"? I believe, in the first place, that it's due to elements of "destiny" and "history" that any cohabitation entails. The connection and love between the two young people was made by chance: a simple meeting at a masked ball. Then the "history" of their passion keeps them from separating. The years lived together can never be abolished. The years were not theirs; they just were. And this "cohabitation," this "history," has reduced them to the proportions of larvae. They suffered because they could not escape from their refuge, from the microcosmic milieu of their bed, their neighbors, their slippers, their quarrels, etc. They were not disintegrated (as happens in a great passion, in a mighty combustion), but they were reduced, diminished, restricted.

I had difficulty shaking off the sadness the book imposed. Can this be man's life? Does the meaning of existence come down to this sad, desperate surrender to chance events? I believe not. The main characters of *Sapho*, as well as the majority of human beings, are sick from what I would call cosmophobia: they have a horror of the universe around them, of all the invitations and suggestions the Cosmos is ceaselessly making to mankind to harmonize himself with it, to sense a solidarity with all life, to realize his exceptional situation, etc. A cohabitation, like any microhistory, resists these appeals. The hero can't even guess that life is not reducible to their unfortunate love, to youth and sexual vigor, to family, job, etc. He is chloroformed by his own fatality. It seems to him that everything begins and ends with the "heavenly joys" of the time he met her, etc. No window anywhere—through which he can look outside and can escape.

✳

Recent events, far from shaking my confidence in the primacy of the spirit and the hierarchy of the spiritual, have confirmed it and strengthened it. However the history of the war will be written, it is certain that the victory was achieved primarily through weapons created by intelligence. It was not the Russian proletariat that accomplished the miracle of Stalingrad, but the mathematicians, physicists, and chemists of the USSR and of the whole world who thought and worked in laboratories, conforming to *scientific truth* exclusively, and not to Marxist or Hitlerite ideology. If German savants had discovered the atomic bomb in 1941–42, Hitler today would be master of the world. The heroism of the whole German population counted for nothing. Germany was crushed, just as any power, great or small, is crushed today—not by material and mass, but by perfected weapons invented by scientists. With or without heroism, with or without ideology, etc., etc., Germany would have been the master of the planet if she had discovered the atomic bomb first. Hitler lost the war, to be sure, due to the enormous errors he made in 1940. But all those errors would have been erased from history if in 1941 he had had only a few dozen atomic bombs at his disposal.

Now, as for the future, it is certain that the fate of mankind depends, this time, directly on the weapons of intelligence. Of course, another war—that is, the final catastrophe—if it comes, will be declared by politicians. But the *catastrophe* will be the work of human intelligence. Without atomic bombs, without V-1s and V-2s and however many more there will be in the series, humankind could have withstood several more wars. This time a new element enters in—the extinction of the human race. And this element is the work of the spirit. Whether it is good or bad, I'm not discussing. The fact is that intelligence, the *spirit*, and not the mass, not the proletariat, not the mystique of the people, not political ideologies, not economics and the class struggle, etc., etc., can alter history and definitively modify the fate of humankind. The terrestrial paradise or Atlantis will be exclusively the work of the spirit.

World peace, if it is ever realized, likewise will be attained through the coercion exerted by those *who can* because *they have known*—more than all the others.

11 August

Japan accepts the conditions of surrender laid down at Potsdam, if the Allies will guarantee the prerogatives of the Emperor.

Someone says, "The essential thing in life is . . ." and he begins to enumerate: the hunger instinct, or sexuality, or the will to power, etc., etc. Certainly, each of these is an essential for the particular species of "life" the individual has chosen. If you reduce yourself to the physiological level of all living beings, both hunger and sex are "essentials." The problem is not here—not in the regression of man to the zoological plane. That's easy, and it's been done since the world began. We have seen the results. The problem is to discover and realize that which is essential to man *qua homo*: that which is not "essential" to ants or apes or the mentally retarded; that which only man, insofar as he is a whole man, can realize. When things are seen this way, the absolute reductions of man to sex, hunger, power, etc. reveal immediately their falsity and absurdity. And if the life around us seems to validate those who argue for hunger, sex, etc.—then so much the worse for that life and for us!

13 August

Brutus tells me that the Americans are beginning to wake up, and according to his information the Anglo-Saxons have resolved to firmly oppose Soviet imperialism in Central Europe. The atomic bomb and some things Truman said in his speech are warnings. One of the American diplomats here told Brutus that the USSR has reached its apex in the world; from now on it will be in decline.

All these things concern me—in the first place as a Romanian, but also as a European. I'm horrified at the idea of "zones of influence" that will lead, inevitably, to our assimilation, politically and culturally, to the Soviet colossus. I'm horrified too by the idea of the "Chinese Wall" between Western and Eastern Europe, which would constitute the germs of a new war. In the equilibrium between the Anglo-Saxons and the Germans, I see again the hope for a Romanian autonomy. We cannot let ourselves fail to take account of *all* the political powers that surround us. But to adhere totally to one of them (as we did to Germany) means to risk our existence. The atomic bomb has saved the world, for the time being, from a Soviet supremacy. But this does not mean that the world can return to the bourgeoisie, etc. I see no other way out than socialism.

16 August

Reading Aldous Huxley's latest novel, *Time Must Have a Stop* (so much like his other novels that I have the impression sometimes that I'm reading a new chapter from *Those Barren Leaves* or *Eyeless in Gaza*), I happen upon these striking words: "But out of all those galaxies of eggs, how many herrings ever become full-sized fish?" (p. 102). And it seems to me that a truth of childlike simplicity is suddenly revealed to me: only those who succeed in discovering and possessing themselves totally, who obtain a minimum of spiritual autonomy, who realize the grandeur of the human condition—only those can be called *mature*, grown-up, *"full-sized"* human beings. The rest, even if they attain the age of ninety, can be compared to the millions of herrings that perished soon after leaving the egg or when scarcely grown. Man must not be judged according to his physical age, but according to his mental and spiritual age. A man forty or fifty years old, if he has remained at an infantile mentality, must be considered as having died in childhood. From the human point of view, he is nonexistent, just like a herring that dies before reaching two centimeters in length. The idea must be made clear that only those mature examples constitute the species *Homo sapiens*; that the millions of individuals who survive in subhuman modalities do not represent it and do not obligate it; that, in fact, they are dead before maturity, as billions of individuals from all other zoological species die. If these "dead" continue to exist morphologically individuated in our environment, it means no more than does, to the mature herrings, the temporary "survival" of herrings that died at a tender age in the form of organic matter in the process of decomposition in their watery environment.

17 August

One of the leading characters in Huxley's novel *Eustace* continues his role in the story even after death. Several chapters are devoted to his *postmortem* experiences. How I regret now that I didn't write, at the time, in 1936–37, that novel in which I proposed to describe the after-death conditions of some of my characters! . . .

20 August

Nine months since Nina's leaving. One of the saddest days I've had since then. Already last night, a great sorrow and weariness. This morning I woke with the sentiment of Nina's presence on her last day. I saw the room on Elias Garcia, I saw her again, exhausted but still fighting, I heard her last word, over and over: "Tired . . ."

I made a donation of soup for the poor. Didn't go to the church, which I knew would be closed, as always, at this hour. I reproached myself for not having gone to pray by her side, at the Anjos Cemetery. But I didn't want to do anything to cause her to *identify* herself with the crypt. I didn't want to force her, in her present spiritual condition, to project herself into that space around the crypt. Since 20 November, I've been to Anjos only once, nine days after her departure. At that time I did my best to separate her from her body, to set her free, to invite her to be beside us as a pure presence, not through the medium of her body.

Today I was overcome with grief for not taking flowers there. Still, I believe I did the right thing. I sense her near me all the time.

22 August

At 4:30 Mica calls from the Legation to tell us that our French visas have arrived. Giza goes wild and jumps up and down like a child. I'm so happy I don't know what to do. *Incipit vita nova!*

25 August

I've reserved places on a sleeping car for 13 September. We have berths only as far as Hendaye. From there on, to Paris, in a regular coach. We'll have to leave our baggage on the sleeping car—and may God take pity on it!

We must keep our visas a "big secret" lest certain Romanians here make trouble for us—persons who requested French visas long ago, and who might protest that a "fascist" like me is granted one, while they, who have "suffered for democracy," etc. I note here the names of Alexandrescu, former SS, Olariu, former supporter of Ică and millionaire, etc.

26 August

We take our passports to the Consulate. How happy I am to be able to present a passport on which is written: "Professor, writer"! Having lost all diplomatic privileges (finally!), I must get my own visa; I present myself at the window and wait my turn—like all the other happy mortals. *This* is my life. This is the life of all Europe: difficulties, penury, patience, and despair steeped in optimism.

27 August

I have obtained the visa. Time of residence in France: "illimité."

I've written nothing in the past week about world political events, the crisis in Romania, etc. Am paralyzed by the thought that these pages might fall into someone's hands, that they would be read in bad faith, etc. I had hoped that, as a result of the atomic bomb, war would be abolished. Now I'm beginning to have doubts. I hoped for a balance of power in our country. But Groza doesn't want to cede anything. What it will come to, probably, is the political situation of a century ago: a Russian party, an Austrian party, etc.

29 August

In the struggle he has been carrying on with ex-king Carol, Brutus has emerged triumphant. I note, for the time being, only this date. When I'm able to write everything without fear, I shall complete this note with some very interesting details.

30 August

Have I written here about this house where we've been living since 19 July, to which we came intending to stay two weeks, and where we will remain until the eve of our leaving for Paris? It is the last house on Rua de Saudade, directly opposite the fish market. It will be torn down in October. It is incredibly decrepit. When you go out the front door, you step on fallen plaster, bricks, and other debris. When I saw it, I said to myself: "This is the image of Europe. I must get used to it!" A constant cacophony. Massive steamrollers, sewers being replaced, children, donkeys. On the main exterior walls of our house hang several hundred containers for fish. Beside them, in the evening, are tied the donkeys that after midnight will leave laden with fish. On Rua de Saudade, the house next door is a kind of storehouse, full of bags of salt. In front of it the sardines are salted temporarily on days when the little truck does not come to transport them to the factories in Sétubal. The alley here is constantly inundated with streams of dirty water, reeking of fish.

In our living room, the wallpaper is peeling beside the couch. There are so many flies that after chasing them with a swatter for an hour every afternoon on the first few days, we resigned ourselves to enduring them. I defend myself as best I can when I'm working. In this large room I situated my books and desk. I've been able to work, with difficulty, until I received my visa. Since then, I've gone to Lisbon almost every day. So far, I've sold more than one hundred volumes, realizing some 4,000 escudos. Two hundred more volumes will be sold at auction in November. I had to make lists, bundle the books, and put them into boxes. It was with a light heart that I sold them, even those I know I'll never replace! . . . What a liberation, to be free of a library!

1 September
    Six years ago today I woke Emil Bulbuc[77] from a sound sleep to tell him that Germany had declared war on Poland. How I wish I could read again the pages of the newspapers of that time!

I shall have to find a few hours someday to write here a balance of the four years and seven months spent in Portugal. I've calculated this balance mentally several times, just for myself. It was always negative.

4 September
    What curse hangs over Romania? Premier Groza persists in continuing in power, even though King Mihai asked him two weeks ago to step down, so he could form a new coalition government on which to base national unity and conclude the peace treaty. This evening we hear on Radio Romania Groza's official statement: that he is "popular," that he has "saved the throne," that he does not "give in to tools of the reactionaries," that he is "not retreating." And now they have gone to Moscow—the head of state and the vice-premier, etc. Everywhere in Southeastern Europe national coalition governments have been realized—everywhere except in Romania. Even in Slavophile and pro-Communist Bulgaria, there have been four ministers who withdrew from the government, protesting an attempt at dictatorship. In Hungary, the present government is constituted of representatives of all the parties—outside of the Black Arrows![78] In Yugoslavia, with Tito at the helm, a bloc composed of opposition parties has been formed. We, however, go to Moscow to obtain support against the "reactionaries" Maniu and Brătianu.

    Is it the fault of Ana Pauker? Is she alone to blame? Or, as I am inclined to believe, is it the old Romanian disease of "power at any price"? A compromised politician like Tăttărescu (Tătăr-Bunar!)[79] and a national traitor like Mircea Solacolu are ready to cede anything in any amount, if only they can continue to "exercise" power. They are simple instruments—both they and others. And the sinister thing is, the game of the parties with foreign support (the "Muscovite Party" and the "Western Party"), now being played, has returned to the old system of pretenders to the throne. The Russians and their peons support Carol, because, through an unpopular king like him, it would be possible to liquidate the monarchy forever. Carol, of course, is valuable to them.

This is all the Romanians have learned from the global war: how to exchange masters.

5 September

The "past," which I feel weighing upon me constantly, is the clearest sign that I'm a human being; that is, I live in *time*, I have a "history," I exist insofar as I am made out of the past. I can no longer enjoy "the moment." As Berdiaev admirably observes: time is the curse of fallen man; this man cannot experience the plenitude of the present, having always a past behind him.

To be related to my observations about the regeneration of man through the abolition of time, through the return to the auroral moment, "to that time." What meaning can *incipit vita nova* have: beginning Creation all over again. Man's struggle against "history," against the irreversible past.[80]

✳

The last swim at Cascaes. For the past several days I've done nothing but mark "last times"—from a series of actions and habits that have somehow gotten into my blood. Four years and seven months of Portugal! Tomorrow I go to Lisbon, to spend the "last" week. Thursday, 13 September, at 8:40 a.m., the train for Hendaye departs. I promise myself that on the train I'll make a balance of these years. Here, I leave behind—Nina, one-eighth of my life, and much, much suffering.

APPENDIX A

Journal of the Novel *Viață Nouă*

Oxford, 1 November 1940

Have decided to begin [writing] *Viață Nouă* (New Life). The plan—such as it was—I left with my notes in Bucharest. Now I know nothing more than that I intend to write a very large and very long novel. The whole sad drama of modern Romania must be reflected in it. Of course, the Legionary tragedy[1] will play the essential role. But I mustn't forget that *all* of Romania has to be presented in my novel.

I don't know how long I'll work on it: maybe a few years, maybe the rest of my life, as long as I still have to live. Ordinarily, I write very fast. But this time I'll work with deliberation.

Since I left the homeland, 19 April, I've written nothing. I haven't had a good table for writing—or any peace. Nor do I have them now, but I've made up my mind to start.

My hand tires quickly. I'm writing in a park. Splendid day!

3 November

My passion for the novel is growing. I have nowhere to write—no room, no peace. As usual, I can't "plan," properly speaking. I see only people and events, but where they'll lead me I don't know. In three days I've succeeded only in establishing the beginning of the action: evening, in the house of Băleanu-Sion, his friend who comes to take him to Sug, and the priest with red hair. The house I know from Danielopol's[2] stories.

4 November

At a distance, gone from home for six months, the action of the novel can encompass an unlimited space, my Romania, and the characters spread themselves out now throughout the provinces. (Rewrite that last sentence properly!)

Now I can see the Romanian world better, and I see it as a whole.

The model for the novel: *War and Peace*.

5 November

I begin to write at 2:30 in the afternoon in room number 8 of the "Private Hotel Oxoniensis," 67 St. Giles Street, a room that Danielopol took a week ago. Nina and I have been living here since 15 September in room number 7, but today Danielopol is in London, and I have his room to myself.

I write seven and a half pages, with which, without rereading them, I'm satisfied.

6 November

Unfortunately, I'm invited by Tilea[3] to lunch today at his place in Wheatley.[4] This evening, Danielopol returns. I won't be able to work except in the afternoon.

7 November

I write four pages. I've reread what I wrote yesterday. Not satisfied. Clumsy prose, with no luster. I'm afraid of repeating that unsuccessful prose of *Ştefania*,[5] which I abandoned precisely because of its lack of life, movement, pathos.

8 November

I've been writing well. So far, I have twenty pages of manuscript. I interrupt the work, because tomorrow Vardala[6] and Munteanu[7] are coming for the weekend, and in the next days we'll be guests of Florescu,[8] Pilcher, Sassoon,[9] etc.

15 November

Yesterday and today I've written well: fifteen pages. I left Chapter I unfinished and have begun the second (dinner at Moscopal's), in which I introduce David Dragu—the first step made to connect with the action and characters of the preceding novels. How I regret that I can't reread *Întoarcerea* and *Huliganii*, especially the latter! I don't remember now what Dav looks like, for example. And the manuscript of *Ştefania* would be useful too.

18 November

I reread Chapter 1 today and am unexpectedly pleased. I correct certain discrepancies. There remain a few details to be verified, an operation I make by talking with Dumitrică Danielopol. This evening I undertake to finish Chapter 1. I write a scene with Lonică Sion and Trandafir's parents, and the whole scene of the introduction of Sion's friends. Satisfied.

20 November

Yesterday I wrote little because I reread and corrected Chapter 2. Today I continued the scene with David Dragu at the Colonnade, and I got involved in a long discussion about the Book of Revelation and Petrache Lupu.[10] Although these things are interesting and I had planned long ago to have an occultist, Tuliu, in Part I of the novel, after I'd written some six pages of discussion I began to reproach myself and wonder if I ought not discard them.[11] Again discussions, again theory, again the atmosphere of abstraction from *Întoarcerea din Rai*! On the other hand, I can't mutilate the intellectual characters of the novel—Dragu has to discuss and say intelligent things. Otherwise, he wouldn't be himself, he wouldn't be authentic. I reassure myself by recalling that a quarter of *Zauberberg* is given over to discussions.

23 November

Sick for several days: fever, dizziness, headache. Had to interrupt the novel, to my great disappointment. I tried to resume work on it last evening, although I still had the flu. Moreover, it's annoying that for the last three nights Oxford has had long air raid alarms, between 7:00 and 2:00. Yesterday, the "all-clear" was at 6:00 a.m. I still haven't accustomed myself to writing during the alarm periods. Too many German squadrons are passing over. We hear the bombs exploding far away, at the airfields.

25 November

Day before yesterday I resumed work—although ill—and I've written five more pages. The act of creation in *Viață Nouă* is constantly being impeded on account of my scruples: (a) not to let myself be drawn into excessively fluent writing and effusive dialogues; (b) not to hurry with the presentation of characters, not to give too rapid a rhythm to their actions in the first chapters (a rhythm that could put me from the outset on the false track of a "cardiac novel" of the *Huliganii* type, in which every chapter begins with a sensational episode or introduces a character who, as soon as he appears, says or does extraordinary things; on the contrary, I want at least the first part of this enormous novel to flow slowly, with a rhythm corresponding to the movement of Romanian society in 1935—so different from the rhythm of changes in 1938–40); (c) to be as objective, as impersonal, as possible in the presentation of characters who, although not structurally antipathetic, will play debased roles in the last parts; and (d) not to "introduce" too many actions and groups of characters at the beginning. Besides all these things, although I have the feeling that I've begun the most important book in Romanian literature, the novel by means of which I'm attempting a regeneration of my nation, I am constantly obsessed by the idea that it won't have the universal circulation it deserves to have on account of its actions.

27 November

I'm over the flu, but I still have a fever this evening, a suspicious 37.4° C. [99.2° F.]. Exactly what it was two years ago, when I was writing *Nuntă în Cer* in the prison camp at Cuic. Tomorrow I intend to see a chest specialist. I sent a terrible telegram to Bulbuc,[12] who is Undersecretary of State for Propaganda.

Yesterday I wrote only one page. Today, so far (at 6:00), I've written two pages. It's going awfully slowly, but it continues that "longue haleine" [drawn-out] rhythm. Even if it won't be inspired, the novel will gain by precision, colors, and force.

7 December

Have been sick almost the whole time. Work on the novel was suspended on account of the illness. Dr. Lloyd, 140 Harvey Street, London, has found my blood pressure very low. At Oxford I had an X-ray made; am waiting for the results. In the meantime, my evening temperature continues suspicious: 37.3, 37.4 degrees C.

24 December

I interrupted work on the novel on 10 December, on account of my illness and the state of constant agitation into which events have thrown me (the disaster of the Italians, events in the homeland, etc.). My passion for philosophy of religions is aroused, and I'm starting work on the plan for *Introducerea în istoria comparată a religiilor*, a book I've been carrying in my head for some two years.[13]

✳

Lisbon. 7 May 1941

The manuscripts from London arrived yesterday, and tonight I reread the entire novel. In general, I'm satisfied. The action is well connected, the characters hold together. Certain pages, however, must be changed completely. I want to see if I can get back to work on it this evening.

3:00 a.m. Have written four pages.

Cascaes. 14 June

At Lisbon, between 7 and 16 May, I wrote twenty-three pages. Then I left for Madrid and met Nina, who was returning from Bucharest. A week later we moved to Cascaes. Since coming here I've been able to work at the novel only two evenings—on which, in fact, I contented myself with correcting, rewriting, and transcribing the beginning. Anyway, I have to reread *Întoarcerea din Rai*, *Huliganii*, and the fragment of *Ştefania* in order to know how to solder the new novel to the old ones.

I notice that in the process of transcription, the consistency of the prose becomes firmer. I add here, there—a sentence that fills out a character, a rejoinder, a description. No longer do you have that impression of something "sketched" that strikes every reader of my novels.

I must combine this journal with the notes on the novel that are in the folder with the manuscript.

Cascaes. 22 July

Between 8 and 17 July, [Pamfil] Şeicaru's visit. Couldn't work. To my great amazement, I took up the novel again on Sunday, 20 July, and I wrote eight good pages. Between 30 June and 6 July I wrote sixteen pages. I was very well disposed, then—but Şeicaru's visit put an end to that.

Today, I start again. I count up the total number of pages: 126, in almost nine months of work. For my fecundity, it is humiliating. But for a novel that will have two to three thousand pages—it's a true disaster.

I'm glad, though, that I could introduce Ştefania. The failure of the summer of 1935 paralyzed me. I didn't want to abandon Ştefania, but I didn't write a single page about her, for fear of sterilizing everything, of turning it all to ashes. Ştefania's appearance in the first hundred pages of the book gives me courage. One big hurdle has been cleared.

If I intend to keep this journal current with the progress of the novel, I ought to copy the notes that are in the box with the manuscript. They have much to say about the discoveries I'm making.

Without rereading it, I'm very well satisfied with the Nadina-Barbu-Ştefania fragment. But the tone and density of this episode forces me to review the previous chapters, so summarily sketched.

Another thing, something that doesn't flatter me: too many teas, dinners, group walks. You have the impression that my characters don't know where to meet one another.

23 July

Something I mustn't forget when I'm working on this novel: that my purpose is not to get to the bottom of the page as quickly as possible, but to overcome difficulties on the spot, to persist in struggling on every page, not to proceed if I know that the last line was written simply because it had to be written. Any negligence will cost me enormously more later when, rereading it, I will feel depressed or will have to redo something that, with a little effort, I could've written properly the first time.

But my great defect, as was the case with my earlier novels too, is that I still don't have the courage or strength to struggle with difficulties. When something doesn't please me, I stop writing, smoke a cigarette, daydream—and then I go on, or I write just as I would have written in any case—that is, without the meditative repose I granted myself.

And then too: my exasperating method of discovering almost everything in the process of writing, instead of forcing myself to know beforehand approximately what's going to happen and with what sort of persons. Of course, the overall vision of the novel I have clearly in mind. And I know too the principal dramas. But still there are a great many gaps. I sense that many characters are going to appear about whom as yet I know nothing.

—Keep returning constantly to this notebook!

—Have the courage to modify the text already written! For instance, the passage with David Dragu at the Colonnade must be redone. And a whole chapter after the scene with Mac is needed. A chapter with Dragu alone, that night, before he leaves for Cluj. Concern yourself with how he lived, what he did up to the present (what followed after *Huliganii*). Many things are still obscure.

24 July

If the reader of my novel doesn't have the sentiment that all the characters in *Viaţă Nouă*, even the odious ones, are right—then I've failed completely.

26 July

I write the chapter with David Dragu, in his room, before his leaving for Cluj. Without realizing it, I regain the introspective fervor of *Întoarcerea din Rai*. No regrets, though. This character—full of ideas, bookish reminiscences, in continuous struggle with his thoughts—cannot resemble the hundreds of other characters in *Viaţă Nouă*. But I wonder if the Dragu text will not contrast too strikingly with the rest of the novel.

And then there's something else that bothers me: Dragu resembles Petru Anicet too much.

But one thing I must note that pertains more to the history of this novel: I'm writing under exasperating conditions. Even when I'm not going to Lisbon on Legation business, I waste several good hours a day in reading newspapers (eight—Portuguese) and magazines, in writing papers, reports, etc. Both yesterday and today I worked some four hours at the stupid business. In the evening, when I sit down to work, I pray to God I won't have any visitors. Yesterday and today Antohi[14] and his family came. They stayed till 11:30. At midnight, I'm at my writing table. Tell, me, when am I supposed to work?!

27 July

I absolutely must return to Tuliu, in a special chapter, where I explain his philosophy, lest the reader think that he's nothing but a simple sideshow "occultist." Actually, his theories are not entirely foreign to me. Tuliu will say things that, for various reasons (there isn't space to elaborate here), I've never had the courage to express publicly. I have just, at times, confessed to a few friends my "Traditionalist" views (to use René Guénon's term).

I'll have Tuliu attend the opening of Nae's course. Another opportunity for a critique—from the metaphysical, antihistoricist viewpoint—of Nae's theories. I'll follow Tuliu back to his house. Description of his rooms, books, etc.

※

When it's going hard and I'm trying to find something to do to let me take my eyes off the page barely begun, I remember a piece of advice from some writer or other: all that matters is that you spend five hours every day at your writing table.

If only I had, not even five, but just two or three good hours for work per day! But how can you work when you're kept in suspense by communiqués from the Eastern front, and when you read ten newspapers (the number has increased again!) and you have to make I don't know how many reports, etc., etc.?!! I find myself torn between two temptations: that of working as much as possible for my country (articles, propaganda, etc.) and that of concentrating on this novel, which is also a great act of Romanianism.

3 August

Something I mustn't forget in writing the novel: that Petru Anicet is a genius, that his drama has universal valences—like those of *Manfred* or *Faust*—that he dares everything, and his capacity for suffering and for making others suffer is formidable.

5 August

Yesterday I took up the work again. With great difficulty I wrote a page and a half. I begin the chapter with Nae's opening lecture. These are things I know so well that I hesitate to write them. I have the impression that I'm working on a chapter of memoirs about Nae. I try to bring some "romance" into the text, and immediately I have the sentiment of sadness, of vulgar "literaturizing."

9 August

I've spent the whole day today in an awful struggle with inspiration. Twice I abandoned the manuscript and threw myself, furious, on the couch, trying to go to sleep. The evening began under a bad sign. The chapter with Nae's opening lecture is going hard. I'm depressed by the sensation of artificiality, of essay. The prose is descriptive, lifeless. Tuliu's presence in the Titu Maiorescu Amphitheater, instead of helping me reconstitute the lecture and the atmosphere, paralyzes me. I abandon it, and return to the Sion-Bordei-Lenuța chapter, to the central plot at which I always work with pleasure. It's almost midnight when I return to this chapter. I write two pages, and although I don't know what time it is (maybe 2:00, maybe 3:00) I intend to continue. More important than the two pages are the details of these unfolding Sion-Bordei actions which I have "seen" in their totality.

22 August

For two weeks I've made it a rule to write fifteen pages per week, no matter what happens. So far, I've held to it.

The chapter with Nae's opening lecture is going hard. One thing, though, is gratifying: on rereading them, I find the pages written slowly, torturously, are the ones most "in the tone" of the novel—which I don't want, in any event, to resemble *Huliganii* in rhythm.

An observation: the secondary plots (Băleanu, Bordei, etc.) are acquiring too large a significance. In the later parts, when they will be abandoned, the reader could be disappointed.

28 August

I've written almost 190 pages, and I still can't tell if the novel has the density I intend it to have. I'm afraid that the action doesn't unfold slowly enough. I'm afraid I've continued the agitation of *Huliganii*, which would be fatal to this novel with its slightly inclined planes, in which masses move slowly, episodes don't "flash by." A novel of two to three thousand pages that begins briskly and accustoms the reader to read fast, expecting a new character or episode every twenty to thirty pages—is a catastrophe.

For what I want to make, I need a listless, dull, even viscous prose in which the reader must struggle hard, so that when the cascade of dramas begins, he will be tired already and will sense the qualitative difference between the time of 1935–36 and that of 1938–39. Unfortunately, I've been accustomed to writing fast. The lively rhythm I impose on my prose is suitable for *Maitreyi* or *Nuntă în Cer*, but it's totally detrimental here. I must find again the loose, obscure, but spicy prose of *Isabel* and *Lumina ce se stinge*. Without, of course, slipping into the excesses of analysis (the interior film—the psychic automatisms that you never find satisfactory or sufficient in the end)—excesses that mar *Întoarcere*, but which here would be catastrophic.

29 August

I don't know if this "journal of a novel" will ever be published—in my lifetime or after. But I should like to call to the attention of the potential reader that, ordinarily, I don't record here anything but generalities and, especially, criticisms that I'm forced to make of a text that doesn't convey precisely the ideal image of the novel (more simply: that which I have in mind). Naturally, I don't record here the things with which I'm satisfied. Therefore, this journal does not contain the total opinion I have about the work in the course of its creation. I've written nothing, for example, about the excellent chapters with Lenuţa, Bordei, Sion—or Ştefania and Nadina, which I consider much superior to all I've created up to the present time.

I have made this clarification lest the reader be prompted by my reservations to say, "Of course, that's the way it seemed to me too! The novel has such and such a defect"—forgetting about the perfectly realized parts.

2 September

On the night of 31 August I wrote the two hundred and first page.

I reread this journal. I regret that many of the things I proposed to do, I haven't done. For example, because Nina and Giza are typing the manuscript for me and I'm not losing time now correcting and recopying—I've left the chapter with Dragu at the Colonnade in the first version—with which I'm not satisfied. But I'd have lost two nights redoing it. And since I have to write fifteen pages per week, and since I have only four nights available for this—I couldn't permit myself the luxury of working so long just to rewrite and transcribe one chapter. Moreover, it wouldn't have advanced the typing of the manuscript.

I'm suspicious of all I've written in the past two or three weeks. I haven't had the courage to reread it. But I'm afraid the prose will be too "dynamic" and episodes will be described too summarily, without the reader's having the sentiment that all these things are happening in time.

And then, too, the secondary actions—which won't contribute anything to the great drama of the novel—take up too much space.

I'm struggling with a dilemma: if I slow the narrative pace, the peripheral episodes will acquire an even greater amplitude, but if I reduce their natural stature, the novel will lose its density, turning into a series of sketches of unequal value.

It may be necessary to reduce the number of actions, allowing the novel to become "fluid" only after some thousand pages.

5 September

This week, mediocre work. I'm far from the fifteen pages I've set as my minimum. But this still is not too serious. I'm a little worried by the ineffective "sprawling" of the novel. Completely secondary characters and actions have acquired impermissible importance. They have won rights for themselves (they've become "substantial"), which will not allow me to proceed in the future with an easy indifference to them.

More precisely, I'm at the episode, now, of Lonică Sion—his dream of Brazil, the visit to Chirică. In the original plan, everything would have taken fifteen to twenty pages. Already I've written thirty, and I haven't reached the end yet; I still have the following stages: his illness, his failure to leave, the visit of friends, the reconciliation with Bordei, his first defeat in Lenuṭa's presence (the beginning of his debasement). If I were to "slight" any of the stages now, I'd give the impression of sketchiness and haste. But if I treat the material left with the same detail, the episode will acquire too much importance.

This is just one example. Unfortunately, there are others. While the principal episodes—with Ştefania, Nadina, Dragu, Anicet—remain, for the time being, embryonic, all the peripheral actions have developed into monsters. And I understand why: my hesitation to make a frontal attack on the major dramas of the novel causes me, by way of compensation, to expand laterally. Another thing: my desire to write, at any price, a certain number of pages each week makes me exploit secondary episodes in order not to have to start a new chapter, a new plot theme (more correctly, not to have to return to the main themes of the plot).

7 September
I return to "the center," Ştefania. Pretext: the Sunday teas at the Nestor family's place. On this occasion, I complete Ştefania's psychology and I paint an amusing Bucharestian milieu.

Nina and Giza began typing the manuscript several weeks ago. They tell me they're not enthisastic about the seventy to eighty pages they've typed, but this delights me. It means that the novel doesn't "charm" the reader from the beginning. That's a good sign that the reading goes hard—exactly what I wanted.

One observation of theirs disturbs me though: they don't like the characters' names.

8 September
Sometimes the thought of the unparalleled greatness of this work that I've proposed to give my nation paralyzes the creation process. I sit staring blankly, contemplating the unfolding of future actions, incapable of continuing the page begun.

30 September
I interrupted work on the novel on 11 September on account of a cold that hung on for ten days. Then nuisances. Tomorrow I'm moving to Lisbon.

Lisbon. 20 May 1942
Although I'm not finished writing the book on Salazar, and I'd have to work intensely for another eight or nine days in order to send the last chapters to Bucharest through the Romanian diplomats who are returning from Brazil[15]—I leafed through the manuscript of the novel today, dreaming melancholically about the many things I still haven't begun to write, asking myself when I'll

ever find time to return to the hard labor of *Viață Nouă*. If I finish *Salazar* by 28 May, I must then immediately take up a book about the Romanian philosophy of history, to be published in Portuguese, ordered for 15 July. This means another summer lost for the novel.

26 May

Obsessed again by this novel, whose qualities and defects I see better now, from a distance. And my great sadness, that I can't start to work on it . . .

What depresses me is the narrative concerning David Dragu, at least as much as I've written, and the immediate sequel (the life at Cluj, etc.). This man, the real hero, has almost nothing to do in my novel, while dozens of mediocre personages sprawl over tens of pages. Only in 1937–38 does Dragu become interesting. And we're in 1933 now . . . [16]

First Impressions of Portugal

Lisbon, 1941[1]

On these afternoons of late spring, I like to stand here in Praça do Comercio at the railing above the Tagus. I watch the many kingfishers that, untiringly, keep trying their luck in the river's turgid, yellow, oily waters. Following their short, plunging flight from a cry to a splash and then aloft again, I find, after a while, that I'm carefree, peaceful, detached from myself, wondering when the world around me was transfigured, when it became so beautiful.

Nowhere, in any country, have I heard a cry more melancholy, more heartrending, than that of the grinder man in Lisbon. This craftsman has the habit of announcing his passing on the streets by blowing notes of infinite sorrow on a short reed pipe: long, lingering notes, suddenly ending in a sharp, piercing cry, like that of a wounded songbird. The grinder pipes most despairingly on hot afternoons, when the sun puts the great trees to sleep and a glassy vapor hovers over the pavement. It is as though he were the last man alive, passing in sorrow through a deserted city.

And again I hear him toward sunset, when the air recovers its transparency and the trees begin to exude their fragrances. It is, undoubtedly, the most consummate expression of *saudade*.

This is a sad people. A Portuguese friend told me this once, but I didn't want to believe him. The better I get to know them, the more convinced I become that *saudade* is not an invention of Coimbra,[2] the poets, and romantic travelers. The Portuguese don't possess the expansiveness of the southerners; they have no vehemence of any kind, no cry that bursts forth from a surplus of emotion. I think of all my friends, all the Portuguese I have met, the people I've seen in trains, city squares, seated at tables in cafés, in theaters. All have a strange, awkward ponderousness about their movements, although they aren't apathetic either. They are melancholy, they smile absently all the time; they are affable, like all who carry about a vague, unmotivated sorrow.

Buçaco

I have left the window open. Far away, beyond the forest in the valley, the flame of a fire can be seen. A fine drizzle. Mountain air, at night, when rain is beginning to fall.

I throw myself on the bed. I try to memorize two strophes from Camões' sonnet *Alma minha gentil* [My Noble Soul]—but I read with mounting discouragement, knowing that I'm attempting something impossible for me. Never have I succeeded in memorizing more than three or four stanzas of a poem, no matter how hard I labor. And the second strophe seems less beautiful to me than the first.

It reminds me of a night I spent long ago in Allahabad, a guest of Major Basu. I was then, as now, alone; it was drizzling, a little chilly (January nights in Central India—and my great naïveté to travel dressed for spring). Old Major Basu had given me that same day a book of travel impressions from a journey he had made in Europe in 1880. A modest, provincial edition, printed at his own little press in Allahabad. I believe I must still have that book somewhere, bound in soiled green cloth: *An Indian Traveling in Europe*, I think he called it. I know I stayed up quite late that night in order to read it. And I couldn't understand how a man so intelligent and cultured as my Major Basu came to mention in his book things of such little interest, commonplaces one meets in any handbook of history or geography: the population of each country, the names of the major rivers, the size and activity of the ports.

Very late, past midnight, someone tapped timidly on my door. It was old Major Basu himself, all wrapped up in a blanket. Someone in the house had seen the light burning and had wakened him. He remained standing shyly in the doorway, seeing that I was reading—and his own book, at that! He seemed to want to say something, because several times I thought he was about to begin. Finally, when I was trying to make a flattering commentary, he saluted me with exaggerated politeness and left. The next day he seemed to have forgotten the visit completely.

I don't know why I remembered all this and why I felt I needed to write it down here, in this hotel room in Buçaco. Maybe, because it's raining and cold. Maybe because I'm expecting the door to open and someone to appear who will stare at me a long time, bewildered, will listen to those few sentences that I will, undoubtedly, say about the volume I'm holding—and then will withdraw, mute, into the shadows, with steps as soft as felt, before I can get a good look at his face.

Luso

There are old houses with foundations of granite, with green-tiled roofs and little windows seemingly designed for a puppet theater, next door to this grandiose, modern hotel that resembles a solarium, which averts its eyes in embarrassment from all that constituted, before it was erected, the true Luso:

fountains, a few family boardinghouses, the restaurant with its pool hall and rooms for parties, the promenade, the public garden.

An abandoned mill somewhere. And the park, with kiosks, terraces, gravel. No one is walking now beside the pool where, with a gentle bubbling, the water of Luso springs, although the flowers are still fresh, the grass tender, and the trees as green as ever. A summer resort town after the departure of the last vacationer.

I understand now the wave of melancholy I've felt continually tempting me ever since we stopped in Luso. I find here the nostalgia for that lost paradise of worlds that have perished: bathing resorts from my parents' time, that semireal life that lasted only for the summer months; friends, idyls, solitary strolls, and martial music on Sunday afternoons in the bandstand in the middle of the park; the parties, dances, paper lanterns, confetti.

Among the many books waiting their turn to be read are the two volumes of Ramalho Ortigâo, "*a Ramalhal figura*" [the Ramalhal figure], as Eça de Queiroz called him. He wrote, among many others, two curious volumes, which together constitute a kind of "Guide for the Visitor to the Baths and for the Easygoing Traveler," containing all sorts of useful and specific information: train schedules, hotel rates, details about the baths themselves, doctors, and culinary specialities. The books are called, respectively, *Banhos de caldes e aguas minerals* [Hot Baths and Mineral Waters (1875)] and *As praias de Portugal* [The Beaches of Portugal (1876)]. They seem pervaded by a limitless, almost fanatical enthusiasm for the possibilities of science, and especially of medicine and balneology. His touristic and balneological guides, today, are said to constitute the chief source of documentation for the social life of three-quarters of a century ago.

Vizeu

We pass through a great hall, the former episcopal dining room, with marvelous *azulejos* [glazed tiles]: Alexander the Great, Titus, Vespasian; the same distinct, glossy blue, which one must learn to like.

From a window, a view of the whole city, nestled between forested hills. Oaks, pines, and cork trees descend almost to the *campo dos toiros*, recently built on the outskirts of Vizeu. Houses of an identical red brick, with roof tiles of red or brown. A few white villas, with windows the color of wet granite, which seem out of place here in this kingdom of clay nuances.

How beautiful is this street from the foot of the cathedral, which drops from wall to wall, propped up at intervals by the foundations or corners of houses, turning abruptly and disappearing in a jumble of rooftops, far away, in the heart of the city.

Before Entering the Museum

Admit it: no place enters into your blood and your memory if you don't travel through it unhurriedly, without any precise thoughts, without trying to reconstruct its history. Take, for instance, this broad square in front of the cathedral, about which for the time being I know nothing, although I'm sure it must be laden with history. With what melancholy I shall remember it always, just because I have walked through it very slowly, looking upward constantly and viewing the cathedral's battlements, its old eaves, its windows . . .

✳

The first thing I observe in the Cathedral are the Manueline knots attached to the arches. This detail seems to arouse my interest. I begin to look in a more friendly way at this vast cathedral with its ascetic nudity, which is nevertheless warm, intimate.

The young man with a proletarian face and hair style, dressed shabbily, has been gazing for some time at the altar. Now he kneels, rather shyly, and starts to pray.

And there are two women, old ladies, who undoubtedly observed us as we entered, and who haven't let us out of their sight, following us with a mute malice all the while they're reciting their prayers and calmly counting their beads.

The abbot shows us to the great stairway that leads to the choir. From above, the cathedral acquires more depth and, seemingly, has a different light. It's another atmosphere, a less certain space, as if those granite columns had acquired imperceptibly a strange musical animation.

But what is truly extraordinary are the choir chairs. The backs and arms are decorated with faces and bodies of a rare, surprising beauty: demons, chimeras, goats, dragons, fish, and heads of the damned. The hand that rested for many years on the chair back has rounded the profile of the devil, giving him an even more sinister expression. How troubling is that old man's head, with mouth half-open in some unknown lewd sigh, with his eyes almost on his forehead—situated so high to enable him to see as much, and as soon as possible, now, on the threshold of death. The incomparable courage and genius of the carver who has animated the hard, smooth wood of the chairs with all these stares and grins and monsters! The men who sat here, of course, were full of piety, and piously they sang, caressing the horns of the devil beside them, or the stupid, cynical face of a guilty monk, or the chimera with a bold tail, or the lizard suddenly risen from out of the wood, or the dragon that for years has striven to detach itself from the chair back and seek a refuge elsewhere.

No image is exactly like any other. No expression is repeated on any of those faces that stare at you from all sides. By what miracle have these characters from fairy tales, myths, and bestiaries, from popular farces and monastic legends, come to exist in the choir loft of the Vizeu Cathedral? And what an unbounded spirit of tolerance, and how much understanding and irony on the part of the clerics who watched while these wooden images—quite as tempting as theological virtues—came to life beneath the master's chisel!

The choir loft is full of surprises, because over each chair, supporting a chain of trumpets and seaweeds, there bends the body of a woman with bare and well-rounded abdomen. I wonder what they could possibly signify—these women whose bellies remind me of prehistoric idols, the Venus of Willendorf or some other Eurasiatic Magna Mater. It means nothing that I discover, fastened to their backs, pairs of angels' wings. The protruding curve of the naked abdomen, the breasts of glorious maturity, and, above all, the smile—so feminine, so impenetrable—prevent me from discerning angelic essences in these bodies!

Japonia

Also in the choir loft, on the walls, several curious wood panels, fashioned in a Japanese manner. They are, indeed, Japanese. A curious mixture of styles: colonial Portuguese and Japanese. I have seen somewhere the reproductions of several oriental works of art—Persian rugs, faience from the Far East—on which Portuguese boats and sailors are represented. I need to get the documentation of these things.

The Grão-Vasco Museum

There are so many art museums about which I've written nothing in this notebook that I can't let myself forget the Museum of the Great Vasco Fernandes. Perhaps because, although it is entitled modestly a "regional museum," it is one of the most beautiful in Portugal—the most beautiful, undoubtedly, if the Janelas Verdas in Lisbon did not possess the triptych of Nuño Gonzalves.

To this Vasco Fernandes so many canvases are attributed that for a long time modern criticism believed that the man was a myth. Recently, however, his historical reality was definitively validated. And in this museum—located in a building of the sixteenth century—there have been assembled his principal paintings, along with canvases of other northern artists plus numerous other precious objects, from a marvelous Byzantine pectoral cross to a curious modern collection of watercolors and gouaches.

What bothers me about all of Vasco's paintings is not the realism with which he treats his subjects—although this realism, in itself, is full of mystery—but the ugliness of his characters. From the Savior in *The Baptism* to the soldiers and Pharisees [*sic!*] in the extraordinary *Calvary*, Vasco's visages reflect the same great, entrenched ugliness. There are only two exceptions, to which I shall return. But I approach each painting individually, and I find Vasco's genius expressing itself in ugliness, as if it were a predestined spiritual dimension. Take, for example, *Calvary,* the great canvas that greets you when you first enter the museum, which is, undoubtedly, one of the masterpieces of Portuguese art—for its boldness, its conception, its skillful execution. But how much ugliness there is in those twenty-five personages! What twisted faces, what opaque grins distort the countenances of the Pharisees[3] who are casting lots for the Savior's garments; what a bloated profile that centurion in the foreground has, like that of a greedy merchant, wrapped in his red mantle, and how much bestial vanity is in the eyes of all those witnesses to the Passion! The unrepentant thief writhing on his cross, the soldiers with asymmetrical faces bursting with mediocrity and villainy; Longhin on his white horse, the lance almost slipping from his hand—apparently, the miracle is taking place in his soul—and the holy women, in the foreground, crowded around the Lord's Mother, who is fainting with melancholic hands pressed together—all these images partake of the same bitter, sinister, or pathetic ugliness, gorged with suffering or exhausted from fruitful efforts. Because the ugliness of Vasco's personages is not always caricatured or demonical, like the faces painted by Bosch or Breughel. In most instances, it is only the result of a lifetime of labor, it is the lack of charm, the opacity and callousness that a hard life gives one, the longing for the good life, the craving for power.

The same outlook has distorted also the numerous other faces, with the exception of those of St. Sebastian—surrounded by hideous executioners—and St. Peter. Almost everyone considers this painting of St. Peter to be Vasco's masterpiece. It is, at any rate, the most popular. The throne on which the saint is seated looks like the immense baldachin of an Asiatic despot. His imperial mantle falls in rich folds onto a mosaic floor. Bathed in gold, with a sumptuous tiara, holding in his left hand, which rests on an open book, the enchanted key to Paradise, and raising his right in an apostolic benediction of dreadful simplicity—St. Peter is represented to us as a true Cosmocrator. Never, it would seem, has a painter lavished more genius, more gold, and richer colors in order to honor the victory of the Roman Catholic Church in the image of St. Peter: an august, slightly weary, but nonetheless apostolic Peter. Everything here shows him as the true master of the world, as the Universal Monarch who establishes law and order everywhere. And if I weren't tempted by other reflections on this art, so full of the secrets of maritime discoveries—what an excellent excuse this would be for meditations on the archaic symbolism of Melchizedek, the Priest-King, the Universal Monarch, the Chakravartin, the one who stands at the center of the world and turns the Wheel, through which all things are possible and obtain being.

Maritime Discoveries

Vasco Fernandes, who represents people, saints, and even Jesus as he sees them in his fellow countrymen returned from rugged Atlantic voyages, is the most bitter of realists. But that realism, which characterizes the whole contemporary Portuguese school, is a creation, along with many others, of the spirit of the era of maritime discoveries. Nothing is further from the graphics of the Renaissance than this Portuguese painting which—perhaps before the Dutch, and in any event independent of them—discovered realism in art. The canon of classical Mediterranean beauty, with difficulty reactualized by the Italian Renaissance through humanism and the cultivation of the classical taste, never became popular in Portugal. The age of maritime discoveries created here a different canon: that of the Atlantic, of the *mare tenebrosum*. The Manuelin style, with all its secrets, with the exotic and maritime influences that strike the eye and disturb, is the most perfect manifestation of that canon.

But no less interesting and suggestive is the realism of Portuguese painters of the sixteenth century. Because all these artists were contemporary with the incredible efforts expended in crossing the oceans and discovering new worlds. Many of them lived in the colonies along the African coast. There they viewed new landscapes, alien images; they were introduced into dangerous geographies, they knew a harsh life; at every step they encountered death and the terrible diseases of the Orient, they lived the hard life of sailors, and, above all, they saw men who were scowling, straining themselves in an exhausting effort, locked in a discouraging struggle with the unknown—men overworked, drained dry, drunk on glory, vice, and the sense of power: in a word, ugly men. The hardness and bestiality of the faces painted by Vasco Fernandes were those he met everywhere on his contemporaries. He had no chance to glimpse the seraphic, contemplative, Mediterranean beauties of the Italian Renaissance. He had no way of preparing his spirit to perceive these lovely, peaceful faces. The brief intervals of creativity of the Portuguese were always situated between such expeditions.

Exoticism

Another great painter, a contemporary of Grão Vasco—"Mestre do Retábulo da Sé de Viseu," as he is called until his name can be identified—has his whole oeuvre collected here. The influences of maritime discoveries are, in the case of Mestre do Retábulo, even more evident. One of his best-known paintings, *The Adoration of the Magi*, portrays a Brazilian Indian as the black king who comes to worship at the Savior's manger. That it is an Indian of Brazil there can be no mistake, since he is preparing to kneel in his varicolored costume, with rings and a string of pearls at his throat, with multihued feathers around his head and his wooden spear. Undoubtedly, he is the forerunner of exoticism in European painting, the prototype of the "noble savage" that, for over two centuries, was to obsess the imagination of Continental writers and moralists.

Portugal can be proud of being the precursor of exoticism and the entire romantic literature. Was not Camões the first European to praise an Indian slave,

Barbara, as "the captive who held him captive"? The poem, "Aquela cattiva" [To That Captive], in which dark skin (*pretidão de amor*) is exalted over blond beauty, opened the road to a whole exotic literature, promoted triumphantly by romanticism. It was not for nothing that Chateaubriand was so fond of "Aquela cattiva," in which he thought he found validation for passion for non-European, unsophisticated beauties pertaining to geographies that his fervor and that of all the other romantics assimilated to Paradise.

Thus begin all the currents later to become popular, and thus begins every mass fashion and every mass snobbery, whether that of a great poet or of a great painter. Because, the fashion that began to be popular after 1920 of bronze, swarthy beauties, the fashion that forces the youth of the white continents to "negritize" himself or at least to "bronze" himself by any means possible, is a serious deviation from classical Mediterranean or Nordic canons of beauty that praise the blond Helen and the beautiful maidens with hair of gold, Blanchefleur or Margareta. It is true that the mode of swarthy skin invaded Europe simultaneously with Negro music and jazz. But its origins are in Romanticism and in the *pretidão de amor* of Camões. Several hundred years had to pass before it would be not only accepted by the elite of Europe and America, but also promoted by art, philosophy, and sports on both continents. The "revolt against white skin" is, of course, complex. One can also identify proletarian elements in it—the revolt against the aristocracy and classical canons. But what is the "proletariat" of the admirable dreamers of the last century if not "le bon sauvage" of Rousseau multiplied into a collectivity? And is there not, perhaps, some connection between the apology for the "primitive" of the eighteenth and nineteenth centuries and the messianism of the proletariat elaborated by socialist idealogues in the last hundred years?

Vouga

From Figuerro we keep ascending continually amid forests in which the pine mingles with birches, cork oaks, and maples. We ascend on this marvelous road with endless, dizzying curves, penetrating more and more deeply into a mountain landscape. And all at once, at our feet, we see the Vouga Valley. It opens from here, a few hundred meters to the left of the bridge we are crossing. And then it spreads out beyond, wider and wider, victorious and fertile.

Everything is different. The bald crests of the mountains begin to resemble granite blocks, steep and hard. We come upon villages with houses of severe, dark colors. Soon the houses are found isolated or gathered in small clusters: self-sufficient farms.

We escape from the rain. The strong, fresh fragrance of rocks and forests reaches our nostrils. The valley is terraced and well-cultivated. Here the greens have riper, brighter tones. No longer are they the pale, sickly shades of the South—those greens faded by the sun, soon vanquished by the clay and

APPENDIX C

Official Communiqués

I.

Lisbon, 11 February 1941
The Royal Ministry of Foreign Affairs
Directorate of the Office of the Code
Decoded Telegram

At the Bristol Airport I was searched, on the morning of 10 February, for three hours, down to the skin, even though I had a diplomatic passport. My wife was isolated and stripped. The lining in my suitcases torn, the soles of my shoes ripped open. The baggage ransacked, seen by witnesses at the airport in Lisbon. The diplomatic valise was confiscated and returned to the Romanian Legation in London, on grounds that it had not been passed by the censor at the Foreign Office.

I protested and refused to leave, but I was threatened with having to pay seven hundred pounds sterling to the airline for the delay caused by the search.

I was not permitted to call London. They refused to let me burn the courier. I was given a document confirming that I had handed over the valise. At London, the bank effected a transfer of funds to Lisbon to cover the expenses of our travel.

Mircea Eliade

II. Notes about the Former King Carol at Lisbon[1]

Lisbon, May 1941

As is well known, I believe, [ex-king] Carol fled from Seville,[2] leaving his hotel bill unpaid. The Spanish newspapers took note of the fact. It is not known who arranged the flight, because I cannot believe that López (his host in Lisbon), Urdăreanu[3] (who had fled long ago), or Pangal[4] and Helfant were able to foil the Spanish police and the German agents. Rather, I believe that, after the breech between the Legion and General Antonescu, Serrano Súñer, fearing that the Falange[5] might face the same situation someday with respect to

Franco and the army, wanted to create difficulties for the Romanian government. I base this hypothesis on the sympathy the Falangist newspapers showed for the "Legionary rebels,"[6] attacking the General violently; on the esteem Ghenea enjoys in Spain; and on the fact that the retaining of Carol by the Spaniards was done in spite of their sentiment of honor, and only in order to do the Legion a service.

Carol's presence in Lisbon was rather amusing for us at the Legation— although poor Cămărăşescu,[7] when he delivered General Antonescu's communication to him, suffered like a dog, because he was forced, following Urdăreanu's instructions, to dress in a frock coat and not be a minute late. Amusing, yet irksome, because we ciphered and deciphered telegrams for as long as six hours a day. Sometimes we didn't get to bed till 2:00 a.m. The communication he had to make to Carol on behalf of the government was rather drastic. He was pointedly reminded that the recent plebiscite had proved again that the whole Romanian populace did not want him. He was told to keep quiet, not to attempt any sort of political action, since his first gesture would endanger the dynasty itself. In an earlier telegram, General Antonescu had asked poor Cămărăescu to present himself to Salazar and to protest energetically against the fact that the Portuguese government had received Carol, demanding further that it pledge itself to forbid his leaving or engaging in any political activity. Cămărăşescu was received by the Secretary General of Foreign Affairs, Sampayo, who replied that his government considered Carol a political refugee and as such it could not make any pledge. Protests were made, following dispositions from the respective countries, by the ministers of Germany, Italy, and Spain. Ambassador Franco [of Spain] also repeated his protest through a verbal note. Sampayo replied to all of them, however, in the same way.

To return to the communication Cămărăşescu made to Carol. He presented himself, in a frock coat, exactly at 4:00, and was received in a salon by Pangal. He sat there some five minutes before Urdăreanu appeared, who conducted him into another salon. (Protocol, of course: both of them are, or were, chamberlains.) Finally, he entered a third salon where Carol was waiting for him, standing. He found him aged, tired, without éclat. Carol asked, "What do you wish?" and Cămărăşescu read him the text of Antonescu's telegram, loudly and clearly. He tells me that Carol listened without moving a muscle. Only when he heard that any political action would place the dynasty[8] in danger did he frown slightly. At last, he said: "Tell the Romanian government that I will respect the obligations imposed."

Cămărăşescu started to withdraw, but Carol invited him to be seated and initiated a conversation that lasted fifteen minutes. He said that he would be staying for some time in Portugal, that he is slightly related to the Bragança family[9] whose history he would like to write, that he wants to visit the countryside, that he will purchase a house for himself. There was no hint in anything he said that he was intending to leave Portugal. Next he asked who else was at the Legation, and when he heard my name, he exclaimed, "But I know him very well! We published several books of his at the [Royal] Foundations!" He added that *Yoga* is a very good book and that *Maitreyi* is the best modern Romanian novel, and he called me "the leader of the young generation." Cămărășescu tells me that out of the fifteen minutes, seven or eight were devoted to me. (Imagine how flattered I feel!) He knew that Nina was the niece of General Condeescu,[10] and he even said that I am under her influence (this made me indignant). He added: "I know, too that many mistakes have been made. Much could be said . . ." With this, the audience came to an end.

Cămărășescu met then with Urdăreanu (to whom he is "distantly" related, he tells me now), who asked him why he was "yelling" in the salon (when he read the General's telegram). Urdăreanu, too, did me the honor of talking about me—and about Nina, whom, probably, he had not forgotten from the time of the famous audience at the Palace.[11] He repeated that people say I am under Nina's influence. (This is something many people believe who don't know me, and I explain it in this way: Nina is a woman who, especially in recent years, since we have taken part in and have found out so many exceptional things, enters passionately into discussions, supports her opinion, is intransigent with scoundrels, and is very straightforward about her Legionary faith—whereas I, in public, usually seek to conciliate, to excuse weaknesses, etc. My "diplomatic" attitude and her unbending vehemence give the impression that I am, if not dominated, at least influenced, by her. Which is far from true.)

Other information about Carol obtained from Georges Oulmont, a French journalist who knew him well at Bucharest, who admired him a great deal and wrote about him in 1939. Oulmont, together with his wife, was invited to dinner by Carol once. He told me about an awkward scene when Carol, embarrassed, flustered, pointed toward Lupeasca,[12] saying, "Oulmont, I believe you've met . . . it seems to me that . . . you know Mme Lupesco." Oulmont found him depressed, discouraged—while Mme Oulmont left with a rather mediocre opinion of Lupeasca. Both had been great admirers of Carol. Now they are no longer, and they even hesitated to accept a second invitation—although they are refugees here and without funds. As Oulmont put it to me: "Carol's exile has no grandeur about it. You don't sense his tragedy when you see him with his mistress beside him. He doesn't even have the courage of the Duke of Windsor to marry the woman who has ruined his throne. That's why he is not looked upon well at all in Lisbon, and no one dares to invite him to dinner. Sometimes he is invited, alone, but he comes with Mme Lupescu. I know what happened in the house of an acquaintance of mine. When Mme Lupescu was announced, one minister started to get up from the table to leave."

About Urdăreanu, I found out six weeks ago that he gambles heavily at the Casino in Estoril. One evening he lost 110,000 escudos—some five thousand dollars—that is, at the real rate of exchange, more than six million [lei].

The English minister, Campbell, saw the king at his house, and it seems he informed him then that he would not grant him a visa, either for England or for Canada. The United States has taken the same stance. The explanation: they don't wish to upset Franco or create difficulties for Salazar (who would, of course, be reproached by us and the Axis for not keeping watch over Carol, for letting him engage in political activity, etc.).

Three weeks ago, Carol obtained visas for Cuba and Argentina. An Argentine woman with whom we are friends, Isabel de Monda, tells me that this news does not please her in the least.

And, suddenly, Carol left on an American ocean liner[13] for South America. It was a bolt of lightning, because no one had been forewarned. Pangal, whom Cămărăşescu saw the same afternoon that Carol flew with Lupeasca to the Bahamas, told him: "My dear sir, that gold is completely liquidated. There's no use for General Antonescu to keep worrying about him. Carol has no wish to return to the country, even if the whole populace were to acclaim him on their knees."

Pangal showed him with pride the check for $3,500 that Carol had signed that morning. Pangal had been engaged for $1,000 per month, but Carol had not paid him his salary for three months. He cursed him for being tightfisted: he had had to struggle for I don't know how long to get the money out of him. "But I didn't let up! I didn't let him go without getting that check! He wanted to put me on the rack, man!"

Pangal said that Urdăreanu and Lupeasca had fought to convince Carol to begin an immediate "action." He claimed that his conflict with Urdăreanu was due precisely to this matter. He, Pangal, advised Carol not to do anything for a while. Carol suddenly decided to take the plane for the Bahamas. He decided in the morning, and at 12:00 he left.[14] (This I can't believe. Seats on the plane are hard to get. Probably the ex-king didn't want to reveal his plan for leaving, lest he be betrayed.)

Before leaving, Carol was received in audience by Carmona and then, for an hour and a half, he talked with Salazar—who found him to be an extraordinary man, cultured and clear-sighted in international politics. The audience was an official one. The Minister of the Interior came to Carol's residence and took him by automobile to the Presidential Palace.

Mircea Eliade, 1941

APPENDIX D

Preface to *Salazar și Revoluția în Portugalia*

This book of political history[1] is written by a man who is not professionally engaged either in history properly speaking or in politics. It was born out of a state of perplexity and it was written to answer a question that the author has not tired of asking for the past ten years: is a spiritual revolution possible? Is a revolution historically realizable, made by men who believe, above all, in the primacy of the spiritual? The Portugal of today, the Portugal of Salazar, is perhaps the only country in the world that has attempted to answer such a question. The study of its history is all the more instructive in that the Portuguese political experiment—inaugurated with the first liberal constitution and the civil war at the beginning of the nineteenth century—is today concluded. Salazar, by reintegrating Portugal into the line of its historical destiny, ends a disastrous cycle, which was nourished by all the influences and all the ideological conflicts of the nineteenth century, which knew the latent preparation for the revolution and the proclamation of the republic, the struggles between parties, the political anarchy, and finally the counterrevolution of 28 May 1926—he ends this cycle and begins a new cycle, oriented around completely different principles and validated by a different tradition. Salazar's moral and political revolution has succeeded; the best proof is the serenity and fecundity of today's Portugal, as compared with the chaos of the last regime. Who does not remember the refrain, "Encore un révolution en Portugal!" with which a famous Parisian couplet of twenty years ago ended?

The modern history of Portugal has seemed interesting to me from another point of view also. How was it possible to arrive at a Christian form of totalitarianism, in which the state does not confiscate the lives of those who constitute it, and the human person (the person, not the individual) preserves all his natural rights? So much has been spoken and written about the function and limits of freedom—but to me it seems that the ancient Christian formula is closest to the truth: "Love—and do what you want" (St. Augustine). But first, *love*. Love assures man of a state of grace in which the brute instincts are at least asleep. Brotherly love purifies, and a man so purified can exercise at will all his freedoms; they will never endanger the peace of his neighbor nor harm society. Freedom preceded and nourished by *caritas* is the optimum climate allowed for the perfection of man. But how far is this Christian freedom in love from the Rabelaisian maxim, "Fais ce que tu vouldras!" that obsessed so many doctrinaire dreamers of the eighteenth century!

The Salazaran state, a Christian and totalitarian state, is founded, first of all, on love. This assertion can seem, in the eyes of the competent, an irresponsible exclamation of a dilettante. But it is nothing other than a reduction to its ultimate elements of the revolution and reforms undertaken by Salazar. Because what is meant by the replacement of the *individual* (the "citizen") by the *family*, the irreducible nucleus of the nation, and the return to the corporation, considered as an organic social collective; and what does it mean to say: "We do not question the nation . . . no son ever wants to be the child of a different mother"? All these are but variations of the same organic community of love: love that creates, unites, and places value on the family. This organic and irreducible unity—and, as such, the one thing that can exercise political rights—only comes into being through an act of love, with all that that entails: humility, sacrifice, renunciation, creation. The whole social and governmental concept of Salazar is based on the family, and, as such, on love. The corporations, towns, and nation are nothing but elaborated forms of the same Portuguese family. The "Unitary Nation" means, for Portugal's dictator, a community of love and a community of destiny—terms that define the family precisely.

In the light of these specifications, one can understand the miracle that Salazar has achieved: a totalitarian and Christian state, constructed not on abstractions, but on the living realities of his nation and its traditions. This creation is all the more remarkable in that it has been accomplished at the end of a political evolution that was violently antitraditional, anti-Christian, and passionately "Europeanizing." Entire generations of Portuguese youth—some of them in good faith, others simply out of snobbery or spiritual drought—sought to divert Portugal from its traditional course and transform it into a "European country." This book relates the history of these men and the results of their efforts. When Republican and democratic Portugal wanted to "enter" Europe, the moral misery and administrative chaos reached unimaginable proportions—and the presence of Lusitanianism in European capitals made itself noticed in couplets. For a hundred years Portugal struggled to become a European country, borrowing from the Right and from the Left, imitating Parisian models especially; and much blood flowed in order to put an end to the "specter of reaction," by which was meant tradition, monarchy, Christianity. And when the liberal ideas had triumphed and Portugal had become a country, at least by constitution, just like other European countries—the only reward was the refrain, "Encore un révolution en Portugal!"

Europe did not begin to take account of Portugal until the day when it became itself again. The prestige this little Atlantic country enjoys today in Europe is simply amazing, if we think about its situation of twenty years ago.

It seems that "Europe" can be satisfactorily assimilated only by the elite; more precisely, only a few personalities can allow themselves to assimilate the genius of one or several European cultures, while remaining themselves and continuing to create in the spirit of their own people. (What the Spanish genius meant for Corneille, the Italian for Ronsard or Sa de Miranda, the English for Voltaire and the Romantics, the Greco-Latin for Goethe, and the German for the Anglo-Saxon Romantics—are well-known facts.) But when whole nations try (or are forced) to imitate one or another European government—then they either fail disastrously or they produce hybrid, weak, standardized forms, which mean, besides their own sterilization, the death of "Europe" as well.

Thus, I believe that I have not digressed too far from the problems of our nation and our time in bringing out this book, which deals with the recent history of a country at the other extremity of Latinity. Addressing the Portuguese youth of ten years ago, Salazar said, "Times are becoming increasingly harsh . . . I tell you that you are the sacrificed generation, the generation that must make atonement . . ." The great conflict of today, in which the youth especially are being sacrificed, atoning for the sins of so many well-intentioned generations, reduces to the problem of the restoration or the disappearance of Europe: of that Europe which takes account only of those countries that have not betrayed their destiny and have not suppressed their history. Salazar has tried to save Portugal through a Christian revolution, that is, a revolution that begins with little things well done—but which ends, naturally, in the reintegrating of man into the organic unities and the cosmic rhythms. He has tried—and he has succeeded. This historic experiment compels us—as Christians, as Latins, and as Europeans—to revise a whole series of concepts: tradition, nation, freedom, etc.

This book is based on true and, insofar as possible, complete information. I have, first of all, allowed the facts to speak, but not only the facts that seemed significant to me (although this is the case also with the majority of historians, even when they don't say so). However, in order to make an accessible book, I have dispensed with the scholarly apparatus, being content to print at the end a bibliography for each chapter individually. Perhaps later, if there is need, I will bring out an amplified, more erudite edition.

Undoubtedly this book would have had fewer shortcomings had I been able to profit in time by Jesùs Pabòn's admirable *La Revoluciòn Portuguesa* (Madrid, 1941). Unfortunately, the first chapters were already written when Pabòn's monograph appeared.

I wish to express my thanks to the head of the Secretariat of Propaganda in Lisbon, which put at my disposal a large number of inaccessible works, as well as to Antonio Ferro, Dr. Tavares d'Almeida, Dr. Manuel Mùrias, Pedro Correa Marquez, João Ameal, and Eduardo Freitas da Costa, who assisted me—through publications, documents, or personal information—in the redacting of this book.

I thank also Minister Victor Cădere, who read the volume in manuscript and suggested several improvements in the text.

M. E.

Lisbon, May 1942

✳

Compare, however, this excerpt from Eliade's journal for 14 October 1946:

The news from Portugal seems to confirm that Salazar is in a state of extreme exhaustion. That man, who worked sixteen hours a day, can't work even one hour now. A complete nervous breakdown. When he is advised to rest, he replies: "It's too late now. The rest that would have done me good a few years ago could change nothing now. It's too late!"

I wonder if he regrets his personal life—love, marriage, studies interrupted, the works he hasn't written—his life as a man and a philosopher that he sacrificed "para o bem da Patria" [for the good of the Fatherland]. Because, while it is true that he has saved his country from many disasters, it is no less true that his "sacrifice" has profited the rich and retrograde opportunists, Catholics of the worst species, etc. This pure and poor man has done almost nothing for the pure and poor people . . . And nearly all those around him were menials, flunkies, opportunists. The great political thinker could not bear to have any but the most ordinary men around him. He alienated the elite of all generations. Did he do it out of the envy inevitable in dictators? Or as a means of precaution, fearing the brilliant intelligentsia, precisely because he knew, from recent history, the evil they had done to Portugal?[2]

Notes

Translator's Preface

1. Eliade's memory was not accurate on this point. Among his papers preserved by his family in Romania, several such notebooks dating back to 1920 have been discovered.

2. But Eliade told me a rather different story in May 1983, relating that Herescu buried them when the air raids began.

3. Eliade, *Autobiography, Vol. II, 1937–1960* (Chicago: University of Chicago Press, 1988), 96. Footnote 2 on p. 99 of that work refers to the diary as the "Lusitanian Journal," and to a "possible selection" from it that might be published someday.

4. I have not handled the notebooks, but have worked from photocopies, to which I was given access in 1996 by Eliade's widow, Christinel, three years before her death. In the photocopies, the manuscript appears to be on notebook pages. The pages are numbered consecutively. Including ancillary texts, separately numbered, the total is increased to nearly five hundred.

5. Cf. June 1943; 15 July 1943; 15 August 1943; 6 April 1944; 2 February 1945.

6. In fact, a few pages of "impersonal" selections from Portuguese travel diaries were published in 1955 in a Parisian exile review, *Caiete de dor*, no. 8.

7. Gershom Scholem, *Briefe, Vol. III, 1971–82* (Munich: Verlag Beck, 1999), 279–81.

8. Published in English in Eliade, *Autobiography, Vol. II, 1937–1960* (Chicago: University of Chicago Press, 1980; and French as *Mémoire II (1937–1960)*. Paris: Ed. Gallimard, 1998.

Chapter One

1. In his memoirs (*Autobiography, Vol. I, 1907–1937* (San Francisco: Harper and Row Publishers, 1981), p. 4.

2. Eliade's wife.

3. António de Oliveira Salazar, 1889–1970, president of the Council of Ministers since 1927, but in effect dictator of Portugal.

4. Jean Antohi, economic counselor.

5. Ion C. Vardala, last chargé d'affaires at the Romanian Legation in London. He left London at the beginning of May 1941.

6. See appendix A.

7. The *Introduction to the History of Religions*, which he soon began to call *Prolegomene . . .* (Prologemena to the History of Religions). This book would become, when published in French, *Traité d'histoire des religions*, and in English, *Patterns in Comparative Religion*.

8. How badly I can be deceived sometimes! I got to know Oulmont well in the summer–fall of 1941. How much mediocrity and fraud in that man—with 100,000 escudos in the bank! (May 1942.) [Eliade's note.]

9. José Maria Eça de Queiroz (1846?–1900), Portuguese novelist and essayist.

10. Eliade, "Ştefania," *Universul literar* 48, no. 52 (December 30, 1939). "Ştefania" was a part of *Viaţă nouă.*

11. Aron Cotruş (1891–1961), Romanian poet who had been serving in a joint appointment as cultural and press secretary at Lisbon and Madrid. Eliade replaced him as press secretary at Lisbon.

12. *Nunta în Cer* was written in 1938 while Eliade was interned at Miercurea Ciuc; first published in 1939; second edition, 1941.

13. Literally, *The Return from Paradise* (but intended to be the Romanian equivalent of *Paradise Lost*), and *The Hooligans*—the novels to which *New Life* was to be the sequel.

14. Well-known Romanian novels: *Ion* [John], by Liviu Rebreanu (1885–1944), published in 1920; *Întunecare* [Darkness], by Cezar Petrescu (1892–1961), published 1927–28.

15. Pamfil Şeicaru, 1894–1980. One of the founders of *Cuvântul* in 1924 who had invited Eliade to the staff in November 1926; he left the paper a year later and founded *Curentul* [The Current] as a rival daily newspaper. Although a keen political analyst, his name was a byword for blackmailing. He was anti-Semitic, pro-Fascist, and pro-Hitler. Antonescu sent him abroad, with money, to organize counterpropaganda against the Soviets. At the end of the war he sought refuge in exile—first in Spain, then in Germany, where he died in poverty.

16. General (later Marshal) Antonescu; ruled Romania during the Second World War, supported by the army. Shared power from 6 September 1940, to 23 January 1941, with Horia Sima, head of the Legion; thereafter ruled alone. See chap. 2, n. 18 below.

17. "Ică" was the nickname of Mihai Antonescu, minister of foreign affairs, vice president of the Council of Ministers, former professor of law at the University of Bucharest, distantly related to Marshal Antonescu.

18. Armand Călinescu, King Carol II's prime minister, who arranged for the execution of Codreanu and certain Legionary prisoners in custody in 1938. He in turn was assassinated by a team of Legionaries in 1939.

19. Nicolae Iorga (1871–1940), historian, professor, politician, an extremely prolific writer, and a vain man. He was assassinated by Legionaries, who considered him responsible for the death of their leader, C. Z. Codreanu.

20. Eliade's beloved "Professor" (1890–1940); died of natural causes in his fiftieth year.

21. Prime minister, assassinated in 1933 by a team of three Legionaries (claiming to be acting independently). He had ordered repressive measures against the Legion.

22. Former chief of the Security Service of the Romanian army.

23. Not to be confused with the famous novelist José Maria Eça de Queiroz (1846–1900).

24. Mihai Eminescu (1850–99), Romania's most revered poet; and Luís de Camões (1524?–80), Portuguese poet, considered the greatest figure in Portuguese literature.

25. Wife of António Ferro, Portuguese minister of propaganda.

26. Nina's daughter by a previous marriage; at this time about twenty.

27. Title of a famous Romanian folktale.

28. Spanish writer (1882–1954); an early supporter of Franco.

29. Leontin Jean Constantinescu (1911–81), with a doctorate in law, was appointed press counselor to Lisbon in 1941. After 1945 he moved to Paris for a time, then to the University of Saarbrücken in 1954, where he enjoyed a distinguished career as professor of law.

30. Marcelino Menéndez y Pelayo (1856–1912), Spanish literary historian and critic.

31. Eliade, "Menéndez y Pelayo," *Cuvântul* 5, no. 1078 (25 April, 1928): 1–2.

32. See appendix D.

33. West Timor was a Dutch colony; East Timor was under Portuguese rule.

Chapter Two

1. Eliade, "Latina Ginta e Regina" [The Latin Race Is Queen], *Acção* (Lisbon newspaper), 5 February 1942.

2. Alfredo Pimenta (1882–1950), celebrated Portuguese historian, poet, journalist, and political commentator, was, by the time Eliade met him, a staunch Catholic and traditionalist, an anti-Communist, and an ardent supporter of Salazar and the corporatist state.

3. José Ortega y Gasset (1883–1955), Spanish essayist and philosopher.

4. Ion Luca Caragiale (1852–1912), famous Romanian novelist and playwright.

5. "Camões: An Essay in the Philosophy of Culture."

6. João Ameal, leading Portuguese historian of the Salazar regime.

7. Criterion was a small, informal group of about a dozen elite Bucharestian young adults that flourished from 1932 to 1935. It presented two well-attended series of lectures and symposia on contemporary political and cultural trends, and prominent personalities of the day. See Eliade, *Autobiography*, I, 1981, pp. 228–28; Ricketts, *Mircea Eliade, The Romanian Roots: 1907–45*, Boulder, CO: East European Monographs, 1988, pp. 552–564; Philip Vanhaelemeersch, *A Generation "Without Beliefs" and the Idea of Experience in Romania (1927–34)*, Boulder, CO: East European Monographs, 2006, pp. 26–35.

8. Garabet Ibrăileanu (1871–1936), Romanian writer and literary historian.

9. A reference to a cycle of romantic novels, *La Medeleni* [At the Medelins] (1925–27) by Ionel Teodorcanu (1897–1954). Eliade scorned the "feminine" way the author depicted the love affairs of the adolescents and youths in his books.

10. Eliade's father was Moldavian, his mother Wallachian. Thus, he believed he had inherited the traditional characteristics of the two provinces of old Romania: sentimentalism from his father and vitality from his mother. See Eliade, *Autobiography*, vol. I, p. 16.

11. No, the Gestapo! [Eliade's note.]

12. Victor Cădere, current Romanian minister to Portugal.

13. Marcu was minister of propaganda.

14. Voronezh was a key transportation center on the Don River, taken easily by the Germans on May 6, because the Russians were in a strategic retreat, preparing to make a stand at Stalingrad.

15. A British defeat in North Africa by the German General Edwin Rommel on 21 June.

16. D. C. Amzar, Legionary sympathizer; settled in Germany after the war.

17. When the marshal was with the troops, Mihai Antonescu served as president of the Council of Ministers in his place.

18. Actually, January 21–23, 1941. Often referred to as the "Legionary rebellion," it entailed bloody fighting in Bucharest, in which about 120 Jews (the number is disputed) were killed, often in brutal ways, and an approximately equal number of other persons, civilian and military, died. See Dinu C. Giurescu, *Romania in the Second World War* (Boulder, CO: East European Monographs, 2000), 74–75. Legionaries contend that General Antonescu initiated the "rebellion" in order to remove Horia Sima and other Guardists from the government and assume full power for himself. Most writers (including eyewitnesses) say it was started by the Guard in opposition to measures recently taken against it.

19. Emil Bulbuc, who served as secretary of state in the Propaganda Ministry in the Legionary government; was murdered by a gunman in Italy in 1945.

20. The year 1940, when General Antonescu staged a popular coup d'état, forcing King Carol II to abdicate and leave the country.

21. Mircea Vulcănescu (1904–1952), one of Nae Ionescu's students. He was a brilliant philosopher and close friend of Eliade, taught courses and held seminars at the University of Bucharest on sociology, ethics, and so on in the 1930s. Not a Legionary. In 1941 he was appointed undersecretary of state for finance, and after the war was tried and imprisoned for his service to the Antonescu regime. He died in a Communist prison.

22. An artist (painter).

23. Born 1904. A writer for *Gândirea* [Thought]. He obtained a well-paid governmental position soon afterward (see Mihail Sebastian, *Journal, 1935–1944, The Fascist Years* (Chicago: Ivan R. Dee, Inc., 2000), pp. 521–22.

24. Constantin "Dinu" Noica (1909–87), philosopher; one of Eliade's best friends. Joined the Iron Guard in 1940. Sentenced to twenty-five years imprisonment in 1957 for contacts with the West; released in 1964 under the general amnesty.

25. There is a gap in the numbering of pages in the journal manuscript at this point (pp. 65–66). Did Eliade remove two pages?

26. Schmitt (1888–1985), controversial German political theorist.

27. Petre Țuțea (1901–91), philosopher and economist. Imprisoned 1948–53 and 1956–64. Survived Communist era in Romania.

28. This phrase is crossed out in the original manuscript, probably when Eliade was preparing to publish the entry in *Caiete de dor*, no. 8 (1954): 22.

29. René Guénon (1886–1986), founder of an influential school of esoteric thought, often called Traditionalism.

30. Crossed out in the manuscript.

31. Published as "Eminescu, poeta de raca romena," *Acção*, 1 October 1942.

32. Victor Rădulescu Pogoneanu. Director of cryptography in the Foreign Ministry.

33. General N. M. Condiescu, relative of Nina, protector of Eliade in 1938 and until his death in 1939. Writer, president of the Society of Romanian Writers at the time of his death.

34. References to King Carol II and his son, Mihai I.

35. Alexandru Busuioceanu (1896–1962), former docent in art at the University of Bucharest, newly appointed cultural counselor at Madrid. Became professor at the University of Madrid; later known for his poetry in Spanish and other languages.

36. Bogdan Petriceicu Hasdeu (1838–1907), Romanian poet, dramatist, journalist, historian, and statesman. Eliade published an edition of his works in 1937.

37. Central figure in Eliade's planned trilogy, *Viață Nouă*.

38. A member of the Legation.

39. Published in *Acção*, 31 December 1942, and in *El Español* (Madrid), May 1943.

40. Founder of the Legionary Movement (in 1927); born 1899; murdered while imprisoned in 1938.

41. Published as "Lucrurile de taină," *Tribuna Ardealului* 4, no. 689 (11 February, 1942). See Appendix B, "First Impressions of Portugal."

42. Territory Romania had been forced to cede to Hungary in 1940 in the "Vienna Diktat."

43. Drâza Mihailović (1893?–1946), leader of the Chetnic guerillas in both the first and second world wars. Ardent nationalist and royalist, believed Communists were a greater threat than the Axis. Gradually lost popularity, and Allied support shifted to Tito. Executed for treason in 1946.

44. William Joseph ("Wild Bill") Donovan (1883–1959). Served as director of the Office of Strategic Services, 1942–45.

45. Ernest Jünger, 1895–1998; German author, veteran of both world wars, opposed Hitler, wrote about war experiences. Between 1960 and 1972 he and Eliade coedited the journal *Antaios*, founded on Jünger's initiative, as a kind of successor to *Zalmoxis*.

Chapter Three

1. See chap. 2, n. 32 above.

2. "Thanks to love, we all feel how carnal is the spirit."

3. "Passion and sensuality are incompatible feelings: passion is arbitrary, while sensuality is logical."

4. A member of the German Embassy at Lisbon.

5. Member of the Romanian Legation staff.

6. Brutus Coste (1910–96), distinguished liberal Romanian diplomat, served in Washington before the war, then in Lisbon (1942–46). He participated in the peace conference at Paris (1946–47), representing the unofficial (non-Communist) Romanian delegation. In 1947 he moved to the United States, spending the rest of his life in activities aimed at keeping the world aware of the plight of the people in the "European captive nations."

7. *Ifigenia*, a play, was performed in Bucharest in February 1942, but was not published until 1951—at an "exile press" in Argentina. May have been intended to convey the Legionary idea of sacrificial death.

8. Eliade is mistaken in saying that he could have "collected" reviews of the last two books mentioned, since those volumes were not published yet.

9. Mircea Eliade, "Magia şi cercetările metapsihice [Magic and Metapsychic Researches]," *Foaia tinerimii*, 15 February, 1926; Eliade, "Folclorul ca instrument de cunoaştere [Folklore as an Instrument for Obtaining Knowledge]," *Revista Fundaţiilor Regale* 4, no. 4 (October–December 1937): 137–61. The latter was published in French in *Mircea Eliade*, no. 33, ed. Constantin Tacou (Paris: Cahiers L'Herne, 1978), 172–81 and in English in Bryan Rennie, editor, *Mircea Eliade, A Critical Reader*, London and Oakville, CT: Equinox, 2006, 25–37.

10. Eliade's cousin, younger son of his uncle, Costica. Evidently (?) he was arrested for being a member of the Legion.

11. Haig Acterian (1904–43), one of Eliade's close friends from lycée and *Criterion*. He was by profession an actor and stage director, and wrote several books about drama. Married to the actress Marietta Sadova. Openly associated with the Legion. Following his arrest, he was sentenced to twelve years imprisonment. Given the alternative of military service, he volunteered for the Russian front, where he perished.

12. Wife of the Italian ambassador (see entry for 26 July 1943).

13 Jean-Victor Vojen, a good friend from the Criterion group, and a Legionary. Frequent contributor to right-wing periodicals. Ambassador to Italy under the National Legionary government (September 1940–January 1941).

14. Bracketed words represent a probable reconstruction of an illegible place in the manuscript.

15. The sentence in parentheses was also bracketed by Eliade, perhaps indicating that he was unsure of including it. Eliade once wrote an article about Ghose, an Indian "mystic" who had an ashram at Pondicherry: "Un reprezentant al tradiţiei hinduse: Shri Aurabindo" [*sic*] (signed with the pseudonym "Krm"), *Memra*, 1, nos. 2–3 (January–April, 1933). He calls him there "the most realized man in India."

16. Never published.

17. Victor Buescu (1911–71), classicist. Early in 1943 he came to Lisbon to teach Romanian language and literature at the university, and remained there after the war. Translated, inter alia, poems of Eminescu and Eliade's postwar novel *Noaptea de Sânziene* (The Forbidden Forest) into Portuguese.

18. *Euthanasius' Island*, published by Editura Fundaţiilor Regale, Bucharest. Contains a collection of scholarly articles on literary subjects, history of religions, and the like.

19. The reference is to the last Moorish king, who surrendered to Ferdinand and Isabella in January 1492, and who wept as he was forced to leave the beautiful city.

20. Nicky (Nicolae) Dimitrescu.

21. Evidently, he means his travel journal from the summer of 1937: see "Notebook of a Summer Vacation (1937)," published (in English) as an appendix to chapter 15 of Eliade, *Autobiography, Vol. II, 1937–60* (Chicago: University of Chicago Press, 1988), 16–61.

22. Novel by Liviu Rebreanu (1885–1944), a prominent Romanian novelist and dramatist.

23. "The demon of middle age"; the midlife crisis.

24. Eliade altered the wording of this last phrase when he first published it to read: "especially all that could be revealed by the discovery of archaic worlds, myths, and symbols." Cf. "Fragmente de jurnal," *Caiete de dor* 8 (June 1954): 24.

25. Wife of Brutus Coste.

26. Oltania, Romanian province located in the southwest part of the country.

27. Romanian novelist and short-story writer, born 1910.

28. This book was never published, nor was a volume of travel notes.

29. Aleksandr Kerensky (1881–1970), as premier of Russia in 1917, refused to withdraw from World War I and pursued other policies that enabled the Bolsheviks to overthrow his government and come to power.

30. Sir Anthony Eden (1897–1977), distinguished British statesman; at this time secretary of state for foreign affairs.

31. A close friend of Eliade.

32. Correctly, Raïssa Maritain.

33. An expression Eliade often used, meaning a device for gaining knowledge.

34. Crainic (1899–1972) was born "Ion Dobre" and changed his name as an adult. After writing for *Cuvântul* and *Gândirea*, he founded (in 1932) his own daily paper, *Credinţa* [Faith]. Of a strict Orthodox religious viewpoint, he criticized some of Eliade's works as "pornographic." At the same time he supported Codreanu, Hitler, and Mussolini, and served as minister of propaganda under Marshal Antonescu. For this "war crime," he suffered seventeen years imprisonment.

35. W. L. Mackenzie King, thrice prime minister of Canada (Liberal), this time from 1935 to 1948.

36. Giza Ionescu, Nina's daughter by a previous marriage.

37. Published in Bucharest.

38. Paraschivescu (1911–71), militantly Communist poet, published several volumes of verses after 1944.

39. Eliade may have been thinking of an article in *Lumea românească*, 13 June, 1937, "Impertinenţa ticăloşiei" [The Impertinence of the Rascal].

40. Reference to "Mai mulţi feluri de naţionalişti" [Several Kinds of Nationalists], *Vremea*, 5 July 1936.

41. Members of the Romanian Legation.

42. As will be seen shortly, Giza was going on to Bucharest.

43. Former head of the French Institute in Bucharest.

44. Emil Cioran (1911–95), already well known as a writer in Romania, studied in France before the war, returned briefly 1940–41 and, then (despite his being a Legionary) was sent as cultural counselor to Paris in February 1941, after the "rebellion." He held the position only until May, when he was dismissed for unknown reasons. Cioran remained in Paris and never returned to his homelaand. In 1947 he decided to write henceforth only in French. He perfected his skills in the language and published many small books of "pessimistic" philosophy and essays. See Marta Petreu, *An Infamous Past: E. M. Cioran and the Rise of Fascism in Romania*, trans. Bogdan Aldea, with a foreword by Norman Manea (Chicago: Ivan R. Dee, 2005).

45. Constantin Noica (1909–87), Romanian philosopher; remained in Romania after the war and suffered greatly under the Communist government.

46. Nicolae I. Herescu (1903–61), professor of Latin at the University of Bucharest, director of the Royal Foundations, and so on. When Romania was about to fall to the Russians in 1945 he sought refuge with the Eliades in Portugal.

47. This signature suggests that Giza was married then (briefly) to Camilian Demetrescu (b. 1924), artist, who lived in Italy after 1969 (suggested by Mircea Handoca.).

48. And yet he did submit a letter. See Mircea Handoca, ed., *Eliade, Europa, Asia, America*, vol. 3, *R–Z* (Bucharest: Editura Humanitas, 2004), 531–33.

49. Brother of the Spanish dictator, Generalissimo Francisco Franco.

50. R. Labat, *Le caractère religieux dela royauté assyro-babylonienne*, Paris: 1939.

Chapter Four

1. Book first called *Introducerea în istoria religiilor* and published as *Traité d'histoire des religions* (Paris: Payot, 1949).

2. Eliade's article "Nicolae Iorga" appeared in *Acçao*, 24 February 1944.

3. This is the first reference to the book that would become *Cosmos et histoire: Le mythe de l'éternel retour.* See the journal, 6 April 1944.

4. Eliade is referring to his volume, B. P. Hasdeu, *Scrieri alese: Răzvan și Vidra, Poezii, Magnum Etymologicum* (Bucharest: Ed. Cugetarea, 1944), 260 pages; condensed from his two-volume Hasdeu edition of 1937.

5. The reference is to D. Murărașu, *Ediția Mircea Eliade* (Bucharest: Tiparul Universitar, 1938), 67 pages, a harshly critical examination of Eliade's Hasdeu anthology. Reprinted in *"Dosarul" Eliade, Jos farsa!,* ed. Mircea Handoca, vol. 5, pt. 2 (Bucharest: Curtea Vechea, 2001), 112–59.

6. In its final published form, there are no "acts," but only three "scenes."

7. The play remained unpublished until after Mircea Handoca had obtained the manuscript from Eliade in Paris, in 1985. First published in *Revista de istorie și teorie literară*, 33, no. 4, and 34, no. 1 (1985–86). Republished in Eliade, *Coloana nesfârșită, Teatru*, ed. Mircea Handoca (Bucharest: Editura Minerva, 1996), English translation by Mac Linscott Ricketts, "Men and Stones," in *The International Eliade*, ed. Bryan S. Rennie (Albany: State University of New York Press, 2007), 247–80. In its final form it has five scenes: four in act 1 and one in act 2.

8. Victor Cădere, professional diplomat, currently the Romanian minister to Portugal.

9. The Evening Star, or Hyperion, "hero" of Eminescu's most beloved poem; it is about a princess who falls in love with the star and draws him down to earth. In the end, her love proves fickle.

10. "Liberator" was the name of the large American bombers used in air raids.

11. A reference to Molotov's statement to reporters on 2 April that Russia had no intention of annexing any Romanian territory or changing Romania's social system in any way.

12. Portugal's main river; passes through Lisbon.

13. This is the book that would become, in English, *The Myth of the Eternal Return*, trans. Willard R. Trask (New York: Bollingen Series XLVI, Pantheon Books, 1954). Also published as *Cosmos and History* (New York: Harper and Brothers, 1959).

14. "Open cities," in wartime, are cities that have abandoned defensive efforts. The enemy is then expected not to bomb them or attack them, in order to protect civilians and historic landmarks.

15. Lucian Blaga (1895–1961), Romanian poet, dramatist, and philosopher.

16. Romanian on diplomatic service in Berlin.

17. See above, 6 April 1944.

18. "But each moment ought to be snatched from despair."

19. "Why, at certain hours, are we assailed by a black and evil sadness like that which remorse over some crime would induce?"

20. (Bucharest: Ed. Cartea Românească, 1934). Eliade's fourth novel. A second edition was not published until 1991.

21. (Bucharest: Editura Națională Ciornei, 1930). Written in India, it was Eliade's first novel to be published. It was not issued in a revised form during the war years, as most of his other books were.

22. "The noble fatigue of the shoulder blades."

23. "I know I'm going to die, since I've stopped loving everything."

24. On 23 August, the young king Mihai I surrendered to the Soviets.

25. Coste was now chargé d'affaires at Lisbon.

26. The first translation of *Maitreyi* appeared in Italian in 1945: *Passione a Calcutta*, trans. Giovanna Calviieri (Rome: Casa Editrice).

27. Rudolf Steiner (1861–1925), "occultist," who, after following Theosophy for a time, rejected it and developed his own school, Anthroposophy, in which Eliade had a personal interest in 1926–27. Also known for having edited Goethe.

28. Andalusia festival and cold meal.

29. Paloma Martín Baena. (Thanks to Joaquín Garrigós, head of the Spanish Cervantes Institute in Bucharest, for this information!)

30. Correct Castilian spelling, and translation, according to Joaquín Garrigós:

Córdoba, sultana mía,	Córdoba, my sultana,
Tierra donde he nasío,	Land where I was born,
Donde tuve mis quereres,	Where I have known my loves,
Donde yo te conosío,	Where I met you,
Donde passé los dolores,	Where I have suffered the pains
Del primer amor sentío.	Of my first love.

31. "Nights at Serampore." Included in the book *Secretul doctorului Honigberger.*

32. Columbian evocation.

33. This was a recasting of his week in Córdoba in October. It is published as Anexo IV in Eliade, *Diario Portugués*, translated into Spanish by Joaquín Garrigós (Barcelona: Editorial Kairós, 2000).

34. "I reread today my travel notes. For whom shall I publish them?—They will be like the resinous secretions that consent to yield their perfume only when heated by the hand that holds them."

35. "My unlimited daily polygraphy allowed me to collect all the essences . . ." "Any thought, come from God knows where, that knocked on the doors of reflection, was always welcomed, hosted, and served. It seems clear that, in such hospitable conditions, we could receive thoughts of the most varied origin—many undoubtedly of a more humble aspect—than those of other men of the pen."

36. Reference to the Romanian philososopher Nicolae Bagdăzar (1896–1971).

37. "A fashion? Fine, but in the same so-called fashions is there not always revealed—more clearly than in any other aspect of culture—some deep change in the dialectics of the spirit?"

38. In the *Autobiography, Vol. II*, p. 106, Eliade says simply that she passed away in her sleep on the morning of November 20. But cf. the journal, 22 December 1944, and 20 March 1945.

39. Although not married until 25 October 1934, they had lived together since October 1933, and had been intimate since the previous spring.

40. Eliade makes a mistake here. It was actually *fourteen* years.

41. Chestov, or Lev Shestov (1866–1938), was a Russian-born Jewish existentialist philosopher. A disciple of Kierkegaard, he enjoyed long-standing philosophical friendships with Martin Buber, Edmund Husserl, and Nikolai Berdyaev.

42. This entry seems inconsistent with the statement that she died at 12:30 a.m.

43. "Watch out, Mister . . . she's my wife!"

44. The Eliades' housekeeper.

45. Eliade's sister.

46. "He is delivered from the past, he transforms that which has been into that which has never been."

47. "But one ought to reason otherwise: I do not possess proofs of my existence, but I have no need of these: therefore, certain truths, very important truths, go completely without proof."

48. "One believes only when man can no longer discover any possibility. God means that everything is possible."

49. "A wonderful teacher, who knows everything better than you, but who is ignorant of only one problem—yours."

50. "Human cowardice cannot endure what folly and death have to say."

Chapter Five

1. Eliade errs here: Job did not lose his wife and thus did not receive a second one. In the first sentence of this section Eliade had originally written that God gave

Job "another wife," but these words are crossed out in the manuscript, and a question mark is present.

2. Eliade published an article about Kierkegaard under the heading "Glossarium," in the exile periodical *Caiete de dor* 2 (1951): 1–5, with the notation that it was written at Cascaes in 1945.

3. "The crucified is the Son of God . . . and [though] entombed he was resurrected; it is certain because it is impossible."

4. The article was published in 1928 (4 March), not 1926 as Eliade remembered, in *Cuvântul*, 5, no. 1035.

5. The article, "Against Moldavia" ("Scrisori către un provincial. Împotriva Moldovei"), was published in *Cuvântul* iv, no. 1021, 19 February 1928. See Eliade's comments in his *Autobiography*, 1: pp. 16, 73, 135.

6. "It is found again."—"What?"—"Eternity."

7. "Acceptance and endurance—are they really the only responses man can make to the horrors of life?"

8. Miron R. Paraschivescu, 1911–71, prolific, militant Communist poet.

9. 6 September, 1940. After overthrowing King Carol II, General Antonescu was compelled by the large numbers of Legionaries to join with Horia Sima, head of the Iron Guard, in forming the National Legionary State.

10. Sergei A. Yesenin (1895–1925), most popular poet of the early period of the Russian Revolution. Later he rejected the policies of the Bolshevik regime.

11. See the journal entry for 29 July 1944.

12. Eliade is referring to Galaction's Romanian translation of the Bible (1938). In the KJV, *skandelon* usually is translated "stumbling block" or "offense." Cf., for example, 1 Corinthians 1:23. Galaction (1879–1961), an Orthodox priest, was known in Romanian letters mainly for his fantastic novellas and was acclaimed after 1944 for his "democratic," antifascistic viewpoint.

13. "One becomes a savant concerning the person of Christ by illicit means, because what is permitted in this regard is to become a believer."

14. "It happens with Christianity or with the fact of becoming a Christian, as with a radical cure that you postpone as long as possible."

15. Eliade published a number of articles under this title between late 1950 and 1964, which, as he indicated, were written at Cascaes in 1944 or 1945.

16. "Damn it, I can make an abstraction of everyone but myself; I can't even forget myself when I'm sleeping."

17. For the "Journal of Novel, *Viață Nouă*," see appendix A.

18. Ana Pauker, a leader in the Romanian Communist Party since the 1920s, who, having lived in Moscow, enjoyed the favor of the Russians at this time. She did not hold a post in the Romanian government, but was the "power behind the throne."

19. "What is friendship without intellectual exchange? A refuge for weak souls who don't know how to breathe in the ether of intelligence, but only in the vapors of animality."

20. François Henry Spitzmüller, former press counselor of the Vichy French Embassy at Lisbon, and before that (in 1941) French ambassador at Bucharest.

21. "To make poetry: the most innocent of all occupations."

22. Evidently Coste had delayed showing this to Eliade, because of Nina's death.

23. Ioan Alexandru Brătescu-Voineşti, respected author of novellas and other short prose works, was born in 1868, and thus would have been seventy-seven at the time of his arrest. He died the following year.

24. "For a long time and in our own day, it has been completely lost to sight that to be a writer is to act, to have the obligation to act, and, for the rest, to have a personal mode of existence"

25. Eliade did in fact publish a number of excerpts from this journal, some of them in a revised form, in 1954, in *Caiete de dor* (no. 8), a mimeographed exile periodical, at the request of the editor. They were chosen, as he says, in such a way "as to not reflect any events of a strictly personal interest, or the history of that tragic era."

26. "The philosopher must be a grammarian, and the grammarian must be a philosopher."

27. Former Romanian minister to Great Britain; had resigned in October after the Legionary government took power, but continued to live in England.

28. Although Eliade had been appointed to Lisbon while he was still in England (mid-October), he did not expect his duties at the Legation would begin immediately.

29. The (presumed) rebellion of the Iron Guard against Antonescu, 21–23 January 1941.

30. Gh. Munteanu, in press and propaganda (later sent to Lisbon); Alecu Bianu, commercial attaché; Victor Cornea, specialist in economic affairs, representing Iuliu Maniu in England (not on Legation staff); Radu Florescu, counselor of legation, later chargé d'affaires.

31. When certain territories were ceded to Russia, Bulgaria, and Hungary in the summer of 1940.

32. Cisck, evidently, had replaced Bulbuc (a Legionary) as secretary general at the Ministry of Propaganda at Bucharest after the Iron Guard rebellion. Cf. Dumitrescu-Borşa, *Cal troian întra muros* [The Trojan Horse inside the Walls] (Bucharest: Ed. Luchman, 2002), 402.

33. English in the original.

34. David Mitrany, Romanian-born professor of international relations, formerly of Princeton University, then teaching at Oxford University, with close ties to the Ministry of Foreign Affairs.

35. Victor Cornea, representative of Iuliu Maniu (National Peasant Party), lecturer at the University of London, involved with the British Labour Party, loosely connected with the Legation.

36. Gabriele D'Annunzio's journal; citations from 8 September to 5 October 1908.

37. Sir Reginald Hoare, British minister to Romania.

38. One of several military attachés at the Legation.

39. A banker who had come recently to London; not officially connected to the Legation.

40. Nichifor Crainic, 1899–1972, poet and director of the review *Gândirea*, one of the most influential interwar periodicals.

41. "The greatest reality corresponds first of all to what one eats."

42. Michelet (1798–1874), eminent French writer of the romantic school.

43. "These nourishing waters are thick with all sorts of rich particles suitable for the soft nature of the fish, which lazily opens its mouth and breathes, nourished like

an embryo at the breast of the common mother. . . . The microscopic nourishment is like a milk that comes to it. . . . The infants for the most part resemble fetuses in the gelatinous state that absorb and produce mucous matter, filling the waters, giving them the fertile sweets of an infinite matrice from where, ceaselessly, new infants come to swim as in tepid milk."

44. Part of *Stages on Life's Way*, a continuation of *Either/Or*. Contains the Diary of Quidam, who, like Kierkegaard, has broken off his engagement.

45. "Terribly in advance of your own people."

46. "How can you keep from being enraged at not living in the hours when you are working, and agitated at not working in the hours when you are living?"

47. "The daily dilemma, and that of fatigue, old age, or sickness, by forbidding us to live, can find its solution."

48. General Nicolae Rădescu, prime minister of the last Romanian government that was not entirely Communist, September 1944–February 1945. Having taken refuge in the British Embassy on 11 February, he was able, after several months in hiding, to slip out of the country in disguise.

49. "Would a naturalist who has never studied the elephant other than with a microscope believe he knows that animal sufficiently?"

50. "Thus, although the bird would have been dead a long time, although the little cubes of muscle separated from its heart could not, either by the circulation of the blood or by the nervous system, be connected to a central network, they recognize each other, one can almost say, when they come in contact, and they persist in performing the work for which their cells were created, not haphazardly, in an independent way, but together and in coordination. Need I say that there does not exist the beginning of an explanation for this curious phenomenon?"

51. In a radio address of 24 February, Rădescu had attacked the Romanian Communist leaders favored by Moscow: Ana Pauker, of Jewish origin, and Vasile Luca, an ethnic Hungarian from Transylvania.

52. General Constantin Sănătescu, Romanian prime minister, August–September 1944.

53. Iuliu Maniu, Uniate theologian of Transylvanian origin, the head of the National Peasant Party, had been prime minister from December 1928 to October 1930. Remained active in politics throughout the thirties and war years. Widely respected. Died in a Communist prison.

54. A term of endearment used by lovers.

55. Vasile V. Rozanov (1867–1919), Russian philosopher and writer.

56. "That which I want and demand of every man whom I claim to know truly is that he thinks in the daytime only of the guiding category of his life, and that he dreams at night."

57. The ceremony formally installing Petru Groza as head of the government. The king was Mihai (Michael I, b. 1921, still living, 2009). See note 75 below.

58. Andrei Y. Vishinsky (1883–1954), Russian diplomat and jurist. Appointed deputy commissar for foreign affairs (1940–49) with special authority in the Balkans (1944–45).

59. Petru Groza, head of the Ploughmen's Front, a radical peasant party with ties to the Romanian Communist Party. President of the council of ministers, March 6, 1945–December 39, 1947, under imposition of the Soviets.

60. "So bitter the years since then! / O wisteria, throw down thy flowers." From a poem by Tudor Arghezi, highly popular Romanian poet at that time.

61. A member of the Romanian Legation.

62. Eliade, *Passione a Calcutta*, trans. by Giovanna Caroncini, was published at Casa Editrice la Caravella (Rome) in 1945, Eliade's first work to appear in translation. The Portuguese translation to which Eliade refers never appeared (a different one was published in 1961), nor did the Italian translation of *Huliganii* cited here.

63. Eliade and some twenty other men in diplomatic posts across Europe were recalled at this time by the Ministry of Foreign Affairs. M.A.F. Archives, cited in Florian Turcanu, *Mircea Eliade, Le prisonnier de l'histoire* (Paris: La Découverte, 2003), 339.

64. Young publisher of *Credința* [The Faith] a conservative newspaper (December 1933–March 1944) to which Eliade contributed briefly (1933–34) under a pseudonymn.

65. Brilliant member of the "young generation" (born 1901); although educated in economics he was an excellent Orthodox theologian. Died in a Communist prison about 1947.

66. This journal is not included in the present volume.

67. "The secret of almost all my weaknesses is that dreadful modesty of which I do not succeed in curing myself."

68. A converted Jew of Romanian origin, teaching at the University of Manchester, England, whom Eliade met while attending the Oxford Group Movement (Moral Rearmament) meeting in 1936.

69. Jewish novelist, playwright, and journalist, once a close friend of Nina and Eliade. He became estranged from Eliade after the latter's association with the Legion. See Sebastian, *Journal*, 1935–44. Chicago: Ivan R. Dee, 2000.

70. Farewell greeting, comparable to "I'll be seeing you!"

71. This Portuguese translation was never published.

72. An expression coined by the Romanian philosopher Lucian Blaga, for Romania, alluding to it as the land of the popular ballad, "Miorița" [The Ewe Lamb].

73. Theodore Besterman, an English bibliographer whom Eliade met in England in 1940. After the war, they were reunited when Besterman came to Paris on a mission for UNESCO.

74. Mussolini's son-in-law, who was executed by Il Duce after voting against him in 1943.

75. Clement Attlee (1883–1967), liberal statesman, head of the Labour Party from 1935 on. While he was prime minister (1945–51), many "socialistic" reforms were carried out.

76. Portuguese translation of the Italian book [*History of a Year*].

77. A Guardist friend who later held a post in the Ministry of Propaganda in the National Legionary government.

78. National Socialist, anti-Semitic party founded in 1935 by Ferencz Szálasi (b. 1897). Correct name: the Arrow Cross (*Nyilaskereszt*) Party.

79. Gheorghe Tătărescu, head of the National Liberal Party and prime minister from 1934 to 1937. In 1925 a peasant revolt occurred in Tatar-Bunar (located today in the Republic of Moldova), which was violently suppressed. When the repressors were tried and declared innocent in 1936, Tătărescu was believed responsible for the verdict.

In 1945 he joined the Communist Party and was appointed vice-premier and minister of foreign affairs.

80. In a revised version of this journal entry published as "Fragmente de Jurnal" (*Caiete de dor* 8 (1954): 29, Eliade added:

> To be related to my observations about the regeneration of archaic man through the abolition of Time, through the return to the auroral moment, in *illo tempore* of the beginnings. The meaning that *incipit vita nova* can have for a modern man: not the repetition of the cosmogony as in the case of primitives, nor the resumption of Creation—but the abolition of "the past," the transcendence of History, in the sense that, through a desperate act of freedom, i.e., through a maximum living of the Spirit, you "denounce" first with respect to yourself, all the conditionings of the past, all the "bonds and chains" of your own and of others, and you endeavor to be as at the beginning of the World.
>
> Poets, in their way, do this through every act of creation. They try to "speak" as no one has ever "spoken;" they try to rediscover the language and they conduct themselves—when they are "inspired" as if the language did not have a history, had not been worn out, consumed, and profaned by Time. They look over Time to God, as if they, the poets, were contemporaries with the beginnings of the World, were witnesses of the Cosmogony.
>
> When the last poet shall surrender his liberty to the conditionings of History, there will occur, probably, what one of the Goncourts foretold in his journal (in connection, I believe, with what will result inevitably from the progress of the sciences): God will descend to earth and will say, "Messieurs, on ferme . . ." ["Gentlemen, it's closing time!"]

Appendix A

1. Reference particularly to the execution of Legionary leaders in 1938 and 1939.

2. Dumitru G. Danielopol (1908–82), banker, concerned with Romanian-British financial relations; loosely affiliated with the Legation. He left a manuscript account of his London years that was published in 1995: *Jurnal londonez,* ed. V. F. Dobrinesc and V. Dumistrşcel (Iaşi: Institutul European, 1955). The MS is preserved at the Hoover Institute, Stanford University.

3. Virgil Viorel Tilea (1896–1972), minister of the Romanian Legation, 1939–40. Resigned soon after the National-Legionary goverment came to power in early September, and founded (with others) the Free Romanian Movement.

4. Besides having an elegant official residence in London, Tilea owned a farm at Wheatley, near Oxford. See Danielopol, *op. cit.,* p. 85.

5. An extract from this text, once intended to be part of *Viaţă Nouă,* was published in *Universul literar* (Bucharest), 48, no. 52 (30 December 1939).

6. Ion Vardala (1907–85), career diplomat from 1936 to 1947. Resided afterward in the United States, worked on behalf of Romanian independence on the Romanian National Committee, and edited the committee's paper, *România*.

7. Ghiţă "Bill" Munteanu, later propaganda secretary at Lisbon.

8. Radu Florescu, counselor at the Romanian Legation. After V.V. Tilea's resignation as minister, he became chargé d'affaires.

9. Mrs. Sassoon, a friend of the Eliades, had rented rooms to them and Danielopol after Christmas. She was the niece of Lord Samuel, head of the Liberal Party.

10. The shepherd who was, supposedly, the recipient of a revelation in 1935 predicting the near end of the world. The site of the revelation, Maglavit, was a prehistoric religious shrine in Romania. Following this "miracle at Maglavit," the place became a pilgrimage center attracting tens of thousands.

11. As revised and published (posthumously), this episode is in chap. 7, pt. 2.

12. Emil Bulbuc, a Legionary whom Eliade knew at the internment camp at Miercurea Ciuc. See Eliade's journal for 27 and 28 July 1947.

13. This is the book that would become *Traité de l'histoire des religions* (1949).

14. A member of the Romanian Legation staff.

15. Cf. the journal, 29–30 May 1942, where Eliade finishes writing Salazar in the wee hours of the morning, in order to send the manuscript "with the Romanians from Rio."

16. The manuscript of this journal is found among Eliade's papers at the University of Chicago Regenstein Library. The journal was published as an addendum to *Viaţă Nouă*, ed. Mircea Handoca (Bucharest: Editura "Jurnalul Literar," 1999): 203–19; also in Eliade, *Jurnalul portughez şi alte scrieri*, ed. Sorin Alexandrescu, vol. 1 (Bucharest: Humanitas, 2006).

Appendix B

1. From a manuscript found in Regenstein Library, University of Chicago, together with Eliade's journal. Published in Romanian in Mircea Eliade, *Jurnalul*, ed. Mircea Handoca, vol. 1 (Bucharest: Humanities, 1993), 9–29. These "impressions" (except for the one in Lisbon) seem to come from one or more excursions Eliade made in Portugal in 1941.

2. Former capital, seat of a famous university, located in the northern part of the country. Among its alumni: Eça de Queiroz (poet), Anterio de Quental (philosopher), and Salazar.

3. Pharisees are not said to be present at the crucifixion in any of the Gospels and only the soldiers gamble for his clothing. But Vasco Fernandes may have included these Jewish figures in his painting.

Appendix C

1. This communique lacks an address, but seems to be directed to someone Eliade knew personally in the Ministry of Foreign Affairs.

2. Carol and his entourage had been living in (pro-Axis) Spain from about the middle of September 1940 until 3 March 1941, when he fled to (pro-English) Portugal by car.

3. Ernest Urdăreanu, Carol's ex-palace minister.

4. Jean Pangal, former Romanian minister to Portugal.

5. The Falange was a fascist type of party, the official party of the state at this time.

6. A reference to the Legionary revolt against General Ion Antonescu, 21–23 January 1941.

7. Mihai Cămărăşescu, Romanian chargé d'affaires at Lisbon.

8. Carol had named his young son, Mihai, to the throne upon his abdication, 6 September 1940.

9. The royal house of Portugal.

10. General Condeescu, 1880–1939, influential retired army officer and writer. Helped Eliade in 1938–39.

11. I don't know to what this refers. It may have happened when Eliade was in the prison camp in 1938. At that time Nina wrote letters to the king and the prime minister.

12. Magda (Elena or Elenuţa) Lupescu, Carol's mistress since the 1920s and his highly influential advisor. Despised by the Romanian people, because her father was a Jew (although converted). Eliade calls her "Lupeasca," meaning "bitch wolf" in Romanian.

13. [*sic!*] They left by air.

14. Carol and Lupeasca flew from Portugal to the Bahamas, then boarded an American ocean liner headed for New York. Refused entrance to the United States, they took another vessel for Rio de Janiero. There they lived for the rest of their lives. Carol married Mme Lupeascu, supposedly on her deathbed, in 1947. She recovered, and outlived Carol, who died in 1953.

Appendix D

1. Volume published 1942 in Bucharest by Editura Gorjan; republished in 2002 (Bucharest: Editura Scara), with different pagination; republished also in Mircea Eliade, *Jurnalul portughez şi alte scrieri*, ed. Sorin Alexandrescu, vol. 2 (Bucharest: Humanitas, 2006), 7–218.

2. Salazar continued to rule Portugal, however, until 1968, when he suffered a severe stroke and was forced to retire. He died in 1970, at age seventy-nine.

Index

Printed in Great Britain
by Amazon

48323880R10169